In Their Own Words . . .
In the Heat of Battle . . .

"They're comin' in, they're comin' in. Help me, help me!"

—Sp4 Charles L. Daniel
527th Military Police Company
U.S. Embassy, Saigon

General William C. Westmoreland—Handsome, confident, ramrod-straight, the theater commander possessed unbeatable mobility and firepower. But tied to a World War II mind-set, he was looking for conventional battle at Khe Sanh while the Viet Cong and North Vietnamese slipped unseen into Saigon.

Senior General Vo Nguyen Giap—The North Vietnamese Minister of Defense was the mastermind of the Tet Offensive. Having baited Westmoreland with a brilliant series of diversionary attacks in remote areas, he thought he could win the war by plunging into the unprotected urban centers of South Vietnam. It was a massive gamble given the superiority of U.S. forces, but communist morale was high.

"I got my attack order from the division commander. We were standing on the patio by the general's mess, and he was pointing right at the VC. It was an unreal situation."

> —Lt. Col. David E. Grange
> Commanding Officer, 2d Battalion, 506th Infantry,
> 101st Airborne Division

Lieutenant General Fred C. Weyand—The corps commander whose operational responsibilities included the approaches to Saigon, he saved the Allies from complete disaster by convincing Westmoreland to pull a number of U.S. units back from the Cambodian border where Giap was creating a diversion.

Sp5 Dwight W. Birdwell—A twenty-year-old tank crewman with Troop C, 3d Squadron, 4th Cavalry. When the unit was shot to pieces on Highway 1 while rushing toward Saigon, Birdwell took the place of his wounded tank commander and laid down a firestorm of cannon and machine-gun fire to keep the enemy from overrunning the column. Birdwell was wounded himself, but his tenacious stand allowed Troop C to regroup and counterattack.

"This time they've accommodated us. They're attacking us for a change."

—Col. Frederic E. Davison
Acting Commander
199th Light Infantry Brigade

Sp5 Richard D. Vincent—A juvenile delinquent turned career soldier. Vincent and his five-man, green-faced reconnaissance team from Company F, 51st Infantry (Long Range Patrol), spotted the Viet Cong battalion that was marching toward the U.S. headquarters at Long Binh, near Saigon. Risking detection from the enemy column passing by only a few feet away, Vincent relayed vital information to higher comand even as his team was caught in a terrible crossfire and surrounded.

Captain Robert L. Tonsetic—Commander of the grunt company dispatched from the 199th Light Infantry Brigade to block the Viet Cong battalion marching toward Long Binh. The two forces met head-on in a point-blank, back-and-forth battle on a night illuminated by flares and burning houses. Tonsetic's bold leadership in the face of overwhelming odds earned him the Distinguished Service Cross.

Books by Keith William Nolan

Operation Buffalo
Battle for Hue
The Magnificent Bastards
Death Valley
Into Cambodia
Into Laos
Sappers in the Wire
The Battle for Saigon*

*Published by POCKET BOOKS

THE
BATTLE
FOR
SAIGON
TET 1968

KEITH WILLIAM NOLAN

POCKET BOOKS

New York   London   Toronto   Sydney   Tokyo   Singapore

An *Original* Publication of POCKET BOOKS

POCKET BOOKS, a division of Simon & Schuster Inc.
1230 Avenue of the Americas, New York, NY 10020

ISBN: 0-671-52287-6

First Pocket Books printing October 1996

10 9 8 7 6 5 4 3 2 1

POCKET and colophon are registered trademarks of Simon & Schuster Inc.

Cover photo by Don McCullin/Magnum

Printed in the U.S.A.

For Kelly

Contents

CONTENTS

Part 3: Bien Hoa

Part 4: Long Binh

Preface

The Tet Offensive was the watershed event of the Vietnam War, and the first day of the nationwide campaign—Wednesday, January 31, 1968—was the day the war was lost in the hearts and minds of America. The public could not reconcile the light-at-the-end-of-the-tunnel rhetoric of its leaders with the news footage of U.S. troops engaged in a full-blown firefight with Viet Cong sappers in the U.S. Embassy compound in downtown Saigon.

Much has been written about the political ramifications of Tet. The Johnson administration imploded in its wake, and given the public's growing opposition to the war, Nixon—sworn in a year after Tet—sought only to extract the U.S. from Vietnam. Much has also been written about more narrow topics, including the failure of allied intelligence to decipher the enemy's intentions and the influence and accuracy of the press coverage of Tet.

Less has been written about the actual combat operations that occured during Tet, with the exception of the Siege of Khe Sanh and the street fighting in Hue. Surprisingly, the dramatic battle for the Saigon Circle—which included the capital itself, the U.S. command centers at Tan Son Nhut and Long Binh, and the vital air bases at Bien Hoa and Tan Son Nhut—has not been covered in any detail. Hopefully, this book will help fill that gap.

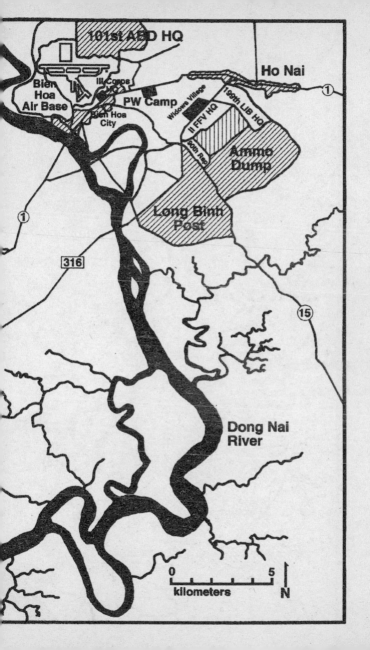

Prologue

Setting the Stage

The decision to launch the offensive was made during a July 7, 1967, meeting in Hanoi between Ho Chi Minh, president of the Democratic Republic of Vietnam—more commonly, North Vietnam—and the highest members of the Lao Dong (communist) Party, to include Senior General Vo Nguyen Giap, the Minister of Defense. The offensive would reclaim a victory denied. The communists had been winning the Vietnamese civil war when, in March 1965, the first U.S. infantry units landed in the Republic of Vietnam (RVN)—South Vietnam—to prop up the Saigon regime. The build-up that followed was massive, division upon division from the best army in the world, supported by artillery and jets, and an armada of helicopters—helicopters to lift a squad patrol or an entire brigade into battle, helicopters to strafe and rocket, helicopters to evacuate the wounded, helicopters to bring in the steak and beer. The U.S. command opted for a war of attrition, confident that sheer technological superiority would pulverize the southern-born guerrillas of the Viet Cong (VC) and the light infantrymen of the North Vietnamese Army (NVA).

The technology provided the U.S. command with the illusion of victory, not the thing itself. To force the drawn-out guerrilla war to a decisive conclusion, senior communist leaders proposed a nationwide offensive—the Tong

1

Cong Kich-Tong Khoi Nghia (TCK-TKN), which translates into "General Offensive-General Uprising."

The world would know it as the Tet Offensive. Tet is the Vietnamese holiday ushering in the Chinese lunar new year. The war stopped during Tet. The first and most holy day of Tet in 1968 was January 30. Using the cover of the celebrations that would begin that night, Giap planned to launch TCK-TKN after midnight on January 31. Tet was also a time of family reunions, and half the Army of the Republic of Vietnam (ARVN) would be on leave when the tens of thousands of guerrillas materialized out of the darkness, hitting cities throughout the country. Generally bypassing U.S. positions, the initial goal of the offensive was to shatter the second-rate ARVN before American forces could rally to its defense. It seemed a realistic objective, given the veteran cadres and highly motivated fighters that filled the ranks of the VC and NVA.

The General Offensive would bring the war to the cities for the first time. Ho Chi Minh and Giap believed that with the ARVN scattered to the winds—and U.S. forces still scrambling to regroup—the fabled General Uprising would sweep South Vietnam. The oppressed people of the south would rally in common cause with the liberation army to overthrow the corrupt puppet regime in Saigon, leaving the U.S. no choice but to withdraw from Vietnam.

It was a massive gamble. Certain field commanders who had seen their units mauled when they faced the U.S. in open battle argued against TCK-TKN, believing that the weak links in the American strategy could be best exploited through protracted guerrilla warfare. The opposing theater commander—handsome, confident, ramrod-straight General William C. Westmoreland, United States Army— possessed unbeatable mobility and firepower, but, mesmerized by the body counts they provided when the communists stood and fought, he had lost touch with certain truths of the Vietnam War. The U.S. could not force the VC and NVA to battle—invisible in the jungle, shielded in the villages, it was the guerrillas who initiated most engagements—and thus the communists were not being bled at the rate required for their destruction. Losses were replaced. The war continued. It could be continued for years in this manner until the Americans finally grew sick of the inconclusive cycle of ambushes and booby traps and body bags.

Playing to his strengths, General Westmoreland fought a conventional, big-unit war in Vietnam. He placed minimal emphasis on civic action. Vietnam was not World War II, however. Battlefield successes were rendered hollow without follow-up efforts to win the goodwill of the people in the areas temporarily cleared of the VC and NVA. Westmoreland's unimaginative search-and-destroy strategy was not only wrongheaded in concept but, given that the sole tactical goal of unit commanders was the production of enemy bodies, it was self-defeating in practice. Units did not protect villages but swept through them time and again in the hunt for an elusive enemy. The resulting carnage— the forced removal of villagers from ancestral lands, the hootches put to the torch by frustrated troops, the shelling, bombing, napalming, and defoliation of what had once been people's farms—ensured the guerrillas new recruits and a rural population that was sullen and hostile, if not actively cooperating with the Viet Cong.

Given its inherent flaws, the U.S. war effort would eventually burn out of its own accord, and once Westmoreland's sand castles had washed away, there would be nothing to stop Hanoi: the theater commander had neither clamped down on the self-defeating venality of the Saigon regime, nor made a priority of upgrading the capabilities of the ill-led, chicken-stealing ARVN. During the July 1967 meeting, however, Ho Chi Minh opted for the decisive TCK-TKN over protracted guerrilla warfare. Giap was placed in command. The first phase was a series of meatgrinder-like battles initiated by the NVA to bait Westmoreland to the remote border areas of Vietnam far removed from the communists' urban objectives—and from the ARVN. The NVA and the 3d Marine Division were already engaged in a horrendous slugging match along the Demilitarized Zone (DMZ) dividing North and South Vietnam when, in August 1967, communist efforts in the area seemed to redouble with convoy ambushes, and battalion-

and regimental-size attacks against marine units. During September and October, the marine base at Con Thien was subjected to heavy shelling from the DMZ.

During the three-week battle of Dak To in November 1967, the elite 173d Airborne Brigade was decimated in the jungled mountains of the Central Highlands out in the middle of nowhere near the Laotian border.

North Vietnamese casualties at Con Thien, Dak To, and other peripheral locations were heavy, but the feint was achieved. The diversionary effort was capstoned in early January 1968 when Giap began sacrificing even more thousands of NVA to lay siege to Khe Sanh, an isolated marine base at the western end of the DMZ. The border battles had played to General Westmoreland's delusions—that the enemy was in retreat and able to make war only in the hinterlands—and he welcomed the prospect of a frustrated Giap trying to turn Khe Sanh into another Dien Bien Phu. United States firepower was a thousandfold that of the French, and if the NVA massed at Khe Sanh in a foolish effort to repeat history, the result would be their annihilation under a cascade of bombs. Westmoreland was so eager for a climatic, conventional battle to break his foe's back that he disregarded the numerous reports of enemy units slipping toward the cities and refused to believe the prisoner interrogations and captured documents that clearly laid out the plans for the coming nationwide offensive. The intelligence did not fit the preconceptions.

Lieutenant General Fred C. Weyand, the corps commander whose operational responsibilities included the approaches to Saigon, was not so sanguine. Less than three weeks before Tet, even as Westmoreland was committing vast resources to Khe Sanh and other border areas, Weyand convinced the theater commander to pull a number of U.S. units back from the Cambodian border and position them in strategic locations around the capital.

General Weyand would be Giap's main foil during Tet. Meanwhile, with Westmoreland focused on far Khe Sanh, the communists were ready to launch phase two of their plan—the urban attacks. The communists had needed the seven months between the time of decision and the time of action not only to mobilize their forces—according to post-Tet U.S. estimates, 67,000 to 84,000 VC/NVA were committed to the attacks—but also to "prepare the battlefield," i.e., to reconnoiter assigned objectives, and to move forward the massive amount of weapons and ammunition that would be required. The process of bringing supplies down the Ho Chi Minh Trail through Laos was torturous and slow. Enemy quartermasters had a much easier time on the Sihanouk Trail in neutral, unbombed Cambodia. Delivered to the assault units in South Vietnam, these supplies were then cached in base camps and villages, and in the targeted cities themselves, smuggled in aboard trucks laden with rice, flowers, fruits, and vegetables, or inside caskets as part of sham funeral processions.

In bits and pieces, Viet Cong units also infiltrated the cities, the guerrillas posing as civilians or ARVN soldiers on leave and joining the throngs of holiday travelers. The population of South Vietnam—both rural and urban—raised no alarm as communist battalions, regiments, and divisions organized in their midst. Their silence spoke volumes about the regime to which the United States had devoted its treasury and the lives of its soldiers.

Because of communication problems, some VC units attacked prematurely, and TCK-TKN began thirty-five minutes after midnight on January 30, 1968, with an assault on Nha Trang. Six other cities in the northern half of the country were also hit that night. This blunder gave the allies a vital heads-up, but the overwhelming scope of the onslaught was shocking when it exploded in the predawn hours of January 31. The communists hit fifty hamlets, sixty-four district capitals, thirty-six provincial capitals, and five autonomous cities throughout South Vietnam. The bulk of an NVA division occupied the old imperial capital of Hue and ran up a red flag with a gold star. They were everywhere along the coast—Da Nang, Quang Ngai, Qui Nhon—and the Mekong Delta was afire from My Tho and Ben Tre to Ca Mau. Most significantly, Saigon thundered with explosions and automatic-weapons fire, too.

The world had turned upside down. According to Hanoi's vision, the U.S. command—about to find itself isolated in a landscape of communist-occupied cities and an aroused, hostile countryside—would soon be debarking. The bulk of the NVA would then march in from its sanctuaries in Laos and Cambodia and join the VC for the final phase—the crushing of diehard ARVN resistance. The war would be over, victory achieved.

Vietnam would finally be reunited.

Part 1

Tan Son Nhut

"Before Tet, we had contempt for the Viet Cong and the North Vietnamese Army."
—Sp5 Dwight W. Birdwell
Troop C, 3d Squadron, 4th Cavalry,
25th Infantry Division

1

We Need Help
Down Here

The breaching of the vulnerable western side of the air base began after a series of diversionary attacks by fire. The first was initiated against the eastern perimeter. When the green tracers started cutting through the night sky there, Captain Carl B. "Bernie" DeNisio and First Lieutenant Melvin G. Grover, Jr., of the 377th Security Police Squadron (SPS), 7th U.S. Air Force, were in a jeep in the main aircraft parking area in the center of the base. DeNisio and Grover had been on the move since guard mount began at eight that night, checking the various security positions along the flight lines, in the bomb and fuel storage areas, and on the twenty-kilometer perimeter of Tan Son Nhut Air Base (AB).

It was now 0321 on January 31, 1968. Lieutenant Grover was in the driver's seat as they headed toward the sound of automatic-weapons fire. "[T]his is [Mobile] 5-6 on the outer perimeter road," DeNisio radioed in, using his call sign, upon reaching the point of contact. The captain was in direct communications with Technical Sergeant James Bloom, senior man at the 377th's Central Security Control (CSC).

Tan Son Nhut Air Base was located on the northwest side of Saigon, and the enemy was firing from buildings just outside the perimeter fence. "Some tracer fire [is] paralleling the east perimeter," DeNisio continued, his transmission being recorded in CSC. "The majority of it, however, is low trajectory into the installation. It's all tracer fire, appearing to be directed at the POL [the Petroleum-Oil-Lubricant storage facilities north of the main east-west runways]."

The fire was heavy. Captain DeNisio was out with Grover precisely because enemy action, most likely a mortar or sapper attack, had been expected. Grover commanded the night guard shift. DeNisio, however, served as the Weapons Systems Security Operations Officer, 377th SPS, and, given his daytime duties, usually made his last inspection of the perimeter before midnight. "But in light of the intelligence, I was still out there," he recalled. Forewarned by the enemy's premature attacks up north, the base was on red alert. "Nothing was going on in our area, but obviously we geared up," DeNisio said. "We planned on working the whole night, checking the sectors, talking to guards and keeping them alert—just plain being out there. If an attack's going to happen, it's going to happen at night."

Twelve minutes into the attack, at which time automatic-weapons fire had erupted at many points around the base, a guard post reported, "There's mortar rounds or grenade rounds landing on the west perimeter fence!" The main attack had started. Moments later, Airman First Class Alan D. Tucker, who manned a little, four-legged observation tower—Tango 4—at the end of the main runways at the westernmost tip of Tan Son Nhut, shouted into his radio, "They're about a hundred yards out directly in front of my post! There's about twenty men out there, they're sending off mortar fire . . ."

"10-4," Bloom said. "Are they coming on base?"

"They're directly in front of my [tower], a hundred yards off the west perimeter!"

The enemy was exposed by the perimeter lighting. DeNisio ordered reaction teams to the area, but Tucker, unsure that anything was being done in the general din and confusion, called CSC again. "This area must be illuminated because they might try and attack the base!" he shouted, sounding frustrated. Tucker's voice suddenly shot up several octaves. "They're ten feet from the base!"

The western side of Tan Son Nhut was paralleled by north-south Highway 1, and faced the open rice paddies and small villages on the rural fringe of congested, polluted Saigon. The unpaved outer perimeter road came to a point here, one branch running northeast behind the perimeter fence, the other southeast. Tango 4 was situated on the inside of this point. Fifteen meters in front of the tower, a little-used service road pierced the tip of the point, running into the base through the 051 Gate from Highway 1.

The enemy assault force planned to enter the base through the 051 Gate, and the initial explosions had not been the grenades and mortar rounds originally reported but satchel charges and bangalore torpedoes utilized by a Viet Cong sapper team that simply pulled up on Highway 1 in a civilian taxicab. The explosives were slipped under the three concertina-wire barriers posted in the grassy median between the highway and the vegetation-covered perimeter fence, blowing gaps in the barriers that the assault troops could stream through from their assembly points in the hamlet hugging the opposite side of Highway 1.

The bareheaded assault troops wore fatigues and sandals, each with his magazine pouches secured across his stomach and lower chest by shoulder straps and a cloth strip that tied in back. Equipped with AK-47 automatic rifles and rocket-propelled grenade launchers—the hard-hitting RPG—the lead enemy soldiers fired as they rushed forward.

"This is Echo 3-7 . . . I've been hit. . . ."

"10-4, Echo 3-7," Sergeant Bloom answered immediately. "Hang on, boy, the ambulance is in route!"

"Security Control, [this is] Echo 1," said Technical Sergeant Billy M. Palmer, the Noncommissioned Officer in Charge (NCOIC) of Sector E, which included the embattled western tip. Palmer gripped the radio handset in his gun jeep. "We need help down here at the Oh-5-1 Bunker bad. . . ."

The 051 Bunker, commanded by Sergeant Louis H.

Fischer and manned by four other security policemen (SPs), was several hundred meters south of Tango 4 on the perimeter road. The entrenched concrete bunker was painted with a camouflage pattern and had a low profile. From under a concrete roof on its sandbagged top, Fischer's M60 machine-gun (MG) team placed devastating grazing fire on the flank of the enemy troops assaulting the 051 Gate. In response, the VC raked the bunker with AK-47 fire, and numerous rocket hits left gouges in the concrete that revealed the stone and brick underneath. The airmen on top immediately took casualties, but those who could continued to fire and to put up slap-flares, which lit up the scene as they floated down, trailing smoke under their little parachutes.

The enemy began mortaring Echo Sector. Meanwhile, Captain DeNisio and Lieutenant Grover had rendezvoused with a reaction team at the north end of the base where another diversionary attack was in progress. Needing to assess the severity of the bigger battle on the west perimeter, they headed toward it with their jeep lights out, their helmets and flak jackets on. Grover roared right down the well-lit perimeter road, but upon reaching the elbow at the westernmost point DeNisio urgently shouted, "Stop—and get out!" Grover hadn't realized it, but the jeep was under fire. Leaving the jeep on the road, which was raised about eighteen inches to prevent it from being washed out during the rainy season, DeNisio and Grover went to the prone on the east side, their feet draped over the tanglefoot wire stretched along the side of the road. Tracers snapped past, the evacuated jeep stopping several rounds.

The 051 Bunker was the focal point of the battle. Tango 4, to the immediate left-front of DeNisio and Grover, also had tracers ricocheting off it. There were VC on the other side of the 051 Gate, which was just across the road. "You could hear them babbling away. You could hear them more than you could see them," said Grover, who opened up with his M16. "I fired some rounds towards the gate, but they hit the crown of the road and ricocheted up. I didn't want to stand up too high, so I stopped shooting. I thought I fired a magazine load, but I was four magazines short when I took stock the next morning. I don't remember firing that many, but I'm sure I did in all the excitement."

Most of the enemy fire also hit the crown of the road. "The VC were doing everything they could to get through that gate," remembered Captain DeNisio, who sprayed the fence line with his CAR15 submachine gun. "They were pulling at it with their hands. They were throwing satchel charges at it. We could see some of them getting hit, but the rest kept trying."

The VC blew the gate down in short order.

It was now 0344. *"We've got VC breaching the perimeter in the vicinity of the Oh-5-1 Gate!"* an SP radioed in.

An assault helicopter company from the 1st Aviation Brigade, U.S. Army, was stationed at Tan Son Nhut, and four UH1C Huey gunships presently pumped rockets and machine-gun fire into the assault force. "He's right on 'em!" DeNisio reported to CSC. The pilots had expected a "suicide squad" sent in to divert attention from a mortar position. They were stunned by the hundreds of enemy visible in the flarelight. The gunships took multiple hits as they rolled in, but continued to thin the ranks of the enemy soldiers rushing through the blown-open gate.

The fire on the 051 Bunker became so intense that the surviving members of Sergeant Fischer's team were forced off the sandbagged top and into the bunker itself. "Tango 1 to Security Control, you have eighty [VC/NVA] in the vicinity of the Oh-5-1 Bunker," reported an SP atop a water tower in the southwestern part of the base.

"The Oh-5-1 Bunker is not firing . . ."

Somebody from inside the bunker called CSC. "Security Control from Echo 37. . . . They're all around our position right now. We're running low on ammo."

Sergeant Bloom called DeNisio to report that "There has been a breach. Echo 37—*they're overrunning his post."*

"10-4," DeNisio answered, helplessly noting that he was "pinned down at the Oh-5-1 Gate."

Reaction teams were moving up, but the VC took the 051 Bunker before they arrived. The fate of the SPs inside the bunker was unknown at that time. In fact, four of them— Sergeant Fischer, plus Sergeants William J. Cyr, Charles E.

Hebron, and Roger B. Mills—had been killed. Fischer was posthumously awarded the Silver Star. The fifth member of the team was so badly wounded that the VC ignored him as they turned around the M60 machine gun on the top of the bunker and commenced firing into the interior of the base to cover their comrades preparing to assault the flight line.

Sergeant Bloom, frustrated with the slow, cautious approach of the reaction teams, finally snapped at one team leader over the radio, *"Get down to the Oh-5-1 Gate directly in front of Tango 4. The VC are overrunning the base!"*

The situation was inconceivable. So large as to appear invulnerable, Tan Son Nhut was the command center of the entire allied war effort in South Vietnam. Generals William C. Westmoreland, Commander, U.S. Military Assistance Command Vietnam (COMUSMACV), and William M. Momyer, commander of the 7th U.S. Air Force, were both headquartered at Tan Son Nhut, as was the Vietnamese Air Force (VNAF). Pentagon East, as the main MACV HQ building was nicknamed, was a massive, two-story, concrete and steel structure with air-conditioned office space for four thousand officers and enlisted staff. It occupied almost three acres on the east side of the base, and came under mortar and automatic-weapons fire during Tet.

General Cao Van Vien, chairman of the RVN Armed Forces Joint General Staff (RVNAF JGS), was headquartered in the built-up area outside eastern Tan Son Nhut. The JGS compound was also hit by a major attack during Tet.

Two months earlier, Westmoreland had told reporters that the enemy could mount major actions only from the remote border base camps into which they had been pushed. COMUSMACV intended to crush these base camps and predicted that the U.S. could begin withdrawing from Vietnam by 1969. Nevertheless, Westmoreland would always contend that the Tet Offensive was not a surprise. Brigadier General Phillip B. Davidson, the chief MACV intelligence officer, later wrote that the premature attack up north had "provided the key tip-off to the waiting Allies." It was thus that January 30 "was a hectic day," the J2 continued. ". . . I briefed General Westmoreland at 0700 hours, telling him about the enemy attacks in mid-South Vietnam and forecasting that similar assaults should be expected throughout the rest of South Vietnam that night. Westmoreland promptly agreed. He called his senior commanders, warning them to expect heavy enemy attacks on the cities and headquarters in their areas that night, and placed his entire command under a maximum alert."

Westmoreland persuaded President Nguyen Van Thieu to order all RVNAF personnel on leave to return immediately to their units. "The evening presented an incongruous spectacle," according to Davidson. While the South Vietnamese people, "refusing to believe that even the Communists would violate the sanctity of Tet, celebrated with parties and fireworks[,]" the U.S. and RVNAF high commands "furiously prepared for the onslaught which they knew was sure to come that night . . ."

Davidson's account is unconvincing. The evidence is clear that the command expected only a smattering of light attacks. President Thieu remained on holiday in My Tho, and the RVNAF recall was a half-hearted affair at best. Having made no effort to shift units to the cities, General Westmoreland retired for the evening to his villa in downtown Saigon. Protected only by a small security element, COMUSMACV would be stranded there when Tet began, unable to return to his headquarters until late morning. In his first conversation with reporters he would state that the fighting in and around Saigon was only a diversion to the main attack still to come at Khe Sanh.

Vien and Davidson were also cut off in their quarters when the battle began, as were most headquarters personnel living in lightly defended billets throughout Saigon, including, ironically, two hundred colonels from the MACV J2 staff who attended a pool party at one of the billets only hours before the attacks started.

As a result, Pentagon East was only partially operational when the crisis began. Davidson's postwar account also clashes with the unvarnished comments Brigadier General

John Chaisson, USMC, director of the MACV Combat Operations Center, made at a news conference on the third day of Tet. "[A]s I read the intelligence it did not indicate that we were going to have any such massive spread of attacks as this," he said. "I've got to give [the enemy] credit for having engineered and planned a very successful offensive, in its initial phases. It was surprisingly well coordinated, it was surprisingly intensive . . ."

Prior to the Tet Offensive, there had been only two attacks on the Tan Son Nhut Air Base—a shelling in April 1966, and a platoon-size sapper raid shortly after midnight on December 4, 1966. The SPs lost three dead and fifteen wounded in the latter action. Twenty-eight VC were killed and four captured. "The squadron was very high on the fact that they had wiped out all the attackers," recalled Major Carl A. Bender, who was assigned as the 377th SPS Operations Officer in April 1967. Bender, however, was concerned less with the heroism displayed by the security police during the firefight itself than he was with the fact that the sappers had cut through the west perimeter fence without detection and had almost reached the aircraft parking area before a sentry dog team finally sounded the alarm. They fired rocket-propelled grenades directly at the concrete revetments in the ensuing battle, damaging twenty aircraft.

"They came right on in, and tore things up pretty good," said Bender. "The VC should never have been able to penetrate as far as they did before they were engaged."

The problem was not complacency at the ground level—the 377th SPS was, in fact, a professional, highly spirited organization—but the low priority assigned to air base defense by higher command. Major Bender got a taste of that attitude during an orientation briefing conducted by an army colonel at MACV HQ on his second day in-country. Standing before the roomful of new officers, the colonel described the U.S. Army and ARVN operations around Saigon, then—turning to security issues—stated that because of this screen the largest enemy force the Air Force would ever have to face at Tan Son Nhut would be a 200-man company. Anything bigger would be detected by the infantry, as would any attempt to preposition the weapons and ammunition needed for a full-scale attack.

Disgusted, Major Bender got up to leave. It was because of just this overconfident mind-set that the 377th SPS had neither heavy weapons, adequate perimeter bunkers, an adequate minefield, nor perimeter lighting when it was needed. The lighting system at Tan Son Nhut was installed only after the successful sapper penetration.

"This briefing isn't over," the colonel snapped.

"If that's the best information you have, I can't feature anything else being of value to me," Bender said.

"Just how long have you been in-country?" the colonel asked, trying to put him in his place.

Glancing at his watch, the peppery, hot-tempered Major Bender replied, "Just shy of forty-eight hours."

"That makes you an expert, I guess?"

"No, sir, but this is my fourth tour to the Orient. I know what these people can do," Bender said. During an earlier assignment in Japan, he had been stunned by the way the locals could sneak in at night, pull up aluminum runway matting, and make off with it right under the noses of the air police, as the security police were then known.

"Oh, is that right?" the colonel said, unimpressed.

"Yes, sir," Bender said evenly.

"Then just what is *your* assessment, Major?"

Bender's answer got him excused from the briefing. "Anytime, day or night," he said, "at any point on the twelve-mile perimeter at Tan Son Nhut, they can put an attacking force of two thousand through the wire."

Lieutenant Colonel Billy Jack Carter took over the 377th SPS in July 1967. He was of the same mind as Bender, and much energy was put into improving the security of Tan Son Nhut AB. Certain problems defied resolution, though. "[L]ivestock grazed in allegedly mined areas," noted one official history. The perimeter minefield had not stopped the sapper raid, nor would it have much effect on the Tet attack. "Old minefields of Japanese and French vintage should be removed and replaced," Bender wrote in his end-of-tour report, pleading for engineer support. The issue was complicated because Tan Son Nhut was a Vietnamese base, and the 7th Air Force was only a tenant unit. Government permission was required for all construction projects. "We should . . . insist on total perimeter minefields even adjacent to housing and industrial areas," Bender wrote, convinced that the Vietnamese were reluctant to approve a comprehensive defensive plan because they wanted to leave open "avenues for pilferage[,] which is abundant."

The 377th SPS divided the base into six sectors. Each sector NCOIC had two gun jeeps, and the troops needed to man a share of the fifty perimeter bunkers and towers, with additional internal positions. The 1,000-man squadron had some fourteen Quick Reaction Teams (QRTs) in reserve, each with an NCOIC, a two-man machine-gun team, and ten troops. "We ran an exercise or two," recalled Bender, "and it took forty-five minutes to roust the QRTs from the barracks and to get them armed, loaded up on trucks, and then out into the various sectors where they would be deployed in the event of an attack. Well, you give these gooks a forty-five-minute head start, there's no sense in going to the ball game because it's over."

Much delay occurred at the armory, where each man had to sign for his weapon by serial number. Under Carter, the troops used presigned gun cards, which they could quickly exchange for their weapons and ammunition. "Eventually, we got the response time down to twelve minutes from our barracks area to any point on the perimeter," said Bender. The SP barracks were in the built-up quarter of the base, southwest of where the main east-west runways intersected the north-south runways. "We got ton-and-a-half trucks out of civil engineering, and we'd line them up on the street in our cantonment area," noted Bender. There were placards with team numbers on the prepositioned trucks. To avoid lines at the armory, the QRTs finally checked out their armaments every night. Each team's weapons, ammunition, grenades, flares, and handheld radios could be neatly fit into a single aluminum military casket. These caskets were then placed on the trucks and covered with a tarpaulin to keep them dry. The trucks had guards posted on them. "Every morning, we had to unload those trucks, unload those caskets, clean every weapon, and put every weapon back in the armory," said Bender.

* * *

For security officers, Tet was always a nervous time. The throngs of holiday travelers, the massive number of ARVN troops on leave, the firecrackers and festivals provided the communists with excellent opportunities for surprise attack. "We did not have intelligence, but Lieutenant Colonel Carter and I had our own indicators, which we would access," recalled Bender. "You get gut feelings—and we both had some gut feelings that *something* might happen during Tet. It was little things. . . ."

Thousands of Vietnamese workers came through the main gates at Tan Son Nhut every morning. There was a civilian terminal in the air base and an old cemetery inside the west perimeter. Carter and Bender were convinced that enemy scouts were among the Vietnamese who used the airport and visited the cemetery. Forged passes were easy to obtain given all the "crap, crud, and corruption"—as Bender put it—among the ARVN, VNAF, and Vietnamese National Police at Tan Son Nhut. "One of our troops at a checkpoint stopped some monks in the traditional orange garb. I said to pat them down before they came on base, but the Vietnamese policeman wouldn't touch them," said Bender. "He's not going to touch the holy man. I wasn't so inclined, and when I got down there I used the front muzzle of my M16 to push the hoods off—and all the heads weren't shaved. They didn't come on base. I caught hell for that, but it was suspicious to me. I said, 'I don't care who they are—it can be Christ and the Twelve Disciples—we're gonna check 'em out if they're gonna come on base.'"

The increased number of burials in cemeteries near the base also seemed odd, and one week before Tet, the Joint Defense Operations Center (JDOC), which coordinated all ground, air, and fire-support elements in the Tan Son Nhut Sensitive Area (TSNSA), held a readiness exercise. (During periods of increased readiness, the 377th SPS had operational control of Task Force 35, a reaction force raised from army support units at Tan Son Nhut.) The exercise concentrated on the west end of the base as it was the shortest, easiest route to the aircraft parking area, the rice-paddy country there allowing the enemy to move up with less chance of detection than in the built-up areas south and east of the base. The area to the north was also open, but an attacker penetrating from that direction would have to move through four kilometers of bomb and fuel storage areas to reach the aircraft revetments.

The Tet cease-fire began on January 29. It was canceled at 0945, January 30, after the first wave of enemy attacks. Westmoreland issued his "maximum alert" at 1125, and at 1730, General Momyer declared "security condition red" for all air bases in South Vietnam. "By then, we'd already made up our minds what we were going to do," Bender said. Alarmed by the local indications of impending attack, Lieutenant Colonel Carter had instructed the 377th SPS to immediately return fire if fired upon that night. "We'd been sticking our necks out until the red alert was declared," said Bender. "[T]he rules [of engagement] usually required that each fire mission [around a city] receive prior political and military approval from RVN authorities," noted an official USAF history. "Many times these officials omitted, delayed, or refused fire-clearance requests—arousing anger and frustration among U.S. forces. Rigid enforcement of the rules of engagement and the glaring publicity given the prosecution of violators made most commanders hesitant about exercising their right of self-defense."

Carter and Bender had also already decided to increase the number of troops on the bunker line, and to preposition the Quick Reaction Teams. "After dark, we had all the QRTs fully deployed at various points on the perimeter," Bender recalled. "You're in a fish bowl. Anything you do they know what you're up to, so we dummied up the trucks and had them sitting in the cantonment area like normal— but we had sneaked the QRTs out on foot. They took the blankets off their cots, and the word was, 'Roll up and sleep. If nothing happens, we'll bring you back at dawn.'"

The 377th SPS was prepared for a guerrilla attack. It was not expecting the Tet Offensive. "We didn't realize what we were facing. Even when we were in the midst of the battle, we couldn't believe the severity of what was going on," said Captain DeNisio. The Tan Son Nhut attack was planned by Colonel Nam Truyen, commander of the 9th VC Division, and it involved one regiment from his division—the 271st

Main Force (MF) Regiment—plus four attached battalions: the 2d Independent Battalion, the D-16 Battalion, and the 267th and 269th MF Battalions. The cadres in these units were southerners, but due to casualties, about half of the soldiers were fillers from the North Vietnamese Army.

The attack force numbered 2,665 VC and NVA.

Disguised as a student home for the holidays, Colonel Truyen, a youthful looking thirty-five-year-old, had entered Tan Son Nhut during the truce on Christmas Day 1967. "One of his regimental commanders paid a call on the 'family grave site' in a government military cemetery near the giant air base," it was later reported. "All of the visitors were supplied with forged identity papers. None reported any trouble at the police checkpoints on their way into the city or on their way back to their jungle posts."

The communists marched to their final attack positions during the night of January 30–31, 1968. The 2d Independent Battalion and the bulk of the 271st MF Regiment were responsible for taking the JGS HQ and for the secondary attacks on Tan Son Nhut. (Simultaneously, two battalions from the 101st VC Regiment seized the ARVN Armored Command HQ and the ARVN Artillery Training Camp in Go Vap, a suburb a kilometer east of Tan Son Nhut. The VC had NVA tank crews with them to drive the captured tanks into the air base, but they discovered that all the tanks had previously been moved out of the compound. Likewise, the ARVN removed the breechblocks from their howitzers before withdrawing, rendering them useless.)

The command post for the main attack was the Vinatexco Textile Mill on the west shoulder of Highway 1 a kilometer northwest of the 051 Gate. The 350-man D-16 Battalion occupied the factory grounds to protect the headquarters group that established itself inside the main mill building and to provide suppressive fires from the roof. The heavy-weapons company from each of the three assault battalions also fell out at the factory and dug hasty machine-gun positions in the surrounding rice paddies that would play havoc with helicopter support during the battle.

The 300-man 269th MF Battalion spearheaded the attack on the 051 Gate. The 267th MF Battalion and the 1st Battalion, 271st Regiment were in column formation behind it. The attack was "on a very narrow front," noted a U.S. after-action report. "The lead battalion's mission was to effect a penetration, the second battalion in line was to exploit the penetration, and the third battalion in line was to destroy the equipment and facilities at TSN. . . ."

Like the army generals, the ten USAF generals headquartered at Tan Son Nhut were in for a rude awakening. "Their living quarters were modular units resembling mobile homes, surrounded by a high cyclone fence," it was later reported. When the base command post hit the rocket siren, the generals ducked into the bunker in their small compound. Only a captain serving as aide to one of the generals had a weapon—a .38-caliber pistol. One VC reached the compound "and climbed a telephone pole next to the fence. Fortunately, he had no idea where he was. Instead of jumping into the compound and running no more than fifty feet to the bunker with all the generals huddled inside, he focused his attention and his automatic rifle on late-night revelers trying to flee out the front door of the officers club [across the street] which was open about twenty hours a day to accommodate the hours of pilots flying missions around the clock." The aide with the pistol "would have been no match for the [VC] with the automatic rifle who was eventually killed [by the security police]."

When the attack began, Lieutenant Colonel Carter was asleep in his quarters, and Bender had just returned to his own room across the hall in the same three-story barracks. Previously, both had been in CSC. With everything still quiet at two in the morning, however, Bender had suggested that the squadron commander should catch up on his sleep. "I'll stay out here for another hour. If nothing happens by three, it may not happen at all," Bender said. There were also several assistant operations officers in CSC. "Half you guys knock off. We can't *all* stay up all night—somebody's gotta run this base in the morning," Bender told them. He went unheeded. The young lieutenants were too pumped up with adrenaline. "Well, I can see how much help I'm going to have in the morning," Bender finally said with a grin. "I'm going to go back and hit the sack."

Awakened by a phone call, Carter shouted across the hallway to Major Bender that the attack had started, then drove to his command post in the white bombproof JDOC blockhouse. Bender jumped in his own jeep and headed for the main gate—Gate 1—on the southeast side of the base. There was a fierce exchange in progress between the SPs at the checkpoint and snipers firing from the multistoried buildings across the street. Ensuring that the metal gate had been closed and locked, Bender started towards an adjacent entrance way—Gate 2—but had to slam the brakes on and bail out when fire from the rooftops began hitting the road and ricocheting into the underside of his jeep. Moving forward on foot with several security policemen, Bender was enraged to discover that the ARVN troops responsible for the gate had deserted their checkpoint, leaving behind a Browning Automatic Rifle (BAR).

Pinned down, Bender's group was unable to reach the checkpoint. "Boy, if we could just get that weapon going," a senior NCO said, referring to the abandoned BAR.

"You got experience with that weapon?" Bender asked.

"I carted one of those around over my shoulder for many a mile," the old sergeant answered.

Bender organized some cover fire, and the sergeant made it to the checkpoint with two other SPs. The NCO began pumping away with the BAR, and Bender rushed back to his jeep. When the major reached CSC, he found that his lieutenants were out with the troops. Sergeant Bloom was the senior man on duty. "Most of the troops never laid eyes on [Bloom], but all knew his [steady] voice—and really were calmed by him," Lieutenant Grover wrote. At that time, DeNisio and Grover were pinned down by Tango 4. Not fully appreciating their precarious situation, Bender was getting steamed. "I was trying to get things organized, and I needed them to feed back quality information—and I wasn't getting it," he recalled. "Instead, I was getting a lot of excited talk from a hundred different radios. The enemy was hitting from all directions, and everybody was chattering on the radio at the same time. The plotter wasn't really able to keep up with things at the mapboard, and I wasn't getting good feedback on where we were, where they were, how far they had broken through, or what we needed to do."

Bender was presently joined by Technical Sergeant Bernard C. Gifford, a liaison NCO assigned to Task Force 35. There were three platoons in the task force, each with its own liaison sergeant from the 377th SPS. Gifford had Army 1. It was the first platoon to respond, and Bender quickly briefed Gifford at the mapboard, pointing first at the west end of the base then slashing a vertical line with his finger at a point to the east: "They're comin' in *here,* and I want you to catch up with the Echo QRT and get on line across *here.* "

Gifford felt his stomach tighten. "Major, I only have twenty-eight days left," he said with a hollow laugh. "Are you *sure* that's where you want me to go?"

Bender told him to get moving, and Gifford got back behind the wheel of his weapons carrier—the army platoon leader, a lieutenant, was sitting beside him—and struck out into the dark, followed by the truck carrying Army 1. "Being that we [liaison NCOs] knew the terrain, we were to respond with [the] soldiers if attacked, and guide them in the right direction," Gifford later wrote, adding that as they headed toward the flash and din at the west end of the base, "[m]y left knee was shaking and I could not stop it. . . ."

Prepositioned near the flight line, the Quick Reaction Team assigned to Sector E had moved in on foot in advance of Task Force 35. "Security Control, [this is] Echo QRT," the team leader radioed CSC. "We have reached the end of the high-speed taxiway. 10-32 [Furnish Data]."

"That's 10-4. Deploy yourself there. Army 1 is in route. Deploy together, and move slowly towards Oh-5-1 Gate."

"10-4," the team leader answered.

"Do you copy, Army 1?" Bloom asked.

There was no answer from Army 1, its entry into the battle too confusing to maintain constant radio contact with CSC. Mortar rounds were exploding as Sergeant Gifford stopped on the taxiway about fifty meters short of where the army lieutenant planned to organize their line. "We didn't want the truck to get blown up," he later explained. "The next thing I realized, my two machine gunners had gotten off the truck and were running up the taxiway the wrong way—not away from the battle, but right into it. There was too much firing and noise for them to hear us trying to call them back, and I never saw them again."

The team was probably cut down. Records indicate that two GIs, a sergeant and his ammo bearer, were indeed killed that night while manning an M60 with Task Force 35. Meanwhile, Gifford and the lieutenant had gotten the rest of Army 1 detrucked and deployed. "These idiots just started shootin', shootin', shootin'," recalled Gifford, who bellowed out, "What the hell are you guys shootin' at?!"

Someone screamed, *"I see 'em, Sarge, I can see 'em!"*

There were only a few flares going off at the time, and Gifford held his fire, unable to see a thing and convinced that the troops were getting panicky. The GIs assigned to Task Force 35—who had helmets and flak jackets like the SPs, but being support troops had old M14s instead of M16s—were mostly from the 1st Signal Brigade. "None of them were infantrymen," noted Gifford. "They were cooks and clerks and supply people, and some of them didn't even know how to load their weapons. At one point, I found a machine gunner who had his ammo belt laid in upside down. If he had fired, he would have just gotten off one round, and then it wouldn't have fed anymore."

The state of confusion was general. "Army 2 to Security Control," the next reaction force leader radioed in after piling up on the taxiway behind the first platoon from Task Force 35. "I seen two people moving east. As long as there's no flare support here [from helicopters or a flareship], I cannot distinguish if its Charlie [VC] or Army 1."

"10-4. Do you have flares?"

"Negative. . . ."

The Echo QRT put up slap-flares for the GIs, and also reported unidentified troops "moving toward the high-speed taxiway from the outer perimeter fence."

"Can you intercept?" Bloom asked.

"10-4," the team leader answered.

As the Echo QRT started forward again, Sergeant Steve Rivers, the NCOIC on Tango 1, called Bloom, "The VC [have seen the Echo QRT] and are now headed towards [it]."

25

"Unable to see anybody," the team leader answered.

Muzzle flashes suddenly erupted in the dark. The security policemen hit the deck on the taxiway and returned fire. The VC/NVA were only about fifty meters away, having advanced over two hundred meters from the breached gate. They had almost reached the edge of the flight line, but stalled by the SPs' fire, the enemy sought cover among the burial mounds in the cemetery where the taxiway curved to the north and was designated Whiskey 8.

"Tango 1 to Security Control," Rivers radioed in. "Tell the Echo [QRT] to fire lower. They're laying right below their fire. . . . The VC are just on the other side of the high-speed taxiway. They're firing over their heads. . . ."

Moments later, Rivers warned that VC were moving down a drainage ditch in an attempt to outflank the Echo QRT. The team's M60 gunner fired a long burst into the group, hitting several of them. "We're running low on ammo," the team leader reported then.

"10-4. Use it conservatively. . . ."

Bender took several calls from 7th Air Force Headquarters and provided what information he could about the penetration at the west end of the base. The decision was made to shut down all air operations. "I've got men and equipment at the far end of the runway," Bender reported. "If you can take off in half the runway length, and break hard to the left, you might clear out, but they've got enough firepower to blast anything out of the sky right now. As far as I'm concerned, I wouldn't take off."

Frustrated, Bender said to Bloom, "I'm going out and find Mobile 5-6 [DeNisio], and get things assessed so that we can plot it on the map. I should be back shortly."

Major Bender never made it back to Central Security Control. The JDOC and CSC buildings faced the aircraft parking revetments along Whiskey 7, the high-speed taxiway that paralleled the main runways. Shortly before Bender moved out, an SP at one of the interior guard posts in Sector D, which included the revetments, radioed CSC, "Be advised, I have personnel out here in the [VNAF] C47 area. They seem to be putting something under the planes, and running back into the bushes whenever there's a flare."

Enemy sappers were, in fact, placing explosives under the out-of-date, prop-driven C47 gunships and flareships in the revetments along the south side of the taxiway, overlooking the valuable RF4 reconnaissance jets lined up in the revetments on the north side. Fourteen aircraft were damaged, either by the sappers or by the Delta QRT, which engaged the enemy, the VNAF personnel in the area, and at one point in the confusion, a guard post, wounding a fellow airman with automatic-weapons fire.

Bender gunned his jeep down the taxiway between the two rows of revetments, with red U.S.-issue tracers zipping past. "This is Warrior," he shouted on the radio. "Cease fire on Delta Row. *You're shooting into friendly air crews!*"

Up ahead, the situation looked even worse. Given the obvious target his jeep was, Major Bender left it on the taxiway after clearing the aircraft revetments, and proceeded on foot to link up with Army 2. "There's too much enemy fire to move up and counterattack at this time," Bender told Bloom. He wanted an ammo resupply immediately brought forward for the Echo QRT. He also wanted the "[p]eople standing by outside [CSC]" to "start picking up additional flares . . . As soon as they have transportation, move them down to Whiskey 7 for immediate deployment in case of a breakthrough [past the Echo QRT and TF 35]."

Bender was in contact with Mobile 5-6 via handheld radio, and he was anxious to get DeNisio and Grover back before it was too late. "Can you start your vehicle. Can you just reach in and *start* it?" Bender asked. Grover crawled up onto the elevated road and got the shot-up jeep running while lying beside it. The starter was on the floorboard. "Okay, hold tight," Bender said while JDOC patched him through to one of their gunships. "I want you to make a pass just outside the perimeter fence, but not past the tower at the elbow in the road," Bender told the pilot, stressing the narrow margin for error. "I've got two officers pinned down there. If you can make everybody keep their heads down, that'll be their opportunity to pull out."

Bender prayed as the Huey rolled in, machine guns

blazing. The scheme worked flawlessly. Meanwhile, the Echo QRT—on line at the curve in the taxiway—was firing furiously from the prone, taking fire from both the enemy and confused members of Task Force 35.

"Security Control, [this is] Echo QRT!" the team leader angrily shouted. *"We need some ammo!"*

Bender jumped on the net. "Echo QRT, this is Warrior. I'm about two, three hundred yards right behind you. I'm moving up with Army Platoon 2. We have M60 ammo."

Major Bender climbed aboard the weapons carrier sitting on the taxiway, and after slinging belts of machine-gun ammunition over his shoulders and stuffing his pockets with hand grenades, he recruited two GIs to leapfrog forward with him by fire-and-maneuver. Moving along the north side of the taxiway, Bender had covered some fifty meters when he realized that he was by himself. The signalmen-turned-riflemen had hung back. Bender screamed at them to come on—then ended up pinned down on his back as enemy fire cracked past so close that one round stung his ear and another caught him in his upper left arm, taking a chunk of muscle with it on the way out. He couldn't bandage the wound. He couldn't move without getting killed. He was convinced that this was it.

Finally able to turn his head a bit, Bender spotted some muzzle flashes. The enemy was in the cemetery. He rolled onto his side long enough to splatter one of the headstones with his M16, then dropped flat on his back again. The burst momentarily silenced the enemy, and Bender sprang to his feet and sprinted the rest of the way to the Echo QRT.

The team was fully exposed on the white concrete, and the M60 gunner and another airman had been shot. The troops had been so busy returning fire that they didn't realize they were being outflanked. Bender wanted them to fall back, but they simply began firing away again with the ammo he had brought. Bender turned to the casualties and bandaged one's leg wound. "I can't do anything for you, not out here," he said to the other man, who had hip and groin injuries. Bender used the troop's web belt to secure his legs together. "You give me cover fire, and I'll get you back," Bender said, handing his M16 to the machine gunner. The other casualty still had his M16. Bender wrapped an arm around each man, and started running backwards, hauling them along, their feet dragging as they fired.

While moving back, Bender shouted to the QRT, "If you think this thirty-eight-year-old major is coming out here with another supply of ammunition, you're full of shit!"

The Echo QRT began pulling back with Bender.

2

Holding the Line

By the time Captain DeNisio jumped in Grover's jeep, he was down to two magazines for his CAR15. It was definitely time to get out. The gunship provided the perfect cover. "We turned the jeep around and breezed out of there," recalled Lieutenant Grover, who sped north out of harm's way before looping back toward the battlefield on the taxiway and linking up with the rearmost element of Task Force 35. "The GIs looked dazed. They were standing in the middle of the damn taxiway, not too sure where they were or what was going on. They needed a little direction. We started forming them up and moving them forward."

Major Bender appeared then, dragging the two wounded troops from the Echo QRT. "Security Control from Warrior," he radioed in. "How 'bout that ambulance?"

Sergeant Bloom could not hear what Bender wanted, given all the radios chattering in CSC, and Warrior exploded, *Get that goddamn ambulance down here!*"

It was unclear when the ambulance would arrive, so Grover ran the hundred meters back up the taxiway to where he had ditched his jeep; he was bringing it down to evacuate the casualties himself when a bullet suddenly hit the center of his steel helmet like a sledgehammer. Stunned, he felt his forehead as he kept driving—it was all wet—then looked at his hand in the flarelight, trying to see how badly he was bleeding. There was no blood, only sweat. His helmet had been dented and blown into the back of the jeep, but it had saved his life.

Grover stopped next to the wounded SPs. Bender had always felt rather fatherly toward this bespectacled, clean-cut, highly motivated lieutenant, and as he loaded the casualties into the jeep, he shouted, "Goddamnit, Mel, where's your helmet? With all this lead flying around, don't you ever come out here without your helmet on!"

Grover was too rattled to explain. "The guy in the back's bad," Bender said, indicating the airman with the groin and hip injuries. "Get 'em to the hospital!"

Lieutenant Grover made a U-turn and sped off, intending to find the ambulance, transfer the casualties, and return to the battle. "I got all the way back into the center of the base," recalled Grover, who was subsequently awarded a Bronze Star Medal for Valor (BSMv). There was a sand-bagged checkpoint that controlled traffic onto the flight line, "and I was just passing through there as the ambulance came roaring through the other way. It had its lights out and our guys fired at it. The rounds either went high or hit the ambulance and ricocheted up because I remember seeing the tracers going up. I just floored it."

Instead of chasing the ambulance back past the trigger-happy guards, Grover turned onto the main road and took the casualties right to the front door of the base dispensary. Along the way, he had another close encounter. "Most of the lights on the base were out by then. I was nearing 7th Air Force Headquarters when I realized a law enforcement patrol had pulled up in front of the building and was deploying off its gun jeep. I flashed my lights because I was convinced they were going to hose me down and blow my ass away, just like somebody tried to do to the ambulance!"

Dodging fire of all sorts, especially mortar shells, which sent everyone ducking at regular intervals, DeNisio managed to get Army 1 and 2 in a north-south firing line that extended into the open area at the end of the main runway, its left flank anchored on the east-west Whiskey 7 taxiway. Bender and the Echo QRT moved into position on the right flank. The line was seventy meters east of north-south

Whiskey 8. The enemy was just on the other side of the concrete strip, silhouetted by the slap-flares popping overhead. "Aim! Aim and squeeze 'em off on semi," Bender shouted as excited SPs and GIs—almost all of them in combat for the first time—sprayed away on full automatic. The troops were at the prone, almost shoulder to shoulder in the grass, and Bender had them number off in groups of four in an attempt to control the firing. "Fire in sequence! Don't everybody be firing at the same damn time—especially if you haven't got a target!"

Major Bender kicked one airman in the ass who had his face buried in the sand as he fired his M16 without looking. "Hey, when you're out of ammunition, nobody's going to be here to save you, friend!" Bender shouted.

The enemy died in bunches at the western edge of Whiskey 8. "They tried to cross the taxiway and never made it," said Captain DeNisio, a cocksure officer on the fast track from upstate New York who won the Silver Star during Tet. The VC/NVA fired AK-47s and RPGs across the taxiway, but only a half-dozen airmen and soldiers were wounded. Bender picked up several superficial fragment wounds, but barely noticed them in the heat of the moment.

Lieutenant Colonel Carter in JDOC, and Grover, who the squadron commander had ordered to take over at CSC in lieu of Bender, kept the reaction teams and ammunition coming. Reinforcements literally piled on at the point of penetration. Lieutenant Colonel Luu Kim Cuong, commander of the 33d VNAF Air Wing, led a composite group of staff officers, air police, ARVN service troops, and National Police into position southwest of the 377th SPS line. Major Phung Van Chieu, the TSNSA Defense Commander, brought up three light tanks from the personal security force of Vice President Nguyen Cao Ky, who lived on base with his family, and who spent the battle in JDOC.

Lieutenant Colonel Cuong was wounded in the leg. Chieu took fragments in his face, and one of his lieutenants was hit three times while manning the .50-caliber heavy machine gun atop one of the tanks. Artillery fire crashed into the VC mortar positions a hundred meters due west of Tango 4. "The barrage was right on target. The ground trembled," noted Bender. There were secondary explosions as the mortar ammo went up. "The enemy was still moving toward their objective, and we were bringing blocking forces in to pinch them in and hold them in the center," DeNisio said. Along with the ARVN and VNAF, the reaction teams deploying north and south of Whiskey 8 put the enemy in a wicked crossfire. In effect, as the enemy advanced toward the main firing line, they entered the open end of a horseshoe of fire. "They could not move to the north, they could not move to the south. They were funneled. To get to the runway and the aircraft, they had to come through us. We were burning ammo, but we had weapons carriers and trucks and jeeps, and there was plenty of munitions being brought up, plenty of munitions. . . ."

The breach was sealed. The enemy appeared to be in retreat. "Is there any reason why we cannot move directly forward towards the Oh-5-1 Gate in a skirmish line?" Captain DeNisio asked CSC. There was, Bloom said. JDOC was organizing an artillery bombardment of the west perimeter, to be followed by a counterattack by ARVN paratroopers presently marching into the area. Their presence was pure happenstance. Two airborne battalions had moved to Tan Son Nhut the day before for transport to the Khe Sanh area. The failure of a staff officer to request the planes on time left the ARVN paratroopers camping on base, and when the attacks started, both battalions were available for emergency use throughout the Saigon area.

DeNisio said that the artillery could not be fired that close because friendly elements were still in the area. For one, there was Airman Tucker in Tango 4. "He was in the enemy's backyard. He was muted on his transmissions and he was careful not to be that visible," noted DeNisio, who was surprised that one of the enemy soldiers hustling past the little tower didn't blow it down with an RPG. The tower was only hit by AK-47 fire, which did not penetrate its armored walls. "I believe he was unconscious for a while because there was a lot of concussion when the fire hit that tower. He went quiet for a while on the radio."

Tucker won the Silver Star when the enemy simply got too close for the airman to continue playing possum. "He was picking them off underneath him," said Bender. Tucker was afraid the enemy would climb the ladder up to his perch. "I was trying to get him to keep his head down. He'd keep his head down so far, and then I'd see him peeping over the side again, and he's blast at somebody else that was approaching the legs of the tower."

Bender and DeNisio were also concerned about the five airmen in the 051 Bunker. "Is there any way we can withdraw these troops?" Bloom asked.

"That's negative. The VC are retreating in their direction. We're firing into them," DeNisio said.

At that point, Sergeant Palmer, the Sector E NCOIC, informed CSC that he was also in the area being targeted for shelling. Palmer was south of the 051 Gate, firing his pedestal-mounted M60 from the back of his jeep. Bloom consulted with JDOC, then called DeNisio again: "We have five minutes to get [Palmer, Tucker, and Fischer's team] out of the area [before the artillery commences fire]."

Under heavy fire, Palmer was only able to make it to the VNAF perimeter bunker immediately south of the 051 Bunker. Meanwhile, the Echo QRT on the right flank of the firing line spotted an enemy squad moving north along the taxiway in an effort to outflank the line. "We have no M16 ammo!" the team leader shouted.

The Alpha QRT had just assumed a blocking position to the north. "Get the lead out," Bloom said. "Go south—there are VC going around to the right of Echo QRT."

Bloom reported to DeNisio that "Alpha QRT is in route now. I don't know whether he's going to make it to head 'em off or not." At this time, First Lieutenant Gerald E. Ingalsbe, an assistant operations officer, was coming up Whiskey 7 from CSC with two more reaction teams. "Attempt to join up with Alpha QRT," Bloom told Ingalsbe. "There are VC sweeping around to the north of the location of Echo QRT."

"Echo QRT! *We need some M16 ammo!*"

Major Bender was with the Bravo QRT, which had just joined the main firing line. The operations officer could see the single-file, ten-man VC/NVA squad, and the RPG launcher that one of them was carrying. "I was trying to point them out to the guys on the line, but the enemy kept dropping down," Bender recalled. "They'd jump up, run about five or ten yards, and drop down in the grass. They kept disappearing." Frustrated, Bender—another Silver Star winner this night—ran after them behind his firing line. "I knew where they dropped the last time, so I popped a flare and waited for them to get up. I was sighted in. I was in a kneeling position, and I was waiting. When the first one came up, I gave him a couple rounds."

The enemy squad immediately dropped down when their lead man was hit, and opened fire in Bender's direction. Unconsciously remembering some old lessons, Bender shot the last man in the file instead of the first man when the VC/NVA squad moved out again. As they leapfrogged along the taxiway, the enemy soldiers were unaware that he was keeping pace with them, pausing to kneel, sight in, and pump two or three quick rounds into each last-place man in turn, hitting them in the waist from the side. Bender got so excited that he stood up once to fire, but he always hustled to a new position as soon as he completed the last trigger pull, his muzzle flash having given him away to other enemy soldiers out across the taxiway.

Bender killed eight of the ten guerrillas. Concerned about getting caught in the Alpha QRT's blocking fires, the major then hustled back to the main line. Renewed mortar fire was impacting uncomfortably close at that time, and he pulled Army 1 and the Echo QRT back about fifty meters to get out from under the shelling. It was a matter, however, of jumping out of the frying pan and into the fire. "We are directly in front of one of the tanks—they're firing over our heads!" the Echo QRT leader radioed CSC.

"You gotta stop that tank!" Bender shouted to Bloom.

"We're contacting JDOC now. . . ."

Two of the ARVN tanks had already been disabled by RPG hits. The third tank was deployed along the southern edge of Whiskey 7, which gave it an unrestricted field of fire to the west. The crew had traversed its guns too far to the northwest, however. "They were going bonkers," Bender recalled. "They were just sweeping with that .50-cal and popping off main gun rounds. . . ."

To get out of the fire, the Echo QRT scooted back toward Lieutenant Ingalsbe. "We've got to get some sandbags under those barrels so that they can't drop the elevation into our lines," Bender said to Sergeant Gifford, the liaison NCO with Army 1. Another burst of machine-gun fire swept past, and they had to eat dirt again. "You see what I'm talking about?" Bender exclaimed. "I think that's Major Chieu up there on the tank. I'm going to give you about five minutes to get over there and tell 'em to stop firing, or get some sandbags under those barrels so he can't depress them into our lines—or I'm going to pick the sonofabitch off myself."

The terrain to the tank was wide open—and under fire from both directions—and Gifford looked incredulously at Bender. "You gotta be shittin' me," he blurted.

"Okay, *eight* minutes," Bender said.

Sergeant Gifford took off and secured the tank fire in short order. Bender could see Ingalsbe moving in from the east then. "It was pitch black, and I was concerned about who was going to be shooting at who," recalled Bender. "I radioed Jerry, 'Okay, I'm going to fire three flares. Just before the third flare hits the ground and goes out'—and this is the damnedest, dumbest thing you'd ever want to do in that situation—'I'm going to stand up with my rifle over my head so you know exactly where we are.'"

Bender stood up with his M16 held up in a two-handed grip like an infantryman guiding in a chopper, then dropped back down. Ingalsbe slid in without a hitch. The battle lulled as a predawn glow lightened the sky. The enemy was pulling out, and the ARVN paratroopers were ready to push forward. Major Bender loaded up with more ammo for his troops, then sprinted toward some bunched-up SPs on the south side of the line. He needed to get them spread out and organized for the counterattack. He never made it. The mortar shell that thunderclapped behind and a bit to his left propelled him some thirty feet through the air. He landed hard, his ears ringing. His helmet was still clamped on, but the back of his flak jacket was shredded.

"Security! This is Warrior!" Bender sounded out of breath. "We've been hit by mortars, including myself. . . . There are three casualties laying down here with me."

Lieutenant Ingalsbe jumped on the radio, too, requesting an ambulance for Bender. "It is in route," Bloom answered. "It should be there any time now. Just bear with us."

Bender was leaking like a sieve from his right leg, unable to control the bleeding with his belt or first-aid kit. There was a quarter-size fragment about two inches deep in the inside rear of his thigh, and a dime-size chunk in his calf. Bender did not realize it, he was so overloaded with adrenaline, but he had fifty-four wounds, to include his previous injuries. Mortar fragments had peppered him from the heel of his right foot, up both legs, in his back, down his left shoulder, arm, wrist, and hand, and up to his neck. Luckily, no bones had been broken, no organs hit.

Fearing an intramural firefight, Bender limped over to the approaching ARVN paratroopers and quickly oriented their advisor on who was where. There was still no ambulance in sight at that point, so several troops helped Bender into his jeep and he evacuated himself. He had a hard time with the vehicle—it was a stick shift, and his right leg wasn't working—and he weaved into the drainage ditch along the taxiway several times. Careening up to the dispensary, Bender bounced roughly over a parking bumper and hit the corner of the building. Medics rushed out with a stretcher. Bender was hurting so badly by then that he waved them away. "Don't touch me," he said. "Let me get out by myself." Bender cranked his left leg out. He could kind of stand on it with a medic supporting his elbow. "Okay, now bring that stretcher up behind me. *Lean* it up against me. Let me lean on it, and then lower me. . . ."

The base commander met Bender in the dispensary. Bender sketched a quick battle map for the colonel—"Get this to JDOC"—then got on the phone with the ops center as the medics worked on him. "Everything's holding," he said. "If we make it to sunup, we've got this thing whipped."

3

Ducks in a Row

The guerrillas usually broke contact before dawn so as to slip away before the full weight of supporting arms could punish them. This modus operandi seemed to be guiding the attackers at Tan Son Nhut. From the box seat on the water tower, Sergeant Rivers watched as enemy soldiers withdrew through a big hole in the perimeter fence in front of the 051 Bunker. "Tango 1 to Security Control," he radioed in. "Would it be possible to spearhead those [ARVN paratroopers] to the flank of Oh-5-1 Bunker? There's about twenty to thirty VC in the minefield, going through one at a time across the road into that village."

Gunships were already rolling in on the village, and only moments after Tango 1's report, Captain DeNisio informed CSC that "The [ARVN] are slowly moving out."

DeNisio stood by in reserve at the request of the advisor with the ARVN. The battles of the Tet Offensive occurred in a vacuum for the U.S. and ARVN troops fighting them. They did not understand the scope of the onslaught or that certain rules no longer applied. The ARVN paratroopers advanced confidently in a skirmish line toward the west perimeter fence. Moving quickly through the thigh-high grass, the ARVN were well out in the open beyond the taxiway when both wounded and able-bodied enemy soldiers who had been feigning death among the bodies suddenly swept the line from behind with their AK-47s.

Eighteen paratroopers were mowed down.

The massacre occurred just before Major Bender departed the scene in his jeep. "I had tried to caution the ARVN about wounded enemy in the grass, and I felt helpless seeing those men shot down like that in the back. . . ."

There were still more enemy ensconced among the burial mounds in front of the paratroopers, putting the ARVN in an intense crossfire. "We're [pinned down] about a hundred feet from that weapons carrier," radioed an SP sergeant who had been bringing his team up when the firing erupted anew. "Have you got enough cover?" Bloom asked. "I hope so," the sergeant quipped, providing CSC its only light moment of the morning. The situation was almost as intense and chaotic as the initial attack. While the paratroopers engaged an enemy squad maneuvering toward them, snipers fired on DeNisio's force from various directions, and, in return, the airmen blasted away at both the enemy and the ARVN. The survivors among the paratroopers began popping yellow smoke grenades to distinguish their positions from the Viet Cong.

When the perimeter was first breached, Major Chieu and Lieutenant Colonel Jack Garred, USA, senior advisor to the Vietnamese TSNSA Security Forces, had "requested reinforcement by at least a US [Army] Brigade" to seal the west flank of the battlefield, as noted in an after-action report. Now, in the midst of the renewed action, Garred called CSC to report that "within the next few minutes, I have an armored force coming down the highway outside the Oh-5-1 Gate. They're going to sweep the area. Hold what you have right now. Don't move anything until they make the sweep. . . ."

"Roger, will comply!" Bloom exclaimed.

Morale soared when Bloom passed the word to DeNisio. In short order, though, the phone rang again from JDOC. Bloom answered it, then got DeNisio back on the radio. "Be advised," he said, "the armored unit that was coming down outside the west perimeter has been engaged . . ."

Engaged—and stopped cold.

The cavalry force rushing to the rescue had been dispatched by the 25th Infantry Division, headquartered at Cu Chi base camp twenty-four kilometers northwest of Tan Son Nhut on Highway 1. The division's original instructions from corps—II Field Force, Vietnam (FFV), at Long Binh—had not been to reinforce the air base but to be prepared to deploy an armored cavalry troop above Hoc Mon, a large village one kilometer east of the highway between Cu Chi and Tan Son Nhut. The enemy attacking the air base might withdraw through the Hoc Mon area.

The 25th Division was the largest combat unit in the vicinity of Saigon, and Cu Chi was hit with rockets and mortars at the same time the Tan Son Nhut attack started. Shortly thereafter, at 0415 on January 31, 1968, the 25th Division G3 telephoned the operations officer of the division cavalry squadron—Lieutenant Colonel Glenn K. Otis's 3d Squadron, 4th Cavalry (the "Three-Quarter Horse"), which was also headquartered at Cu Chi—and relayed the Hoc Mon mission from II FFV. Otis's primary responsibility was securing Highway 1, the main supply route (MSR) between the Saigon–Long Binh depots and the 25th Division positions extending northwest along the highway to the Cambodian border. As such, Otis only had the headquarters and two platoons of Troop C available at Cu Chi, along with Troop D—an air cav unit with scout, gunship, and lift capabilities, and an aerorifle platoon. Troop C's detached platoon was guarding the Hoc Mon Bridge fourteen kilometers southeast of Cu Chi on the highway, while Troop B was at the Trang Bang Bridge fifteen kilometers northwest of Cu Chi, and Troop A was securing an artillery base at Go Dau Ha another thirteen kilometers up the MSR.

Lieutenant Colonel Otis's deployment of his units matched the tempo of the war. The enemy was up on the border, not in Saigon. "We were unprepared for Tet '68," Captain Leo B. Virant II, the Troop C commander, wrote after the war. Westmoreland's "maximum alert" order of the previous afternoon did not carry the gravity MACV later affixed to it to save face. It was, in fact, rather routine. "The most damning thing that happened (rather, didn't happen) was the total lack of combat intelligence available to the men and units that had to fight," Virant wrote. "At our squadron daily briefing, late afternoon the day before Tet '68, we were told: 'Something is going on but we don't know what'—sort of another 'cry wolf' which we frequently received."

Lieutenant Colonel Otis had one unit in reserve, thus only one option to the order from II FFV. Called to report to the squadron's Tactical Operations Center (TOC), Virant received the mission to be prepared to move to the intersection of Route 15 and the Hoc Mon Canal and act as a blocking force along the probable route of VC withdrawal. The squadron was loaded with West Pointers, including Otis and the three line troop commanders—all three captains had been classmates at the academy, Otis their math professor—and because the NCO corps had not yet been gutted by casualties and multiple tours, there were a good number of "old" sergeants down at the squad and platoon level. The squadron was not battle-hardened, but it was superbly led and relatively field-wise. Given his orders, Virant put his two available platoons on short-notice alert—the troops mounted their vehicles to await further orders—and briefed his platoon leaders. The situation was not extraordinary. The unit often operated at night, and there was nothing to indicate that the air base attack was anything more than a hit-and-run raid by a small guerrilla unit.

Charlie Troop had only recently returned to Cu Chi after weeks of field operations. "When we came into camp, we'd blow off a little steam," recalled Specialist Four Albert J. Porter. The GIs had virtually rushed from barracks to bunker with beer cans in hand during the shelling that night. Maybe a quarter of the troop was also buzzed on marijuana. The parties had died down by the time of the mount-up. Standing on their vehicles in the motor pool now, the sleepy, bleary-eyed troops could see gunships making firing runs right down the main street of Cu Chi village, which was nestled between the base camp and the highway. They did not know it, but a VC battalion had seized the village from the local militia unit and, having penetrated the advisory team compound, was proceeding to set it on fire.

Other 25th Division units in Cu Chi were cranking up to clear the village. "Hey, man, I heard a report the Chinese might be coming," one GI said in the motor pool.

"Oh, *bullshit!*" someone retorted.

"Where we going anyway?"

"We're going down to Hoc Mon."

"All right, man—Hoc Mon!" another GI exclaimed, thinking of the Popular Forces (PF) compound there where everything was for sale. "They got good dope, and *women!*"

The troopers were full of bravado because of their faith in their firepower. The two available platoons fielded three M48 tanks and ten "tracks"—M113 armored personnel carriers (APCs). Each tank had a 90mm main gun, and a .50-caliber machine gun mounted atop the commander's cupola. Each track also had a .50 for the commander, plus two M60s fixed in shields on the back deck.

At 0503, the order came to execute the Hoc Mon mission. Captain Virant and Troop C, 3d Squadron, 4th Cavalry were rolling within fourteen minutes, but had not even cleared the camp gate when there was a mission change. Charlie Troop was to proceed directly to Tan Son Nhut and counterattack the enemy force assaulting the base.

Captain Virant loved maps and happened to have one for the Saigon–Tan Son Nhut area in his map bag. It was the only one in the troop because this area was well to the rear of their normal area of operations (AO). Virant's command track moved with the lead platoon, Second Lieutenant James P. Pinto's Charlie Two, which was followed in the blacked-out column by Staff Sergeant Gary D. Brewer, the acting Charlie Three platoon leader. To steer clear of the action in Cu Chi village, which was on the main road connecting the base camp and Highway 1, Virant took a side gate out of camp, then followed the shoulder of a thin laterite road which ran in a diagonal line from the gate to the MSR. (Fifteen minutes later, the reaction force that rolled out the main gate to counterattack the VC in the village was shot to pieces on the main road.) To avoid possible mines or ambushes along the most direct route to the air base, Virant had elected to make a cross-country approach to their objective. Instead of swinging onto Highway 1 at the end of the laterite road, the column crossed over it, then turned southeast onto a back trail that paralleled Highway 1 down to Tan Son Nhut.

Lieutenant Colonel Otis flew over the column in a Huey gunship from Troop D which dropped flares, lighting the way and discouraging possible enemy action. Troop C reached the Hoc Mon Canal without incident. One of the tanks got stuck in the marshy ground there, and after it was pulled free with towing cables attached to another tank, Virant decided to wheel onto Highway 1, which was blacktopped and elevated some five feet from the flat terrain. As Charlie Two and Three passed through Charlie One's bridge position, "the 'word' on our tank was that a squad of VC was attempting to breach the wire at Tan Son Nhut," wrote Specialist Five Dwight W. Birdwell. Other troops had the impression that a few snipers had pinned down the rear-echelon air force personnel who worked on the flight line. Whatever the case, an easy body count was anticipated. "[Two] platoons of [Troop C] could handle a squad of VC any day," as Birdwell put it. "I remember thinking that the 1st [P]latoon was unfortunate because it would not be able to share the experience of teaching this rowdy squad of VC not to mess with one of our premier facilities. This experience would surely prove to be like shooting fish in a barrel."

"We were rolling fast down the road in good spirits," wrote Private First Class John Rourke, a mortar track crewman with Charlie Three. "A lot of guys were joking on the radio that we were going to Saigon for breakfast. . . ."

If the troops were eager for a stand-up battle, it was because their previous operations had been frustrating lessons in guerrilla warfare. The MSR security mission meant that "10 VC held down our 1000 man squadron," Captain Virant later wrote, and the search-and-destroy ops in the hamlet-rice-and-rain-forest country above Cu Chi had been like chasing phantoms. "We steadily took casualties, but rarely saw the enemy. We had overwhelming firepower but couldn't find the enemy to shoot."

It was fourteen kilometers from Cu Chi to Hoc Mon Bridge, another ten to Tan Son Nhut. Two klicks beyond the bridge, as the column "entered the crowded outskirts of

Saigon, visibility greatly improved with first light and I released the flareship," Virant wrote in his report. Lieutenant Colonel Otis's helicopter not only needed to refuel at that point, but when Troop C crossed the Hoc Mon Bridge it came under the opcon of the Vietnamese Capital Military District (CMD) in Saigon. Virant made radio contact with Lieutenant Colonel Garred, the TSNSA senior advisor, and Garred instructed him to rendezvous with an advisor from the Quan Tre Training Center who was waiting on the side of the highway in a jeep. The advisor would guide the troop to the location where it was needed. "This guide was met but could not provide any information on the current situation so I directed that he move his vehicle further back in the column," wrote Virant.

Not knowing what to expect, Captain Virant put a Charlie Three tank on point before proceeding on—the lead platoon had none that were operational—and had his command track fall in directly behind the tank "since I felt I could best command the troop from that forward location[.]" Virant could see tracers in the gray overcast twilight some distance down the highway—"direction of fire, primarily East to West," he noted—and Garred instructed him "to move to the 'West Road' of Tan Son Nhut and to [']fire on anything that moves to the West.[']" Garred was Virant's only connection with the base, and "I asked him the standard questions—Where are they? How many are there? What direction are they going? What kind of weapons do they have?" the troop commander later said. "I was looking for any information—but he was underground with a radio at one corner of the base, and the attack was taking place at the other end. People within the small battle area will send funny messages or panicked messages, and you're in a bunker looking at maps. That's the big problem. He just didn't know what was going on. . . ."

The militiamen at the 53d PF Battalion compound two kilometers northwest of Tan Son Nhut had sand-filled fifty-five-gallon drums across Highway 1. Charlie Troop maneuvered around the roadblock. "Beyond this point, no civilians or any military forces could be observed," Virant wrote in his after-action report. "It was a very eerie feeling," he said later. The houses appeared deserted, and there was none of the usually heavy civilian traffic on the highway.

"It was like going into no-man's-land."

Enemy soldiers on the roof of the Vinatexco Textile Factory on the west side of Highway 1 opened up on Troop C as it passed by. The fire was light, and the return fire minimal as the column continued toward Tan Son Nhut. Captain Virant did not like the standard combat-vehicle-crewmen (CVC) helmet because it blocked out almost all outside noise. Instead he wore a bush hat with a headset clamped over it, one earphone in position, the other pulled up so he could try to hear what was going on around him over the roar of track and tank engines. There was apparently a lull in the attack on the air base. Virant could hear no fire past the factory.

Captain Virant had an M16 across his lap as he sat on the left rear deck of his command track, his legs in the open cargo hatch. First Lieutenant Richard L. Larcom, the troop's artillery forward observer (FO), sat to the right rear. "Virant was a total professional in performing his military duties, always on top of any situation and always thinking ahead," Birdwell wrote. Virant, the lean, handsome, sandy-haired son of an army colonel, was West Point '63. He sported sunglasses and always maintained an immaculate appearance. His manner was precise and clipped. "He tolerated no shortcomings whatsoever and could be incredibly arrogant," according to Birdwell. Virant had once rebuked a GI who reported capturing several banana-style AK-47 magazines, noting caustically that the enemy had no other type. "A lot of the guys didn't like him, but he was damn good. If what you're saying is true, it's not bragging, and by that measure Virant's arrogance was totally justified."

The destruction of Troop C began at 0708. The enemy was concealed among a row of hootches that paralleled the elevated highway thirty meters to the west. The lead tank took an RPG, then was knocked out by more direct rocket hits even as the tank commander (TC) started turning his turret to return fire. Staff Sergeant Patrick J. Strayer was swept off the deck by the 90mm main gun—the Charlie Two platoon sergeant had climbed aboard the Charlie Three tank when it moved to the point position—and if he did not break his neck in the fall, which was how it looked to some troops farther back in the column, he did not long survive the intense fire raking the tank and the highway. The four tank crewmen were all killed in a matter of seconds, too, the commander and driver in their open hatches, the gunner and loader because they were sitting exposed on the outside of the vehicle, not an unusual place to be, given that the greatest fear of tankers was to be trapped inside the cramped turret should a rocket-propelled grenade ever punch through and set off the main gun rounds.

Private First Class Robert M. Finnegan, the command track driver, was shot in the side of the head at the same time the tank was blasted. The track jerked to a halt behind the tank, even as Captain Virant ordered the column to "Herringbone right, herringbone right!"—in other words, to stop in place and pivot to face the enemy—and to "fire at anything to the west!" Virant realized that the lead tank was engulfed in smoke as he dropped down into his track—just as he did not know about his dead driver in the heat of the moment, he found out about the fate of the tank crew only after the battle—and he shouldered his M16 without pause, his head and shoulders exposed above the open cargo hatch. He sighted in on the hootches on the right flank.

Before Virant could fire, Lieutenant Larcom bumped hard against him, and the captain snapped, "Goddamnit, I'm trying to shoot!" He did not realize that Larcom had bounced against him because he had just caught a burst of automatic-weapons fire or that the forward observer had several fingers shot off and a massive hole in his thigh. "I fired a magazine into the little hootches, then dropped down into the track to reload," Virant said. "I always kept extra magazines in a certain place. They were supposed to be right next to the radio. I reached—but they weren't there. Having things in the correct position is always very important, because you reach for it without looking and you grab it. The crew had apparently cleaned the track the previous day and not put the magazines back in the right place."

Captain Virant found the ammo on a little shelf above the radio. At that time, the track commander, Specialist Four Richard J. Rhodes was shot in the chest as he fired his .50-caliber MG. "I saw him sort of slump down inside the track under the cupola," Virant said. "He bled to death there. . . ."

Meanwhile, Virant thumped a fresh magazine in his M16 and popped back up. Squeezing off into another hootch, he got a little secondary explosion. In the next instant—and this was less than sixty seconds into the action—the captain took a skull-cracking wound to the back of his head. There was no sensation of being wounded. "You could hear the pinging of bullets off the aluminum armor—and then all of a sudden, I just got really tired," Virant said. "I had my back against the fuel tank, and I just slid down into a sitting position and thought that I'd better rest for a minute—and I was out cold for the rest of the battle." He had been facing the enemy when hit, his right shoulder to the track behind his, and he later surmised that he caught a ricochet of some sort off that vehicle. "It was probably a metal fragment. It went in the right rear of my head, and out the left rear. It fractured the outer skull and gave me a concussion, but I'm pretty lucky because it went between the brain and the spinal column without damaging either. It was a very clean through-and-through wound—a miracle kind of wound."

When the tank and command track stopped, the third vehicle in line had no choice but to halt, too, as did the track behind it. Both were put out of action by rockets before they could pivot to the right and return fire. "They blasted us so fast and so hard that it was over before it got started. They took the whole platoon at once," remembered Private First Class Richard F. "Fighting Frank" Cuff, whose nickname reflected the fact that he was one of the most tough-minded, straight-arrow soldiers in Charlie Two. Cuff was the driver of Lieutenant Pinto's APC—the fifth vehicle in the column—which survived the initial shock wave because of a big advertising billboard between it and the row of hootches. The top of the sign was about even with the track deck on the elevated highway. "Every time they would try to blast us, the RPG would hit that billboard," said Cuff. "I was firing my M16. The .50 was going, and the 60s were both going, but it wasn't too long before the track commander, a big sergeant, took a round right in the neck and fell down into the vehicle."

The sergeant survived. Cuff clambered from his hatch to the commander's, and put the .50-cal MG back in action. The AK-47 fire was so intense, however, that Lieutenant Pinto and crew finally had to abandon the APC and seek shelter on the left side of the elevated highway.

Moments later, the VC found the angle to get an RPG into the vehicle, and it sat burning on the highway. Enemy soldiers flung grenades over the roadway from the opposite embankment. "I didn't know what was going on," said Cuff, who returned fire with a dismounted M60. "You couldn't see anything over there. The only thing you could see was the green tracers going over your head. I kept low as I fired because you stick your head up, it was gone. . . ."

Specialist Four Russell H. Boehm, another track driver in the lead platoon, had just stopped and turned to the right when the APC in front of him was penetrated by an RPG. The two M60 gunners on the back deck fell forward through the cargo hatch at the impact. The rocket exploded inside the APC with a brilliant flash an instant later, and Boehm was stunned to see the track commander fly out of the cupola like a cork out of a champagne bottle. The sergeant crashed onto the highway, painfully wrenching his back, while the two gunners scrambled back up through the cargo hatch. One's hair was on fire as he jumped down and disappeared into the darkness.

By that time, Boehm, a dependable, level-headed twenty-five-year-old former ranch hand invariably nicknamed Cowboy, had opened up with his M16. After firing all eight or ten magazines that he had in his driver's compartment, he grabbed his backup weapon, an M79 grenade launcher, and unable to clearly make out a single enemy soldier or position in the smoky dawn—he felt like he was just firing into a dark void—he started lobbing shells at a hootch to his left front where he supposed the enemy might be firing from. His third shell went right through an open window—and in response, an AK burst splattered the forward slope of the track in a spray of metal fragments just inches below his hatch where he was exposed from the waist up.

Boehm dropped down before the sniper could raise his sights, and as he slipped through the tight confines of the vehicle so as to resume firing from the cargo hatch he realized that the track commander, a big, gentle-souled black sergeant, was sitting shell-shocked against the rear wall of the engine compartment directly below his cupola. Boehm barked, "You better get that .50 goin'!"

The sergeant mumbled something, and Boehm ignored him as he joined Specialist Four Anthony F. Vanhulle, their one and only M60 gunner. "Vanhulle was bouncing around, trying to get the guns to work. He'd already burned out the barrel on his M60, and the .50-caliber was jammed," remembered Boehm. Vanhulle replaced the burned-out barrel, and when he dropped down for another can of ammo, Boehm said, "How 'bout I grab my grease gun, and get up there and put some grease in that .50-caliber, and we'll get it going?" Vanhulle replied, "Yeah, you do that"—and that was the last thing he ever said because he caught a bullet about an inch and a half above his right eye at that moment. "The expression on his face never changed. He was talking, and his expression froze just as if you took a picture of it. He didn't drop. He just went limp, and I saw this spot on his forehead where the bullet had gone in, and I just reached over and helped him down and laid him down on the floor of the track. He was still breathing, and I shouted at the track commander, 'Well, at least you could try to call the medic for me, I gotta get this machine gun goin'!"

Vanhulle died. Boehm did not know exactly when because as soon as he shouted at the immobilized sergeant to get a medic, he sprang back up to the M60, fearing that the enemy might take advantage of the suspension of suppressive fire by rushing the APC. "I was pretty shook up because when I swung the M60 around and started shooting, I shot a hole right through the shield of the .50-cal there."

4

Keep Firing, Chief

In addition to the tank leading the column, there was one in the middle, and another at the very end. Staff Sergeant Ron E. Breeden, the acting Charlie Three platoon sergeant, commanded the middle tank, which was positioned between the last track of Charlie Two and the first track of Charlie Three. When Captain Virant ordered the column to herringbone right and open fire, Breeden stopped and pivoted a bit to the right to face that part of the roadside village opposite the lead platoon. He did not commence firing, however. The roar of the tank engine and the muffling effect of his radio helmet were such that he could not hear the firing on the lead vehicles of the well-spaced column, and given the dust that had been stirred up by their passage, he could not see well in the hazy gray twilight.

Breeden pulled his helmet off to hear better, and turned to Specialist Birdwell, his gunner, who was sitting atop the turret. "They're saying there's North Vietnamese up there," Breeden said. "Hell, I don't see a damn thing. Do you?"

"Goddamn, man, look—*they're everywhere!*"

It was an overcast morning, but the top of a tank on the elevated highway provided a commanding view. Birdwell could see enemy soldiers both in the village to the right and inside the air base perimeter to the left of the highway, and he urged Breeden to open fire. "Breeden was very reluctant to fire for fear that the people were actually civilians or ARVN," Birdwell recalled. "You had to have permission to fire, or you could be court-martialed. That was always on your mind, especially for a career man like Breeden."

Unaware of the hits on the lead vehicles, Birdwell thought Breeden initiated an ambush when he finally pumped thirty to fifty .50-caliber rounds down range, then fired the main gun. "After Breeden fired into that hootch area, the sky just lit up with tracers," he said. Thousands of green tracer rounds poured into the lead platoon from the ville, along with RPGs that looked like streaming balls of fire in the dim light. Birdwell was thunderstruck. The scene resembled the Mad Minute demonstrations at the Fort Knox armor school in which sixty seconds of intense tank and machine-gun fire would be directed at targets on a firing range. "This looked just like a Mad Minute, and it took me a second to grasp that something was wrong—the tracers were coming at *us*, even though it was always supposed to be that we gave it to *them!*"

Almost immediately, Breeden screamed and collapsed into the turret. Going to his aid, Birdwell pulled the sergeant's hands away from his face and saw that his left eye had been blown away and that he had another ragged hole in the back of his head. Breeden was in agony, but Birdwell encouraged him to stand, and then with rounds ricocheting off the turret he hauled him up through the hatch and down to cover in the ditch to the left.

Taking Breeden's place in the commander's cupola, Birdwell put on a tanker helmet, connected it to the tank communications system, and began returning fire with the main gun and the heavy machine gun. Birdwell's .50-cal MG had no armor shield, and he felt insanely exposed amid the whining, high-pitched buzz of rounds snapping past. "[S]everal RPG rounds were fired at C-35 [the tank's call sign], but they overshot or were to the left of the vehicle. They exploded in the air base," he wrote. To fire the 90mm main gun, Birdwell used a lanyard wrapped around the internal firing handle. "You could sit up top and shoot by sight. You just gave that cord a little jerk, and—*bang!*—you could flat go to town. The main gun was deafening. It was punishing, but after five or six firings, you're kind of numbed over. You don't really care. . . ."

Birdwell's furious fire kept the bulk of the enemy at bay. The big tank on the road also sheltered the tracks behind it from the heavy fire from the front as Charlie Three shredded the hedgerows and hootches on the right flank. "If the unit hadn't reacted so quickly, it would have been a disaster," said Sergeant Brewer, the platoon leader. Even if blindly delivered, fire superiority was the key to survival. After the battle, Brewer discovered a dead enemy machine-gun crew only thirty feet from his APC. They were well camouflaged, and Brewer suspected they had never actually been spotted. "We probably eliminated them with our sweeping fire, coming in close and moving it out again. We just tore up the ground, hoping to hit something."

Specialist Four Ralph Ball, the driver of the APC directly behind Birdwell's tank, pulled up as far as he could to the edge of the road, allowing his two M60 gunners to place fire on the main enemy positions opposite Charlie Two.

This maneuver also exposed the front of the track. As one of the gunners, Private First Class Robert D. Wolford, fired past the front of the tank, there was so much noise—especially from Birdwell's 90mm cannon—that he found out only afterward that armor-piercing rounds had penetrated the hull of his vehicle in two places. There were other spots where smaller-caliber rounds had ricocheted off or were embedded in the aluminum armor. Ball used an M79 at first, then in the absence of a track commander on the undermanned vehicle, he jumped behind the .50-cal and pounded away "until he had burned out the barrel and produced a mountain of brass," Wolford said.

The lead tank of Troop C had just drawn abreast of the 051 Gate when it was knocked out. The rear tank was some two hundred meters past the textile factory at that time. The column on the two-lane elevated roadway was thus squeezed in between the brushy village running down the west side of Highway 1 and the air base perimeter wire running down the east side. What the GIs called a drainage ditch was actually the narrow space between the base of the five-foot-high roadway berm and the first concertina-wire barrier. It was a short distance through the wire to the perimeter fence, which ran parallel to the highway.

Captain Virant's force had driven not into a carefully prepared ambush, as the troops supposed, but into a second wave of VC/NVA forming up in the village to rush through the 051 Gate. "[Troop C] had sliced directly across the path of a three battalion enemy assault," noted a 25th Division report. "[Virant's] column had come to a halt in such a position as to cut off [those] enemy troops who had breached the air base perimeter and occupied the western end of the active east-west runway from the main body of the enemy force which was moving in from the west . . ."

Virant was subsequently awarded the Silver Star for leading the charge that saved Tan Son Nhut. "[T]he shock and boldness of [Troop C's] assault stopped the VC movement toward the penetration," noted a II FFV report.

This is true. It is also true that Troop C lost twelve dead and almost fifty wounded. "We were butchered—I should have done better," Virant wrote. Having been placed opcon to the Capital Military District, he also held that organization to blame. "They didn't tell us anything. We didn't know the bunkers were gone. We didn't know the enemy was on the edge of the runway. We didn't know there was a regiment there. It was only by default that we divided their force and sealed the penetration."

In addition, Virant pointed to an uncharacteristic lapse on the part of Lieutenant Colonel Otis, who had turned back for Cu Chi without having a Troop D scout ship take his place. "Otis basically had a small air force," Virant noted, and during previous operations the line commanders routinely had helicopters providing information from above the action. "We were going into Tan Son Nhut blind, and Otis knew we were going in blind. He had heard the communications between me and Garred."

Otis would have been more protective of his detached unit had he understood that "Capital Military District became almost nonfunctional once Saigon got hit," as he put it. "Virant did not ask me for a scout ship because there was no notion that he was going into a hot area," Otis said. "We were simply chopping a troop-minus to CMD, and once Virant rendezvoused with the guide, there was no longer a Three-Quarter Cav mission. In retrospect, the squadron should have been tasked to provide more than just two platoons from Charlie Troop. . . ."

There was a bigger problem. One report noted that while Troop C was en route to the air base, the 25th Division TOC asked higher command whether it had "clearance to fire all its organic weapons in this heavily populated and developed area . . . no direct reply to these questions was forthcoming." This confusion "led [directly] to the massacre at Tan Son Nhut," Virant wrote. "By the ROE [Rules of Engagement], we were not supposed to shoot or use artillery in built-up areas (villages, towns, cities—especially Saigon!)—therefore the VC got first licks at Tan Son Nhut. . . . The ROE intimidated soldiers who put their lives on the line—deadening instantaneous response . . . Not reconning by fire or being a split-second hesitant to fire or being second to fire can cost you your life. . . ."

Birdwell had fired about ten main gun rounds when his loader began screaming that they had to pull back before they all got killed. Birdwell barked at the panicked crewman between .50-cal bursts to get back to work. The loader finally did, and Birdwell resumed firing the 90mm cannon.

It was at that point in the mayhem that Birdwell finally realized not only that no one was firing from the vehicles ahead of him, and that some were on fire, but also that several enemy soldiers had clambered atop one of the disabled APCs. "They were monkeyin' with the M60s," he recalled. "I couldn't believe it. I fired on them with the .50, and hit about half of them. Every fifth round was a tracer. I knew where my stuff was going—and anytime anybody's hit with a round that big, they're going to react in a bad, bad way, and there were some bad reactions out of those guys. The burst really spread them out."

As soon as Otis landed at Cu Chi, one of his officers ran out to meet him on the chopper pad and report that "there was a confused call from somebody in C Troop, claiming they'd been hit badly and that tracks were burning and people dying and wounded," the squadron commander recalled. Instead of waiting for his helicopter to be refueled, Otis immediately transferred to another Huey on strip alert, pausing only to instruct his operations officer to "crank up" all available squadron assets to reinforce the embattled troop. The S3 had previously secured permission from division to release Charlie One from its security mission at Hoc Mon Bridge, and the platoon was already en route down Highway 1. Permission was granted now to scramble Troop D's gunships, and within minutes they were airborne for the five-to-ten-minute flight from Cu Chi to Tan Son Nhut. From Go Dau Ha and Trang Bang respectively, Troops A and B also joined the race, moving straight down the MSR at top speed, ready to punch through any ambushes by dint of their speed and firepower. It was time, as cavalrymen say, to "re-gas, bypass, and haul ass."

Lieutenant Colonel Otis took control of the entire Battle of Tan Son Nhut. "Theoretically, I had no right to do that because the area was under CMD," he recalled. On the other hand, the intense, low-key Otis—call sign Saber 6—was "an armored commander's commander, who would lay it right out there for his soldiers," as one of his lieutenants noted. "He always went to the sound of the guns."

On the way in, Otis was unable to make contact with Virant or anyone else because a wounded soldier had keyed the radio and was incoherently crying for help. Captain Charles K. "Kim" Flint III, the squadron's artillery liaison officer (LNO)—and another West Pointer—was able to get through to Lieutenant Larcom on the artillery net. "Captain Virant's been hit in the back of the head. I'm pretty sure he's dead," Larcom reported. The FO—who had locked the hatches on the command track and was lying inside it with a mangled leg and hand—was very excited and in great pain. "The driver's dead. The TC's wounded and he's on the floor in here," he shouted on the radio. "The first four tracks in our column have all been hit by RPGs. There's no fire coming from any of the tracks. What fire is being returned is being done by a couple people who have dismounted and are in the ditch. . . ."

Lieutenant Colonel Otis and Captain Flint were wearing flight helmets. The right earphones were plugged into the radio each was using, the left into the command-and-control (C&C) ship's communication system. The Huey followed Highway 1 at top speed, and Otis and crew were in the middle of the battle before they knew what was happening. The copilot on the right side of the ship exclaimed, "You better pull up quick!" The aircraft commander immediately pulled pitch, up and to the right, and as the ship ascended over the big rice paddy "the wave of green tracers going from the west side of the highway towards C Troop changed directions and was chasing us," recalled Flint.

The pilot swung over the air base. The fire kept tracking them, so to get out of it while he tried to get the situation sorted out, Otis had his C&C land inside Tan Son Nhut about a hundred meters east of the line of vehicles on the highway. "It was the open west end of the runway, and there wasn't anything out there but us in the grass," said Flint. Otis made radio contact with Sergeant Brewer, who had taken command of Troop C. Brewer needed ammo—and for someone to call off an ARVN Quad-50 that had driven onto the taxiway to fire into the ville across the highway. "I told Otis that if the ARVN wanted to fight, they should come up even with us," Brewer recalled. "Instead, they were sitting back several hundred yards. If they dipped their fire just a bit at that range, it would have swept right through the lead platoon."

According to Fighting Frank Cuff, the ARVN did indeed walk their fire through Charlie Two. "One of the guys in the ditch said, 'We're going to die one way or the other, *somebody's* going to kill us today!'—and several troops shot back at them. It was either them or us."

The ARVN immediately ceased fire and pulled back. "I don't know if we hit them or just scared them," Cuff said.

Otis instructed his S3 to organize a resupply by Troop D lift ships, then reboarding his command ship, he bounced over to where Charlie One was coming down the highway. "Otis had told them to put some ammo together. We landed beside the column, put it in the helicopter as fast as we could, and brought it back," Flint said. The rearmost tank crashed through the concertina wire and perimeter fence at Brewer's direction, running back and forth over it several times to clear a lane for medevac and resupply; and Otis and Flint, landing there first, quickly unloaded their ammo for a number of troopers who hauled it back to the ditch along the highway.

The enemy fire was unrelenting. Boehm was swiveling his shielded M60 from side to side, blazing away, when he glanced back and saw that among the survivors from the lead vehicles scuttling down the roadside ditch on all fours was a buddy from another APC. "He looked up at me as he went past," recalled Boehm. "His face was as white as a ghost, and his eyes were as big as paper plates."

Moments later, Lieutenant Pinto, whose own track was ablaze, ammo exploding inside it, jerked open the back door of Boehm's APC: "Is your radio working?"

"Yeah, I can hear people on it!" Boehm answered.

Pinto clambered inside to use the radio, then shouted, "We gotta get out of here!"

While Pinto hauled Tony Vanhulle's body to the ditch, Boehm unhooked the M60 and "emptied all the ammo out of the track. I threw the ammo boxes out the back door, and there were guys back there getting it and taking it for the machine guns they had set up on the edge of the road."

Private First Class Philip T. Randazzo of Charlie Two had been peppered twice with fragments at that point, once when he was blown off his track by an RPG while firing his M60 at the outset of the battle, and again when he dashed to a disabled track to grab an M16. Firing now from the ditch, Randazzo watched in awe as a trooper named Martinez knelt atop another APC on the elevated highway to fire down into the village. "He had a pile of LAWs, and he kept popping 'em right at 'em," Randazzo said, referring to the one-shot, shoulder-fired 66mm Light Antitank Weapon (LAW). Martinez didn't last long. Blown backward by an AK-47 burst, he fell through the cargo hatch. Randazzo and Al Porter, who had crawled forward from the second platoon in the column, ran to the track and jumped in through the back door. Martinez was lying inside, holding a towel between his legs. One of his testicles was gone.

Martinez was a movie-star handsome Puerto Rican with wavy black hair. Randazzo and Porter dragged the mangled soldier out the back door and "threw him in the ditch, literally *threw* him in the ditch," Porter said.

One of the medics appeared, and working quickly before rushing to the next casualty, he ripped the packet off a large bandage, shoved it up into the wound, and told Randazzo to keep pressure on it to stop the bleeding. "I lay on top of Martinez with my right knee up his crotch to keep the bandage in place—and I'm firing my '16 over his head. He was going into shock. He was shaking like an earthquake."

When Randazzo ran out of ammo and scrambled off to find more, Porter and another GI started dragging Martinez back down the ditch. Martinez was going crazy from the pain, shrieking curses at his rescuers. "Keep your mouth shut!" Porter shouted back, so scared he was angry. "Just keep your fuckin' mouth shut, you sonofabitch, and we'll get you out of here. Otherwise, *I'll leave your ass here!*"

Lieutenant Colonel Otis touched down to get what information he could from Captain DeNisio, the senior air force officer fighting the battle at the west end of Tan Son Nhut. Airborne again, Saber 6 put the first phase of his impromptu counterattack plan into action. "Here a commander demonstrated the classic defense against an enemy attack," noted a division-level report. "He attacked." Instead of having Charlie One pull up behind Charlie Three on Highway 1, Otis directed Staff Sergeant Roy W. Kennard, the acting platoon leader, to turn off the MSR onto a service road at a point immediately north of the textile factory. This road cut straight to a small gate in the perimeter fence. Charlie One was joined there by an airman who guided the column around the firefight raging inside the base and allowed it to join with the base security forces from the rear.

Charlie One would then lead the attack on the nose of the penetration. Meanwhile, four Troop D gunships arrived on station. Otis gave them to Brewer—"Roger, we need all the help we can get," the sergeant said—and coming in abreast the gunships made repeated north-to-south firing runs down the length of the village. "They could bring the fire in close and tight, and they saved our bacon," noted Brewer. Two of the Huey gunships were so heavily damaged by the ground-to-air fire, however, that the pilots had to crash-land in the grass on the west end of the airfield.

Gunships from the base aviation company rocketed the 051 Bunker. It was presumed that the airmen inside were dead, and with VC/NVA using the position to fire on both DeNisio's force and Troop C, the decision had been made to eliminate it. Having linked up with DeNisio, Charlie One prepped the bunker with .50-cal and 90mm fire. Charlie One was southeast of Charlie Two, so its east-to-west fire did not endanger the cavalrymen pinned down along the highway on the other side of the wire.

Charlie One and the Air Force SPs started towards the 051 Bunker, but diehards among the burial mounds inside the west end of the base knocked out the platoon's only tank. "[It] was struck by three anti-tank rockets, and [the] commander directed the crew to evacuate the disabled vehicle," read the citation to Specialist Four Roger B. Crowell's Distinguished Service Cross (DSC). Instead of evacuating the tank, Crowell, the driver, climbed inside. "Alone, he quickly loaded and fired eighteen devastatingly accurate cannon rounds . . . When continuing enemy rocket fire rendered the main gun inoperable, Specialist Crowell fearlessly exposed himself to the relentless fusillade and raked the hostile positions with a hail of bullets from the tank's machine gun until he was struck by enemy small arms fire and instantly killed. . . ."

Captain Virant thought Sergeant Brewer was the best noncommissioned officer in the outfit, and it was in the natural order of things that he took command of Troop C when Virant was knocked out in the opening round at Tan Son Nhut. Lieutenant Pinto outranked him, but originally pinned down with Charlie Two, this green platoon leader was in no condition to take the reins from Brewer when he finally worked his way down the ditch to Charlie Three. "He was pretty dazed," Brewer recalled, though he did not think the lieutenant was totally shell-shocked. "You could talk to him. I said something to him about helping move munitions or something, and he did respond."

Brewer seemed to be everywhere as he kept Charlie Troop

organized, resupplied, and fighting. He did so with a cool head and good cheer. "Son of a bitch," he joked in the middle of the battle. "I'd have you guys fix bayonets—but they haven't issued any yet for the new M16!"

Coming across a distraught GI who was still holding the dead buddy he had dragged down the ditch, Brewer got him refocused and back in action by gently telling him, "If you leave him here and help me, I'll make sure he gets home."

On the second of three Vietnam tours, Gary Brewer was a laconic old soldier of twenty-six who had joined the army at seventeen rather than follow his stepfather down into the coal mines of Jasonville, Indiana. He was a powerful man with a big handlebar mustache and a beer-keg build. "Brewer had kind of a young W. C. Fields-type body. It was built more for comfort than speed," mused Birdwell, who further described the NCO as a "slow-mannered, easygoing, frumpy-looking guy—his fatigues were as rumpled and wrinkled as an old washrag—and a good, intelligent soldier who we all respected. He was always on the lookout for goods we could use, such as steaks, extra weapons, etc."

Brewer was known to his troops as "Brew-baby," and Captain Virant had previously taken him to task about such informality. "Brewer never took stuff seriously. He wasn't a heavy lifer," recalled Porter. "When you're down at the bottom, going on patrol every night, you pick up who cares about you and who doesn't give a shit. Brewer cared about us. It just came through in everything he did."

Sergeant Brewer won the DSC for Tan Son Nhut. His tenacity was such that when Lieutenant Colonel Otis ordered him to pull back, he refused. "We got too many wounded," Brewer told Otis over the radio. "I can't leave 'em, and I can't pull 'em all back—so I'm going to stay put."

Early in the fight, Brewer climbed aboard an APC to momentarily take over an unmanned M60. That was all the firing he did, and as he worked his way up and down the line he didn't even unholster his .45-caliber pistol. His job was not to shoot but to bring order to the chaos. This he did. When an excited cry went up over the radio—*"They're coming at us from behind!"*—and some of the Charlie Three

GIs firing into the village swung their machine guns around and opened up on a skirmish line of troops moving slowly toward the perimeter fence from two hundred meters back inside the base, Brewer instantly got the situation back under control. "Don't fire toward the base," his voice boomed over the radio. *"That's the air force coming to help us!"*

At some point in the battle, Brewer climbed inside the Charlie Three mortar track. The TC had already taken a fragment in the leg while manning the .50-cal MG, and the driver had taken his place. He was blasting away as Brewer produced a bottle of Old Crow and turned to Rourke, the only other crewman still on board. Rourke had been firing his M16 from the cargo hatch.

"John, take a slug," Brewer said.

Rourke took a good one, then Brewer said, "We've got a lot of wounded men at the front. Would you go up the ditch and see what you can do?"

Private First Class Rourke hesitated, took another slug, nodded—then took a third drink. Hitting the ditch, Rourke made it to an old service road that branched off the highway. The service road, which no longer connected with the air base but petered off in the wire, was elevated like the highway. "I backed up in the ditch and got a running start on my hands and knees," Rourke wrote. He scrambled across the hump and back into the ditch on the other side. Crossing another service road behind the knocked-out lead tank, Rourke found a man wounded in his right arm and side. The GI could crawl, and Rourke started back with him. "We'd take our time until we got to those roads, and then we really had to get over them fast. He was hurting, but he pushed with his legs, whatever he could, and I'd be crawling and dragging him as best I could, trying to stay low. The enemy could see us when we crossed those roads, but what saved us was that the highway had a bit of a crown to it and their fire would hit that and ricochet up."

Rourke dragged the GI into his track, then went back for more with several other troops that Brewer had mobilized. "[Before long], we had about eight wounded guys bleeding on the floor of my APC," he wrote. Rourke resumed firing from the cargo hatch, and accidentally stepped on the legs of the first man he had dragged back. "I looked down and realized he didn't feel it, he was gray, he was dead. . . ."

Shortly thereafter, a Troop D resupply ship was shot down while landing in the air base, and Rourke turned to see Brewer running back from it with an ammo box over each shoulder. "The crazy bastard," Rourke later wrote with great admiration, describing how as soon as Brewer dumped off the ammo he turned around to go back for more, ignoring the fire whipcracking all around them. Motivated by such raw courage, Rourke joined Brewer at the downed Huey. "The crew was handing the ammo out to us—and those ammo boxes were heavy, too! Before long other guys were running back and we were completely resupplied."

Sergeant Brewer's closest call came when he medevacked Breeden aboard another resupply ship. Brewer had a grip on his seriously wounded platoon sergeant's arm as he led him to the Huey through the mashed-down lane in the concertina wire. "You had to watch where you was walkin' to keep from falling," Brewer said, "and with all the noise it was hard to hear anything, but I sensed something and looked up—and there's the rear rotor blade. I had almost walked right into it. It scared the hell out of me."

Sergeant Brewer got through Tan Son Nhut without a scratch only to be seriously wounded two days later in a freak-type incident during the clearing of Ap Dong, a village immediately north of the air base where remnants of the enemy assault force had retreated. Brewer was behind the .50-cal MG of a tank when he saw a round flash off the tin roof of a nearby hootch. The ricochet punched into his stomach just below the bottom of his flak jacket. Feeling little pain, Brewer stayed with his platoon. When he finally realized that he was bleeding heavily, he helped load other casualties onto a chopper, then climbed aboard himself. It turned out that the bullet had damaged his intestines and he was medevacked out of Vietnam.

The tank that Specialist Birdwell had hastily assumed command of was the locus of Troop C's desperate battle for survival. The troops crawling down the ditch from the lead platoon found shelter behind it, and thanks to Birdwell's nearly constant machine-gun and cannon fire, the enemy in the village were unable to maneuver decisively against the column after the initial fusillade. "Some guys took to it, and some didn't. Birdwell was part of that ten percent that are good soldiers and understand fighting," said Porter, who was not particularly close to Birdwell, hanging as he did with the more raucous elements of Charlie Troop. Birdwell was more at home with low-key, rock-steady soldiers like Cowboy Boehm and Fighting Frank Cuff. He was a quiet, hard-shelled but warm-hearted kind of man, smart as a whip and wonderfully wry among friends. He was also one of the heroes of the Battle of Tan Son Nhut.

At one point, Birdwell happened to glance down and saw that Sergeant Brewer was in the ditch behind his tank. Brewer smiled up at him before turning around to make his way back down the line, and shouted, *"Keep firing, Chief!"*

Birdwell was part Cherokee and from hardscrabble rural Oklahoma. Thus, the nickname. At another point in the battle, Thomas, the black sergeant commanding the tank at the rear of the column, chimed in appreciatively over the radio, "Birdwell's really feedin' that cannon. It's *smokin'!"*

Birdwell, age twenty, won a Silver Star. Half of his battle was actually with his loader. The man had come unglued early in the fight, but Birdwell had calmed him down. The result was temporary. "He freaked out again. He got on the radio, and he's howling and screaming like a stuck pig— and not loading," Birdwell recalled. The loader was not a draftee, but a balding, good-time, beer-and-frauleins Regular Army (RA) screwup who, with six years in this man's army, was still a specialist fourth class.

The loader, inside the turret, was screaming to the driver over the tank intercom, *"Back up, back up, back up—let's get the hell outta here before we all get killed!"*

Birdwell tried to countermand the order. He got no response from the driver. "I had my helmet on and I could hear, but no one was listening to me over the intercom and I couldn't figure out why," said Birdwell, who did not realize that part of the communications apparatus on the left side of the CVC had been shot off by one of the rounds buzzing by his head. "As C-35 started to back up, I looked into the ditch behind the vehicle. It was occupied by numerous wounded personnel who were yelling and screaming for the tank to stop, as it was going to back over them."

In desperation, Birdwell disconnected his helmet, jumped down onto the road amid heavy fire, and banged on the hatch the driver had closed to protect himself from the concussion and ear-splitting noise of the 90mm main gun. When the driver opened his hatch, Birdwell directed him "to return the tank to its former position, which he did without hesitation. [The driver] was not acting out of fear or stupidity—he simply didn't know what was happening. He could not hear me on the intercom, so it was natural that he would listen to the directions of the loader."

Birdwell was reconnecting his tanker helmet after climbing back into his commander's cupola when he saw a group of enemy soldiers falling back toward the perimeter fence. They were behind him inside the base, and were so close that he could not turn his 90mm main gun on them for fear of hitting the troops piled up in the ditch. "In addition, I had burned out the barrel of my [.]50, so that the rounds coming from it as shown by the tracers were flying in several directions, none of which were directly at my targets. Therefore, if I placed [.]50 fire on the enemy, I would probably have killed more of our own than the NVA," Birdwell wrote. The main gun's coaxial machine gun was jammed, so he was reduced to shouldering his M16 and quickly sighting in on the group from atop his tank.

Birdwell squeezed off a burst. "Two or three dropped to the ground and did not get up," he wrote. The others changed direction, and Birdwell held his fire as they slipped through the perimeter fence in front of him where Charlie Two had left its vehicles as the survivors pulled back.

It was a traumatic withdrawal. There were wounded men who kept up the fire, and Birdwell was especially impressed with a new medic, a round-faced Indian boy with a shock of black hair, who completely ignored the enemy fire cracking all around as he hustled up and down the ditch to treat the casualties. Others had ceased to function, however. *Why in the fuck aren't you doing something?* Birdwell thought furiously when he noticed the numerous stunned troops hunkered down like turtles in the ditch behind his tank. He recognized a GI from his own platoon, a real problem child, sitting there, too, cradling a bloody arm and beaming broadly about his million-dollar wound.

Why aren't you returning fire?! . . .

During a brief lull, Birdwell saw a jeep coming south on the perimeter road on the other side of the perimeter fence. There was a young troop behind the wheel, a man of field-grade age beside him. Neither wore a helmet or flak jacket, the older one sporting only a baseball-style utility cap. The jeep stopped, and the older man got out and began shouting. "I could not make out what he was saying, so I again disconnected my helmet and went to the rear of the vehicle to ask if anyone in the ditch knew what he was saying. I was told he was calling us cowards and demanding that we charge the enemy," Birdwell wrote. The troops were too numb to be offended, too numb to respond. "Most of the guys in the ditch were in pretty bad shape, and in no condition to do much of anything but to hold on."

Ignoring the unrealistic order, Birdwell resumed firing from his tank. The jeep continued south—and got splattered with a burst of automatic-weapons fire. "[T]he passenger slumped over. The [driver] made a hard left movement and drove away," Birdwell wrote. An enemy soldier with an AK-47 jumped up from the grass near where the jeep had been hit, and escaped in a flat-out run down the perimeter road, away from Birdwell's tank.

The chaos continued. Birdwell was thundering away with the main gun when one of the rounds failed to fire despite repeated jerks and pulls on the firing cord. The loader wouldn't touch it. Instead of removing the defective round and putting the 90mm gun back in operation himself— Birdwell was also afraid that the shell might explode in his hands due to the intense heat building up in the gun chamber—he replaced the burned-out barrel in the .50-cal MG, and opened up with that instead. He fired without let up, burning the replacement barrel out, too, even as several soldiers in the ditch screamed at him to fire the main gun, unaware of the dud round still sitting in the chamber.

It was then that the loader flipped out once again. *"We're being overrun,"* he shrieked on the squadron net. *"We're out of ammo . . . please help us . . . !"*

The loader also contacted the driver again on the intercom, screaming, *"Get out, get out, get out!"*

The driver started backing up just like before. Still unaware that the communications apparatus on his tanker helmet was damaged, Birdwell was completely baffled that he could not get through to the driver. Infuriated, and thinking that the driver should know better than to listen to the hysterical loader, Birdwell tore off the helmet and jumped down onto the forward slope of the tank. He beat on the driver's hatch and was so angry that when the driver opened it, he kicked the man right in the head, furiously motioning at him over the roar of the engine to pull the tank back into position. The driver complied, but not before glancing sharply up at Birdwell with blood in his eyes. He looked so angry that had he been wearing his sidearm, Birdwell thought he would have unholstered it and shot him in the heat of the moment.

The driver was a pretty tough soldier in his own right. Birdwell was really angry at the loader, and dropping inside the turret, he proceeded to slap him across his face while shouting at him that they would all have a better chance of getting out of this alive if he would do his job. It worked. The loader calmed down. At that point, Birdwell "faced the fact that I had to do something about the main gun." The longer he left the dud in the chamber, the more heat it absorbed, and the likelier the chance of the cook-off he feared. Birdwell got the loader out of the turret, then worked the 90mm breechblock lever several times to extract the jammed-up round. "I placed my hands on it, and it burned. However, I was so anxious to get [it] out of the vehicle that I just bore the pain. I slid out the top of the vehicle with the round next to my body. All of a sudden I heard a loud explosion and thought the dud had exploded. I was confident I was dead. . . ."

The dud was intact. It turned out that Sergeant Mike Christie had just let fly with a shoulder-fired 90mm recoilless rifle from the left side of the tank. Getting reorganized, Birdwell, who wasn't about to throw the round into the paddy to his front for all the fire coming from that direction, waved away the GIs in the ditch behind his tank and heaved it into the wire. Climbing back into the cupola, he noticed the asbestos gloves he had used to change machine-gun barrels and cursed himself for a dummy for not using them when he handled the hot shell.

Birdwell finally saw that his radio helmet was damaged, so he stood bareheaded in the turret as he resumed fire. Christie added to the roar with his recoilless rifle. "He was fully exposed to the enemy, but exhibited no fear whatsoever," Birdwell wrote. Meanwhile, Birdwell got another dud round, but "I was better able to control my emotions, so when it became apparent that it would not fire, I got the loader out of the tank, and quickly removed the dud, throwing it in the same area where I had thrown the other round. This time I wore the asbestos gloves. . . ."

5

Firepower

Birdwell used up everything he had. "The tank carried sixty-four main gun rounds—and we fired every damn one of them except for the two duds," he recalled. Having also expended all his .50-cal ammo, Birdwell told his loader and driver to evacuate the empty tank while he remained up top, firing his M16. "We were in a very serious situation. The fire from the NVA was intensifying, and there did not appear to be many troops left who could fight."

Thankfully, artillery support had been organized. From Lieutenant Colonel Otis's C&C Huey, Captain Flint, the Arty LNO, laid it in as close as he dared to the roadside village while the command ship orbited over the air base to avoid the worst of the ground fire. "Otis was getting a little more adventuresome now, wanting to know the size and organization of the bad guys, so we began to expand our orbit further west," Flint said. The new orbit used the highway as a dividing line, and on the second pass over the west side of the battlefield, the door gunner pointed out an enemy .51-caliber antiaircraft position, then opened fire on it with his M60. The .51 crew had dug a chest-deep circle in the field outside the ville and mounted the weapon on the earthen pole that remained in the center. "It looked like a lifesaver from the air," noted Flint, "and the crew could run

69

around and traverse three-sixty—and they were following our helicopter."

The command ship was hit on its third pass over the enemy-occupied village, the big green .51 tracers making contact with jarring thumps. "This baby's not flying much longer, boss," the pilot told Otis over the intercom.

"I don't care how you do it, but get this sonofabitch back *east* of the highway," Otis answered on his boom mike.

The pilot made a rough emergency landing in the wire directly behind a tank on the road—it was Birdwell's—mashing the concertina down with its skids. Fearing ruptured fuel tanks and fire, Otis, Flint, and the four-man crew instantly unstrapped their seat belts and jumped out. "I had nothing but a .45 and a radio. I thought, what the hell am I going to do now?" recalled Flint, who grabbed the nearest piece of cover, "and plunked my radio down because I was still coordinating the fires of two artillery batteries."

Otis had a whole battle to run but no communications. Luckily, he and Flint were picked up shortly by Centaur 6—the Troop D commander. Meanwhile, Birdwell hustled over to the crashed Huey and salvaged its two M60s despite the protests of the crew chief. After giving one of them to Wolford, Birdwell climbed back aboard his tank with the other—it had twin D-handles and a butterfly trigger—and cut loose into the ville with a renewed fury. The front of the barrel suddenly disappeared in a flash. Birdwell was peppered with fragments in his face, neck, and chest, and bled heavily from his head. The wounds were actually superficial. Whatever had slammed into the machine gun had been relatively small—an RPG would have blown him away. The only problem was that the blast had left him with nothing but his sidearm, and at that point he finally abandoned his tank on the highway.

After moving forward to scrounge ammo from several tracks, Birdwell ended up with his driver and the platoon mechanic near a big tree just behind the knocked-out lead tank. The mechanic, Specialist Four Dean A. Foss—a gravely RA troop from Bar Harbor, Maine, who could pass for Popeye—had ridden into the battle on the back of Birdwell's tank, and had proven a tenacious on-the-spot infantryman, firing his M16 from the ditch after Birdwell shouted at him that he was too exposed alongside the turret. He had been scorched across the side of his neck by a red-hot rocket fragment.

While Foss popped up to fire his M16 in quick bursts, Birdwell and the driver, having collected some fifteen hand grenades between them, started heaving them across the highway. In response, the enemy turned a machine gun on them. It ferociously chipped away at the tree trunk above their heads, completely pinning them down. They could not move back. They could not even rise up to return fire. It seemed clear that they were about to die.

"My mama begged me not to volunteer for any more overseas duty," Foss said grimly. "By God, if I get out of this one, I'm going to listen to her the next time."

"With certain death appearing imminent, fate, or [Troop B], depending on your point of view, intervened," Birdwell wrote. Gunships took out the machine gun that had them pinned down. Other helicopters swooped in to lay a smoke screen between the village and the paddies, "and then [Troop B] began moving towards [Troop C] with the NVA in the middle. At that point, we were out of the barrel, and it was now the turn of the NVA to be the fish. . . ."

Hauling straight down Highway 1, Troop B had covered the thirty-nine kilometers between Trang Bang Bridge and Tan Son Nhut in an hour. "We were a good troop. We were always in a high state of readiness," said First Lieutenant Joseph A. Gallo, Jr., whose platoon—Bravo Three—led the race to the air base. "We got the call, and were able to pack up and move out in about ten minutes. It being the cavalry, when I'd signal the platoon to get rolling, I'd say, 'Okay, guys, *boots and saddles!*' That was my war cry, so to speak."

Captain Malcolm D. "Mac" Otis—no relation to the squadron commander—commanded Troop B, 3d Squadron, 4th Cavalry, 25th Division. He was a low-key, highly regarded West Pointer. The enemy had constructed hasty, moundlike roadblocks at various points on the highway. Gallo's lead tank encountered the first one some five kilometers past the Trang Bang Bridge on the north side of the An Duc Bridge. Otis joined Gallo at the roadblock.

Unable to simply smash through it for fear of mines, and having no time to stop and carefully clear the area, as was the usual procedure, Otis instructed Gallo to bypass the barricade and the potentially booby-trapped bridge itself along a seldom-used detour road, and then to jump back on the highway and continue at top speed.

"We'll have to take a calculated risk," Otis said. "Don't worry about mines—just *go!*"

The next roadblock was south of Cu Chi, in the middle of picturesque Tan Phu Trung. It was bypassed, as was a third roadblock in the next hamlet down Highway 1. "We didn't stop for nothin'," said Private First Class Thomas F. Higgins. "We went right through the villes, knocking over hootches. There were no civilians visible in any of them. It was real eerie."

Smashing through the hamlets slowed the column down, so at the next set of mounds on the highway, Otis radioed Gallo, "Screw it—just go through 'em." The lead tank had an attached dozer blade. It plowed through that roadblock, and the next, which turned out to be the last. Neither were mined. Troop B, in fact, came under no fire of any kind, even when roaring past enemy-occupied towns like Cu Chi and Hoc Mon. "We probably went through faster than they could react," said Captain Otis. It was an incredible situation. Tan Son Nhut was a primary communist objective, but the enemy had made no serious effort to cut the most obvious route the allies would use to reinforce the air base. "If they had just blown the Hoc Mon Bridge, it would have kept us out of the battle until half the day was over, which would have been too late for Tan Son Nhut," noted Otis.*

---

*This lapse in the enemy's plan may have been linked to a battle that began on the afternoon of January 29, 1968, when a D/3-4th Cavalry gunship rolled in on three guerrillas in the Ho Bo Woods some fifty-five kilometers northwest of Saigon. The area was inside a loop of the Saigon River known as the Mushroom. The Aerorifle Platoon (ARP) was inserted to search the bodies, but ran into a hornet's nest. Five ARPs were killed, the rest pinned down in a bomb crater. Two companies from the 2-27th Infantry, 25th Division, were combat assaulted in at dusk, and following close-in

THE BATTLE FOR SAIGON

Lieutenant Colonel Otis and Colonel John R. Thurman III, the division artillery commander, had arranged for a towed howitzer battery—C/6-77th Field Artillery (FA) (105mm)—to join Troop B on Highway 1 outside Cu Chi. Troop B's rearmost platoon, Bravo One, fell out of the column to wait for and then escort the battery to the battle area. Thurman had already lined Flint up with two other batteries—eight-inchers from II FFV, and 155mm howitzers from the 1st Infantry Division, since the 25th had none in range. They were forced to divide their missions between several battles, however, and were of such heavy caliber as to make close-in support somewhat hazardous. The towed battery would be able to provide direct and uninterrupted supporting fire.

Captain Otis had no map coverage below the Hoc Mon Bridge, so Lieutenant Colonel Otis guided him into his final attack position from his helicopter. With Troop C's burning, smoke-shrouded column in sight up ahead, Bravo Troop made a column right off Highway 1 just past the Vinatexco Textile Mill. Saber 6 warned Otis to fire on the enemy-occupied building but to waste no time—he was to just get past as quickly as possible. Moving southwest across

---

night fighting, linked up with the ARPs an hour after midnight. Total U.S. casualties were eight dead and fifteen wounded, as against a sixty-eight VC body count.

During the battle, a misplotted illumination round burst on the wrong side of the Saigon River. There was a gunship making a turn over the area at that moment, and in the sudden light the pilot "saw a huge column of NVA going south along the river," remembered Captain Otis. "I was listening to the radio, and the pilot said, 'Holy shit—look what we got down here!' and they called in artillery and everything else they could on that unit." The enemy unit—tentatively identified as the 88th NVA Regiment—was infiltrating toward Saigon under the cover of darkness, and appeared to be trying to slip past the fight in the Mushroom. Reportedly, the 88th had been responsible for blowing the Hoc Mon Bridge but had been too badly mauled in the night battle to complete its mission. If true, then "that one artillery illumination round that went long saved Tan Son Nhut," said Otis.

the open ground there until the whole column had cleared the highway, the two platoons then halted and executed a left flank so that the well-spaced line of tanks and tracks, which was oriented from northeast to southwest, faced the top and upper rear of the north-south village from which the enemy had Troop C pinned down.

Lieutenant Colonel Otis landed to brief Captain Otis, whose command vehicles were deployed behind the firing line, the factory several hundred meters to the rear. The colonel provided Otis and his forward observer, First Lieutenant Rolland Fletcher, with maps, then ran back to his chopper. With Troop B blocking the enemy from the north and west, Saber 6 was now "ready to apply the final blow to his hastily devised plan to destroy the enemy attack," noted a battle analysis. "[Otis] directed [his] helicopter gunships to take up positions on the southern flank of the battlefield and to seal that escape route by fire. . . . The headquarters element of B Troop was instructed to direct its fire on the enemy located in the factory complex to the north of the contact area. The remaining two platoons were ordered to . . . attack to the south through the enemy. . . . In the meantime, C Troop was to maintain its position on the road and support B Troop's movement across its front by fire."

Captain Otis was in direct radio contact with Sergeant Brewer. "B Troop just moved in behind the village, and they're going to open fire," Brewer shouted to his troops in the ditch. "Whatever you do, *keep your heads down!*"

Troop B commenced firing with everything it had. "Stuff was hitting the barbed-wire fence behind us and making it *ting*," remembered Specialist Porter. "If you would have picked up your head, you would have got it blown off."

The firestorm was incredible. "Enemy soldiers started coming out of spiderholes, trying to get away," recalled Lieutenant Gallo of Bravo Three, who excitedly unholstered his sidearm when several black-pajamed Viet Cong broke cover about fifteen meters away. "I emptied my .45 at the closest one. I don't really know if I hit him or not because I was a lousy shot with a .45." The most effective weapon in that situation was a 90mm main gun loaded with a canister round—a can-shaped shell packed with ball bearings that turned the cannon into a giant shotgun. "One of my tanks blew away a whole NVA squad with a canister round. It was a couple vehicles down from me, but the main gun is very loud and I looked over there to see what had happened—and I saw these guys flying left and right!"

Someone shouted excitedly on the platoon net, "They got 'em, they got 'em—*it's a goddamn turkey shoot!*"

"Hey, 3-0, that was a beautiful shot," Captain Otis chimed in, using Gallo's call sign. *"Keep it up!"*

Bravo Troop tore apart the north half of the village, while those enemy troops withdrawing across the open fields from the south end had to run a gauntlet of artillery fire that Lieutenant Fletcher called in from C/6-77th FA while standing atop the command APC with his binoculars— blissfully unaware, given the outgoing fire and the constant talk on his communications helmet, that the track was taking small-arms hits. "The battery commander was out there *all-by-him-self*—they had absolutely no security," noted Flint. The battery and its ammo trucks were deployed to one side of the highway about two klicks north of the air base. "When B Troop showed up, the artillery was not far behind. It doesn't take a one-oh-five battery long to get laid and ready to shoot, and almost as soon as the attack commenced, they were ready to fire in support."

The battle was not completely one-sided. Troop B took its first casualties in the moment between executing the left flank to face the enemy and actually commencing fire. Everyone was still getting organized when Private First Class Anthony E. Kozlinski—a track driver in Bravo Two, which was on the left flank and closer to the village than Bravo Three—saw an enemy soldier stand up from the brush at the edge of the hamlet with an RPG launcher over his shoulder. The scene unfolded as if in slow motion. The track commander opened up on the man with his .50-cal MG even as he screamed at Kozlinski over the vehicle intercom to move the APC. There was no place to move to. Machine gunners on other tracks also opened fire on the standing figure, but he survived long enough to fire his rocket. Kozlinski had the impression out of the corner of his eye that the enemy soldier was hit and knocked down in the next instant, but what really had his attention was that the rocket was coming straight at him across the open paddies.

The projectile seemed to spin on its axis in flight. It seemed to be warbling off course—but then the RPG suddenly slammed into the left side of Kozlinski's track, directly under his seat in the driver's compartment. The blast was incredible. One moment Kozlinski was standing up in his hatch, and the next he was sitting stunned on his seat. He looked down at his feet to make sure they were still there—then realized that his fatigues were on fire, and his legs were bloody messes below the knees. Moving as quickly as he could, he pulled himself out of his hatch and rolled down the front of the track, right over a big roll of concertina wire that was lashed down on the forward splashboard.

The pain of the wounds and the fall was unreal.

Hitting the ground and putting out his burning fatigues in the process, Kozlinski frantically pulled himself away from the track in case the fuel tanks might ignite, dragging his mangled legs behind him. One of the gunners, Tom Higgins—who'd been blown off the back deck by the RPG—dragged Kozlinski to cover behind the APC. A medic got him onto a stretcher, secured tourniquets around his legs—he had lost a lot of calf muscle, and some shin bone—and thumped him with a morphine syrette that quickly did its job. Kozlinski stopped writhing and thrashing.

Troop B was pouring fire into the village by that point, and Captain Otis ordered First Lieutenant Robert Adamski's Bravo Two to launch a dismounted assault into the north end. Though completely outmatched by the firepower assembled against them, any number of well-disciplined VC and NVA were still holding their ground in the blown-apart village to cover the retreat of their comrades. Hitting a wall of fire from unseen entrenchments, the attack bogged down. Almost immediately, Higgins's M60 jammed, and he ran back toward his track, looking for cover so he could clear the malfunction. Along the way, he was under plunging fire from enemy soldiers atop the factory—and he had just reached the track when a speck of metal, probably a fragment from a bullet ricocheting off the hull, caught him in his left cheek just below his eye like the red-hot snap of a whip. It knocked him down, but when a medic cleared away the blood, the wound turned out to be minor.

Higgins lay beside Kozlinski, unable to hide the you're-really-screwed-up look on his face as he mumbled, "You're going to be okay, man, you're going to be okay . . ."

Higgins handed Kozlinski his rosary.

"Thanks, Tom, this is wonderful," Kozlinski said with an exasperated laugh. "I'm fine—but here's a *rosary!*"

Enemy soldiers were visible as they retreated from the factory, and Higgins, having cleared his jammed M60, fired on them from the prone with his weapon on its bipod. In response, the enemy on the roof opened up again. Near misses thumped into the dirt around Kozlinski's stretcher, spraying him in the face with dirt. The morphine was really hitting him, though—he watched the battle through a detached, surrealistic lens—and with rounds cracking all around, he called to Higgins, "Tom, you got a cigarette?"

Higgins stopped firing his M60 long enough to shake a smoke out of its pack for Kozlinski.

"Hey, Tom—you got a light?"

"Yeah, yeah, here, here, here," Higgins said, fumbling for his lighter. Kozlinski watched nonchalantly as Higgins frantically rolled back behind his M60. Frustrated that his machine gun wasn't doing the job, Higgins finally blurted, "Fuck this shit," and ran to one of their tanks on the firing line. Higgins got the tank turned around, and as it pulled up near his track, the commander was already firing the main gun into the factory. The explosions gave great pause to the enemy snipers. Kozlinski said he needed another cigarette.

The firefight in the village raged on.

Delayed while getting the towed artillery into position, Bravo One finally roared in to join the firing line. One track pulled in behind Bravo Two's disabled APC, and the troops on the back deck began dismounting to take up firing positions along a paddy dike there. "[O]ne of the guys jumped off and, as his feet hit the ground, he accidentally emptied a magazine of M16 rounds point-blank into another GI's guts [and chest]," Higgins later wrote, the scene seared into his memory. The man who was hit—a new guy—had just gotten off the track and had turned to look back toward the others. The shooter—another new man—sank to his knees, his eyes wide in shock and horror. "Guys were trying to calm the wounded man down," said Kozlinski, "but he kept screaming that he wanted to see it, he wanted to see it—he had to see it—and when he ripped his shirt open, you could hear the sucking chest wound."

Specialist Four Willie H. Porter, a black trooper in the wounded man's squad, removed the plastic from a first-aid pack and tried to seal the wound. "He didn't last long before he spit up blood and died," Porter remembered. "The last thing he did was call for his mother. . . ."

Unable to cope with what had happened, the GI who had accidentally pulled the trigger would later be transferred off the line. Meanwhile, Captain Otis—to be awarded the Distinguished Service Cross for Tan Son Nhut—was concerned about his stalled assault force in the village. Needing to assess the situation, the troop commander unhooked his communications helmet, grabbed a steel pot, drew his sidearm, and ran right across the open ground from his track to where he could see pinned-down troops amid the hootches and hedgerows.

Having joined the assault force, Otis realized there was a .51-caliber antiaircraft gun firing on them from the second-floor window of a two-story, brick-and-mortar house nestled in among the thatch hootches. Otis also realized that there was a woman inside the house with the enemy. The village was, in fact, full of people. They had gone unseen during most of the battle, but with the enemy in retreat, some had begun to pop up, trying to escape the crossfire.

Only moments before Kozlinski was wounded, for example, he had seen two small Vietnamese children caught in the open between the two sides. "The medic on the platoon leader's track jumped off the track and ran through this incredible fire we were taking from all directions and grabbed those kids, one under each arm, and dragged them out of there as fast as he could. I couldn't believe he didn't get hit. It was the bravest thing I ever saw."

The woman that Captain Otis spotted was in her thirties and was on her hands and knees at the door of the enemy-occupied house. She waved frantically to Otis, and he waved back to let her know that he had seen her. The woman's husband was there, too. "I tried to work my way back around a hedgerow to tell the platoon there that, 'Hey, there's civilians in that house, let's see if we can get them out,'" remembered Otis. He hadn't gone five meters, however, when the gun crew on the second floor turned their fire on a nearby tank, "and the tank commander took exception to that, and blew the house away with the main gun. He had to defend himself. He probably wasn't even aware that those civilians were in there. . . ."

Captain Otis called in a gunship on another machine gun that was holding them up, and when the pilot minigunned the position into oblivion, allowing the assault to continue forward, Otis exultantly promised to buy him a beer back at base camp. "Let's double-check on Charlie Troop. Make a quick run down their column, and see if they're getting their casualties evacuated," Lieutenant Colonel Otis told his pilot, well satisfied with Troop B's progress. By that time, the colonel's regular command ship—an H23 Raven—had arrived, and Otis and Flint had transferred to it from the Troop D commander's chopper. Otis preferred the Raven to the Huey, which he considered too fast to really see what was happening on the ground—"but, holy shit, a '23's just a bubble with a lawn mower engine, and there were a lot of bad guys down there," said Flint, who was highly concerned as they chugged along at forty knots, half the cruising speed of the Huey they had originally been shot down in.

Lieutenant Colonel Otis was sitting to the right of the pilot, and Flint to the left. The light observation helicopter had no room for door gunners. Although the fire on Troop C had slacked off with Troop B in the attack, "when we made a low pass at about a hundred feet to see what condition Charlie Troop was in, the NVA opened up with AK-47s," said Flint. "There were holes everywhere in the '23—the engine, the windshield, the whole nine yards—so we did a quick left-hand turn and plunked that baby down right on the west end of the runway."

Jumping aboard a Huey gunship that swooped down for them, Lieutenant Colonel Otis and Captain Flint were airborne again in minutes. Saber 6 would be shot down two more times before the battle was over, but because the air cav troop was organic to his squadron, replacement aircraft were immediately available, just as there was no delay in receiving gunship and resupply support.

That was pivotal. Had Otis been forced to rely on an ouside aviation unit dividing its assets between numerous hard-pressed outfits that first chaotic morning of Tet, he would have been stuck on the ground after being downed the first time and "would have watched Troop C die on the gates without being able to help," wrote Lieutenant Fletcher. Instead, Otis was able to bring order to the chaos and orchestrate a stunning counterattack that broke the enemy's back. "To have hesitated . . . would have resulted in a disaster," noted a division-level analysis of the battle, which congratulated Otis for being able "to strike swiftly on the spur of the moment, so to speak, and win without the benefit of detailed plans and preparations. In the final analysis, the challenge to a unit to do so represents the most critical test of a commander, the unit's leadership and its fighting spirit and ability . . . ."

Lieutenant Colonel Otis received the Distinguished Service Cross for Tan Son Nhut, and his command the Presidential Unit Citation. "Otis was the best boss I ever had," Flint said. The thirty-eight-year-old West Pointer—a future four-star general—had originally assumed command of the 3d Squadron, 4th Cavalry, in December 1967. Short and stocky, Otis was in superb physical condition. "I don't think there was anybody on any army post who could beat him at handball," noted one captain. He was a tough, intense, decisive, and hard-nosed commander who was also unassuming and down-to-earth. The troops loved him. "Out of the blue, a sole mechanized vehicle would pull up to your position, and it would be Otis, without any security other than what his vehicle provided," wrote Birdwell, noting that this happened day and night at even the most isolated locations in the squadron AO. "He would ask what we were observing, how we were doing, did we need anything and then be on his way. . . ."

Birdwell thought Otis was "blessed with an abundance of intelligence and courage, with a human heart to match." When the squadron commander addressed Charlie Troop after Tan Son Nhut, "[t]ears flowed from his eyes as he spoke, like a parent grieving for a child. He did not choke up, but those tears were very symbolic of his personal anguish over the loss of so many fine men."

The losses quickly mounted. Tet was never the one-day event portrayed by Westmoreland, but actually the start of unrelenting action for the entire 25th Division as the communists, repelled from the urban centers, clung tenaciously to the towns and villages they had seized in the countryside. From February 6, the first day of the seven-day battle for Hoc Mon, to the end of May 1968—the month Lieutenant Colonel Otis left the squadron—the 3-4th Cavalry lost seventy dead and hundreds wounded. Through it all, Otis's "courage was steel like," Birdwell wrote, impressed that the colonel—shot down and wounded at Hoc Mon—was never more than three hundred feet above the action. "Other times, you would be on line kicking the NVA, or being kicked, as the case might be, and behold— next to you in his vehicle would be Otis, directing the fire, moving back and forth, working to secure the objective. . . ."

Lieutenant Colonel Otis left only after being wounded a second time while atop his command track in the midst of another big battle. He was on the horn at the time, so the RPG fragment meant for his head instead splattered his hand, which was on the radio-intercom switch on the right side of his communications helmet. Saber 6 somehow survived Tan Son Nhut unscathed, even though "we rode four choppers to the ground that day," noted Flint (who won the Distinguished Flying Cross for Tet). Otis's gunship-turned-command-ship was orbiting Troop B's action when it was hit by another circle-shape .51-cal position. "There were four in one belt pretty close to the road, then four more in another belt almost a kilometer farther west. We got too enamored with what we were doing, and we weren't paying attention to where those guns were."

The pilot made a controlled crash inside the air base, and Otis and Flint ended up in a Huey "slick"—a lift ship— from the Aerorifle Platoon. By then the battle had spread some distance west of the highway as a Troop B platoon engaged an enemy force spotted behind an earthen berm.

Otis tried to guide the platoon from the air. "While doing that," said Flint, "we were once again too low, too slow, and within range of a .51 position. . . ."

The slick was too shot-up to make it to the air base, and the pilot had to make an emergency landing in what was, given the circumstances, the middle of nowhere. Luckily, there were no enemy in the immediate vicinity, and within minutes, Colonel Thurman, the 25th DivArty commander, rescued everyone from the isolated paddy in his own Huey. Thurman deposited Otis and Flint at Tan Son Nhut, and another slick landed for them from Troop D.

"We're not really sure we want to pick you up, Colonel, because you've been having a *bad* day," the pilot joked.

Troop D lost numerous helicopters at Tan Son Nhut in part because the weather favored the enemy. "There was about a 400-foot ceiling. If you got up above the cloud cover, you wouldn't be able to see anything, and below it, you were in the kill zone," remembered one aviator. The experiences of WO1 Michael D. Siegel, a lift platoon aircraft commander, are instructive. Winning a Distinguished Flying Cross, Siegel conducted the first medevac for Troop C, landing near the lane that had been cleared through the perimeter wire. The Huey took thirty-seven hits, but Siegel made it to Bien Hoa with the casualties. Leaving the shot-up slick on the medevac pad, Siegel and crew were flown back to Cu Chi, where they immediately cranked up another Huey. Altogether they flew six to eight resupply-medevac missions in support of Troop C. In the process, the replacement ship accumulated enough holes that Siegel lost all hydraulics and had to crash-land on the runway. The third Huey of the day also picked up considerable battle damage but stayed aloft until the battle was over.

The action that resulted in Saber 6's last shoot-down was Troop B's most traumatic during the course of the battle. It involved Lieutenant Gallo's platoon on the right flank, and initially centered on rice stalks randomly piled haystack-like around the field that rolled west from the village. The field was a recently harvested rice paddy, now dry and hard. Enemy soldiers had taken cover under the stacks, and when they exposed their positions by firing, Gallo's .50-cal MG gunners hosed the stacks down, blowing some away completely, catching others afire with tracer rounds. With five or six bonfires going, a squad's worth of enemy soldiers ran from their hiding places with their hands up. They ended up behind the troop commander's track, sitting blindfolded, their hands tied behind their backs.

Lieutenant Gallo could see more enemy soldiers running back and forth like shooting-gallery ducks behind a tree-lined berm some five hundred meters further west, just beyond effective small-arms range. The figures dove for cover when fired upon, only to pop up moments later at different spots. It was later speculated that these enemy had exposed themselves in an attempt to pull part of the armored force into an ambush and thus take some of the heat off their comrades in the village.

When Captain Otis finally dispatched Gallo's platoon to the scene, it had just closed within small-arms range when a terrific amount of AK-47 fire erupted from behind the berm. Bravo Three was out in the open field. Gallo's track was marked as a command vehicle by a big radio antenna, and the platoon leader was probably the first man hit—violently lifted up and blown backward through the open cargo hatch while the APC was still rolling forward. The sensation was so wrenching that when he regained consciousness some moments later sprawled atop the duffel bags on the floor of the vehicle, he thought the track had hit a mine. He had a dull stomachache, and realized that he had been shot once through the guts, the bullet piercing the front of his flak jacket. He was numb, only vaguely aware that he couldn't move his legs.

Lieutenant Gallo's communications helmet was still clamped on, and when he reported to the troop commander that he had been wounded, Otis ordered him to pull back to his position for medevac. In Gallo's stead, Otis turned to his executive officer, First Lieutenant Andrew Gerrie, who, acting on his own initiative, had just come barreling down the highway from Cu Chi with as much ammunition as he could load aboard two radar tracks and a tank retriever. Gerrie's mini-convoy was manned by headquarters personnel who had volunteered to fill the breach in this emergency and troop members who had been back at base camp for various administrative reasons when the battle began. Otis viewed their dash through the enemy-controlled countryside as nothing short of heroic. They were needed, and they came.

Otis immediately fed them into the action.

When Lieutenant Gerrie reached Bravo Three, one of its tanks had been disabled by an RPG and the platoon sergeant had been shot through the chest. Specialist Four Vernon C. Wilderspin—a conscientious objector medic—had patched the sucking chest wound and saved the sergeant's life. Wilderspin himself was hit moments later, one of two troops killed in the continuing battle on the far right flank.

Captain Otis also sent in elements of his command group. "I jumped on the communications track, and we hauled ammo out to them," remembered Specialist Four David W. Garrod, the troop commander's radioman. While GIs ran over to the APC to pick up the ammo, Garrod ran to the disabled tank. The loader's legs had been shredded by the RPG hit, and the inside of the turret was "splattered with blood and meat," said Garrod, who helped pull the unconscious loader out. "We carried him to the communications track, then headed back. The smell of blood and burning flesh from the hot shrapnel that tore through the loader's legs still comes to mind when I think back to that day. . . ."

6

Mopping Up

Captain Otis's maintenance track faced the factory to Troop B's rear, and whenever muzzle flashes winked from the roof, the motor sergeant in the commander's cupola suppressed the fire with his .50-cal MG. "We were right out in the open, but the saving grace was that there were no windows on the south side of the factory," noted Lieutenant Fletcher. "To fire on us, the enemy had to get on the roof, and that made them ready targets for Troop D. The gunships would sweep the roof, and then sweep it again whenever the enemy crawled back out there."

Fletcher estimated that Lieutenant Colonel Otis called twenty gunship missions on the factory. Meanwhile, VNAF A1E Skyraiders were scrambled, using the secondary runway at Tan Son Nhut. The Joint Defense Operations Center contacted Captain DeNisio through CSC, asking, "Where do we drop the napalm, where do we drop the bombs?"

"Right on the factory," DeNisio answered.

"Where?"

"Right *on* the factory."

Higher command was hesitant to blow up such a major installation and radioed that "the forward air controller over the area doesn't see anything at the factory."

"Hit the factory!" DeNisio insisted. "I'm telling you, we're getting fire from the factory. . . ."

The mission was approved. Coming in one at a time and using the highway as a guide, the low, slow, prop-driven Skyraiders sailed through tracer fire, released their ordnance, then pulled up through the smoke belching up from the bombs of the planes that came in before. "The bombs floated right over us as if in slow motion before hitting the factory. We were hoping they wouldn't drop one short!" remembered Captain Otis. "There didn't appear to be much external damage to the factory. The bombs went through the roof. The inside of it must have been rubble."

Buttoned up and cut off inside the command track, Lieutenant Larcom and the unconscious Captain Virant were finally rescued by a group led by Specialist Four Steve Uram, a Charlie One track gunner. Uram ran to the vehicle under fire from the roadside ditch and opened the door built into the back ramp of the APC. "The lieutenant had his .45 out because he didn't know who was opening that hatch, but when he saw it was us, he relaxed," Uram recalled. After pulling Larcom to the ditch, Uram ran back to look for the driver, his good buddy Bobby Finnegan. "Bobby was dead at the driver's handles, sitting up in his seat. When he got hit, he pulled back on the handles, but they weren't locked back, so the engine was still running. It was still in gear, and the only thing keeping it from moving was his weight."

Specialist Uram won the Silver Star for the rescue.

Interestingly, Uram had been in Cu Chi when the battle began because his track had hit a mine while rolling over a paddy dike three days earlier. The APC was demolished, and the entire crew injured. Uram suffered a concussion and took fragments in his head. Nevertheless, when word came that Charlie Troop had been ambushed at the air base, Uram's crew cranked up their new APC. "We were just a single vehicle on the road," he said. "We went right through villages that we found out later had been overrun, but somehow we didn't get any contact. . . ."

Pulling up behind the last vehicle on the highway, Uram had moved forward with cans of M60 ammunition. After helping get Virant and Larcom to the ditch, he climbed aboard their track and, ignoring the dead driver and track commander, swung the .50-cal MG into action. "I fired up everything on that track. I fired until it was all over. There were lots of dead enemy soldiers along the side of the road. The live ones were still right up close in the bushes. They'd get up every now and then and rush into view. I had no idea what they were trying to do. I was just shooting. You could put the .50 on them, and it would break a dike, it would break whatever cover they were behind. . . ."

Captain Otis knelt beside Kozlinski's stretcher and asked the maimed track driver how he was doing and if he could do anything for him. "Just get me the fuck outta here!" Kozlinski shouted. One Huey laid a smoke screen near Troop B's command group, and another came in behind it to kick out ammo and take aboard wounded. Kozlinski was quickly loaded aboard, as was Lieutenant Gallo, who had just been carried down the lowered back ramp of his APC. Someone removed the platoon leader's communications helmet, and he was hustled to the waiting chopper on a stretcher before any medical care was provided.

The helicopter landed at the 12th Evacuation Hospital in Cu Chi. The base camp was rocketed throughout the Tet period, and because Kozlinski had too many IVs going to get under his bed, he ended up lying there with a flak jacket and an extra mattress over him. "Those nurses gave up their own flak jackets to the patients," he recalled.

Lieutenant Gallo received last rites from a Catholic chaplain before passing out on a gurney in the triage area. He woke up in bed after surgery, dangling with tubes, a row of rubber-type sutures across his chest and stomach. "Earlier, I had been more in shock than in pain," Gallo said. "Now when I moved, it was extremely painful, so I tried not to move at all—then I realized I couldn't move my legs."

The doctor who came through the ward, checking the patients, asked Gallo, "How you doing?"

"Well, Doc, I can't move my legs."

"Yeah, you were hurt pretty bad," the doctor answered bluntly. "You'll probably never walk again."

Gallo reared up in bed. *Bullshit!* he roared, pulling at his IVs in a panic. One of the nurses quickly administered a sedative that knocked him out.

Lieutenant Gallo, a solid citizen-soldier anxious to get back to his wife and daughter and his high-school teaching position, was awarded the DSC. He was twenty-four years old, and would spend the rest of his life in a wheelchair because the round that went through his guts had bruised his spinal cord. "It rendered me impotent. I lost the function of my bladder and bowels. You really have to adjust. It was like starting your life all over again, and I wouldn't have made it without my wife. I didn't want anything to do with anything that was Vietnam. When my personal belongings caught up with me, I saved a single picture of myself in the field and got rid of all the other photos and souvenirs and my tattered fatigues. . . ."

The most bizarre incident of the battle occurred around noon when the VC in the 051 Bunker, which was by then the last pocket of enemy resistance inside the air base, released the sole survivor of the five-man security police team originally assigned to the position. The iron door at the rear of the bunker was cracked open about a foot or two, and to the astonishment of the SPs moving in on the bunker, the survivor, Sergeant Alonzo J. Coggins, emerged with his hands raised. It had been assumed that everyone in the position had been killed at the beginning of the attack. Being black, Coggins was immediately identified as a friendly, and the fire on the bunker came to a screeching halt. It resumed when the delirious, burned, and badly wounded airman proceeded down the perimeter road and was pulled to cover by troops in the next bunker to the south.

The enemy's humanitarian gesture was never deciphered. Perhaps the VC hoped that by showing mercy, the SPs about to retake the bunker would in turn spare them.

The guerrillas did not surrender, however. Under fire, Sergeant Gifford of the 377th SPS—who was to win the Silver Star—maneuvered to a point on the perimeter fence within hand grenade range of the 051 Bunker. "We used to throw a case of grenades for practice almost every day at the training range, and we would try to get them to detonate in the air," Gifford later wrote. He tried to get an airburst in the doorway, but his first grenade landed about twenty feet to the right of it. "Not so good, but remember at the range we didn't have a helmet or a flak jacket on, so off with the helmet and try again. I pulled the pin, stood up to throw, and immediately dropped back down for all the fire. The second throw was a little closer. . . ."

Peeling off his flak jacket, Gifford popped up to hurl a third grenade, which exploded in midair right in the doorway. The 051 Bunker was thus retaken at 1219, the last three or four VC inside running outside jabbering immediately after the blast. Their hands on top of their heads, they sat down behind the bunker as the SPs moved in to secure the position. "I smoked at the time, Salems to be exact," remembered Gifford, "and later on that day I realized that the unopened pack of cigarettes in my pocket was soaked clear through with sweat."

Lieutenant Colonel George M. Tronsrue's 1-18th Infantry, 1st Infantry Division, participated in the last act of the Battle of Tan Son Nhut. The jungle-fighting battalion had returned to its Lai Khe base camp forty kilometers northwest of Saigon only the day before. "One of our TOC radio operators woke me up in the middle of the night to report that, 'Something big is going on, we're hearing all kinds of stuff on the division net,'" recalled Tronsrue. "We all gathered around the radio, and by the time we got the alert to move to Tan Son Nhut, we were already saddled up."

The battalion flew first to the brigade CP at Di An between Saigon and Bien Hoa. "I got a four-sentence mission order from the colonel and had about forty-five minutes to get ready to lift out of Di An by Chinook," said Tronsrue. It took from 1100 to 1300 to get the entire battalion reassembled at Tan Son Nhut. The pilot of Tronsrue's helicopter reported that they were taking ground fire as they came in, but the infantrymen inside the big Chinook could not see or hear anything. "We landed on one of the runways. People were running every which way, but a lieutenant colonel from whatever headquarters was controlling the battle met me when I got off the helicopter. He passed along an order that my battalion was to attack out the southeast gate and push the enemy back. That was it in terms of a briefing!"

Otis picked Tronsrue up in a scout ship for an overview of the battlefield. The 3-4th Cavalry was mopping up along Highway 1 at that time, while an ARVN unit moved in from the west to cut off the enemy retreat. VNAF Skyraiders and USAF F100 Super Sabers were stacked up, waiting their turn to hit the Vinatexco Factory.

The situation on the western perimeter was well in hand. As such, the 1-18th Infantry, minus Company D, which was detached to secure the MACV HQ, was to attack southeast from Tan Son Nhut. "Fellas, the world has just changed completely," Lieutenant Colonel Tronsrue remarked to his unit commanders as they prepared to deploy out the air base gate. "We're going into a built-up area, and we're going to run this operation just like a Combat in Cities exercise at Benning. We'll put the recon platoon up on the rooftops on either side of the main street, followed by a rifle company on either side as we push through. . . ."

The movement out the gate was by fire team rushes. The GIs proceeded down alleys and through deserted houses. "We had a sharp meeting engagement a block or so outside Tan Son Nhut," said Tronsrue, whose battalion claimed sixteen kills as it pressed on "shucking the VC out of places where they had gone to ground. There was continuing small-arms fire as we moved forward for the next hour, and by the time the enemy broke contact, it was almost dark and we were simply one infantry battalion out in the Saigon streets with no support behind us and no command structure above us. In the absence of any other instructions, we pulled straight back up the street and through the gate through which we had originally left Tan Son Nhut."

Squeezed between infantry and armor and subjected to artillery, gunships, and air strikes, the enemy disintegrated. During the final push through the hamlet along the highway, Staff Sergeant Glen T. Pike, a Troop B squad leader, had never seen such a butcher shop of horrors. He had also never been so scared. At the end of his tour, Pike had been at the Cu Chi airstrip, scheduled for transport to Tan Son Nhut for his flight out of Vietnam that very day, when a jeep pulled up and the driver shouted to him that Bravo Troop was in heavy contact at the air base. The driver explained that he had been told to find Pike, and that he was supposed to load a track with as much ammo as it could carry, and get down to the battle with the sick, lame, and lazy that the driver was rounding up in the base camp.

Sergeant Pike hit the highway behind the .50-cal on an APC. "Oh my God," he thought over and over. "I ain't going to make it home. This is it. . . ."

Captain Otis pointed Pike towards his old APC when he rejoined the troop. It was this track that had been RPG'd at the beginning of the battle, and his driver Kozlinski had yet to be medevacked at that point. "We were all apprehensive about facing such a formidable [enemy] force without our leader," wrote Tom Higgins, who was amazed and relieved when he realized in the middle of the battle that the beloved, big-brotherly Pike had suddenly materialized beside them, firing his M16. "The Sarge didn't leave until it was all over and the enemy had been defeated."

Pike scrambled aboard his track, and turned the .50 on enemy soldiers retreating across the paddies several hundred meters away. "They were trying to get from one treeline to another, and the whole troop was firing at them," said Pike, who won a BSMv. "I'd never seen so many of 'em. You'd see a bunch, you'd open fire—and then they'd be gone, and you didn't know if you hit them or if they just ducked. It was like we couldn't miss, though. The paddy they were in was kind of wet, and you'd walk your fire into these little groups, spraying the water up in a line."

Finally, the enemy disappeared, the fire petered out.

It was then that Pike joined the dismounted sweep through the devastated hamlet. He stared aghast at the human carnage sprawled in the debris. There were enemy soldiers, but also villagers—men, women, and children—who had been ripped apart by canister shells and heavy machine guns. Tom Higgins would never forget the four- or five-year-old girl who wandered past with her mamasan, both of them dazed and whimpering. The little girl was a bloody mess, one arm dangling at her side, shattered bone thrust through the skin.

The sweep flushed the last of the enemy. Sergeant Brewer of Troop C was stunned when three VC/NVA darted out the back door of a hootch previously splintered with machine-gun fire. "They ran across an open area, trying to get to the textile mill," said Brewer, "but I had one of my tracks covering that area, and they cut them down."

All enemy resistance was eliminated by about 1630. The 377th SPS had four killed-in-action (KIA) and eleven wounded-in-action (WIA), while TF 35 had two KIA and an unrecorded number of WIA. The ARVN lost twenty-nine dead, and with the VNAF, approximately fifteen wounded.

Troop B had three KIA and seventeen WIA, and Troop C, 3-4th Cavalry, twelve KIA and forty-eight WIA.

The 1-18th Infantry had one KIA and five WIA.

It was the enemy assault force that paid the real butcher's bill. One hundred and fifty-seven VC/NVA bodies were counted inside the west end of Tan Son Nhut Air Base. There were approximately 350 more in the hamlet along the highway and in the fields to the west. "Some of the bodies had numerous bullet wounds, to include one whose foot had been blown off at the ankle by a .50-caliber round—but the enemy soldiers had tied wire around their limbs for instant tourniquets," noted Specialist Porter of Troop B. "They had wire wrapped just above their ankles, then another piece above or below the kneecap, and more around their arms. If they were hit, they would simply tighten the appropriate wire, and continue to fight. Ingenious!"

Sergeant Pike walked up to a ditch in the hamlet that was stuffed with dead enemy soldiers—and a live one who suddenly stood up. "He could have killed me because he still had his AK-47, but he was hollering, '*Chieu hoi, chieu hoi!*'" Pike remembered. "He laid his weapon down, and I motioned to him, and he came out from the ditch—along with four or five others. Some were wounded, and all were pretty well shell-shocked. They knew they'd had it."

The prisoners were escorted back to the tracks. In all, Troop B captured twenty-four VC and NVA. Pike's squad checked out a hootch in which a dozen shot-to-hell enemy soldiers were sprawled. One was moaning, and Pike jumped on the man and pinned his arms, afraid he might be a diehard with a grenade. He wasn't. He was just another dazed survivor. "As I took him back, I got real angry all of a sudden and I started kicking him in the fanny," Pike said. His emotions were on a roller coaster. Returning to the same hootch, he dragged out a wounded enemy soldier who wore a medical armband. "He needed water, and I started screaming for a medic because I wanted to help the guy. He died in my arms. Even though he was the enemy, it really hurt. I was angry. I hated what they had done. I hated what we had done. I was sick of the whole mess. . . ."

Troop C joined the dismounted sweep. "At one point as we were mopping up, I saw several members of Charlie Troop executing prisoners. There were five or six prisoners in a little clearing in the ville, on their knees with their hands tied behind their backs, and the GIs were shooting them in the head," said Tom Higgins of Bravo Two. The GIs were insane with vengeful anger. "Our platoon leader tried to stop them, but one pointed an M16 at him and told him to mind his own business or he would be next."

The fact that the enemy soldiers in the clearing were all tied and shot in the head was obvious evidence of murder. "I was told to make it look like they had been killed in the firefight, so me and somebody else walked over there and cut the ropes," remembered a Charlie Three trooper who had not participated in the summary executions.

The enemy's hands were bloodier. "One of the [Vietnamese] told us that the NVA had come into the village early that night and killed everyone they could find to keep them from spreading the alarm," wrote Private First Class Ken Hardesty. "The survivors were glad we had gotten there [and] couldn't understand the vicious attack by the NVA."

Presumably, Viet Cong cadre also executed political opponents and their families. During the mop-up, Sergeant Brewer found a Vietnamese family lying face down in a row by size—husband, wife, then oldest to youngest child—all of them executed with a shot to the back of the head.

Many hamlet women were employed as hootch maids at Tan Son Nhut. After the battle, one of them tearfully described to 377th SPS personnel how when the enemy slipped in and prepared for the attack, a VC tortured a family member to death with a knife because U.S. Air Force uniforms were in their home. He thought the family knew secrets about the base. They did not, of course. The uniforms were merely there to be laundered.

Privates Higgins and Hardesty followed a gray-headed mamasan to an unscathed, French-style house in the village. "The old woman kept pointing at a closed door and saying, 'VC! VC!'" Higgins wrote. "I walked to the door and slowly opened it. What we saw was so horrifying that I can't recall the image like I can others. There were several children (one a small baby) and an old man in that room. They had all had their throats slit . . ."

After the wounded were evacuated, the dead went out on a Chinook that landed near the west end of the runway. "There I was, one live guy with all these dead people," remembered Birdwell, who was ordered aboard the Chinook by a lieutenant over his violent protests that his wounds were minor and that he should stay with his platoon. APCs from Charlie One were scattered inside the wire, and as Birdwell hustled to the Chinook, he passed one of his buddies, a black sergeant, who stood atop one of the tracks, laughing and sniping with his M16 at enemy stragglers.

There were twenty-three bodies in the Chinook. "They were uncovered, and they were really a mess," remembered a distraught Birdwell. "Some of them had limbs and parts missing. Some of them were stiffening up. . . ."

Birdwell realized to his horror that one of the casualties—a chubby, popular career Charlie Two NCO with a wife and family back home—was twitching and mumbling incoherently on the floor of the Chinook. He had been shot through his communication helmet while manning the .50-cal on his track. Birdwell grabbed the crew chief, an older black sergeant at a window-mounted M60, and shouted, "This guy's *alive!* He's moving and talking!"

"Aw, forget about it, all bodies do that."

The crew chief refused to look for himself, and Birdwell sat back in his canvas seat, sick and furious. "I knew that sergeant, he was somebody I'd kidded with and palled with. The man was definitely alive, and the crew chief just didn't give a damn. He was totally indifferent. It was no big deal to him, so I just sat there looking at my buddy—looking at his brain where the skull was torn off—and I was thinking, My God, I know he's alive, but how could he. . . ."

When the Chinook landed at Cu Chi, Birdwell explained the situation to the medical personnel that met the chopper. They immediately checked the sergeant—who was indeed still alive—and rushed him into the hospital. The sergeant lasted two weeks on machines before finally passing away.

Bravo Troop's twenty-four prisoners went out on another Chinook. "One of them looked up at me and asked for water," wrote Higgins, who—inflamed about the murdered civilians he had seen—did something he would be ashamed of when tempers cooled. "I walked over, unbuttoned my pants and pissed in his face. I took out all my anger and frustration on that one POW. . . ."

Sergeant Pike was assigned to escort the prisoners back to Cu Chi, where they were packed into a truck. "When we pulled up to the holding compound, an MP opened the tailgate and started grabbing these prisoners and sliding them right off the back of the truck like they were duffel bags," Pike remembered. "All of them were wounded and tied up. If they could land on their feet, fine, if they couldn't, too bad—and I'm thinking that this asshole's probably never seen combat in his life, and he's treating these guys like dirt when they were in the same battle I was but they got the worst of it. I told him to knock it off. I'm pretty sure I pointed my M16 at him, I was that upset."

The 3-4th Cavalry and 1-18th Infantry pulled back inside Tan Son Nhut before dark, where they were joined by elements of the 2-27th Infantry. "The ground troops had to camp right in amongst the bodies between the runway and the perimeter," noted Lieutenant Grover, USAF. "We had gone through and shot every one of those bodies, but the next morning two enemy soldiers popped up and surrendered to the infantry. I don't know where they'd been hiding, but they were two scared fellas."

Part 2

Saigon

"In the Tables of Organization and Equipment of every military police unit, the secondary mission is 'To fight as infantry when required. . . .'"

—Lt. Col. Richard E. George
Saigon Provost Marshal
18th Military Police Brigade

7

Firefight at the U.S. Embassy

The defense of the capital being the responsibility of the ARVN, there were no U.S. combat units in Saigon on the eve of the Tet Offensive. There was no indication that any would be needed. When Westmoreland issued his "maximum alert" order, the best information available to Brigadier General Albin F. Irzyk, CG, Headquarters Area Command (HAC)—which controlled the various support units stationed in Saigon—was that a number of sapper units were already in the city, and that some type of attack might occur in the next twenty-four to forty-eight hours.

Brigadier General Irzyk presently had George report to HAC headquarters, along with Lieutenant Colonel G. D. "Doug" Rowe, commander of the 716th MP Battalion, 18th MP Brigade. As Provost Marshal (PM), George exercised operational control of the 716th MPs, the primary combat support unit available to HAC. The decision was made to convert all foot patrols to jeep patrols for the night, to have reaction forces standing by, and to man additional posts at some of the more likely targets, to include MACV HQ, HAC HQ, the PM Office, and the Armed Forces Radio and Television Station.

Lieutenant Colonel George anticipated that the attacks "would be the usual terrorist hits on one or more of our

99

billets or activities. There wasn't even the slightest hint that the VC effort would be as massive as it was. . . ."

It was later estimated that in addition to the regimental-size force that hit Tan Son Nhut, eleven more battalions infiltrated Saigon. These 4,000 VC went undetected before they emerged. "We had no idea," said First Lieutenant Gerald L. Waltman of the 716th MP Battalion, who ruefully thought that the Viet Cong had probably been able to test fire their weapons amid the Tet fireworks. "It seemed like we'd get a 'maximum alert' every two weeks. You'd gear up—and nothing would happen. When we went to 'maximum alert' during Tet, the feeling was, okay, here we go again. There was not a lot of trepidation that night."

Saigon was untouched, the eye of the storm.

This bubble of invulnerability would be burst most spectacularly by the sixteen sappers assigned to seize the U.S. Embassy in downtown Saigon. The Embassy attack was actually only one head of the Hydra. Major General Tran Do of the Central Office for South Vietnam (COSVN)—the communist high command for the Saigon and Mekong Delta areas—commanded the attack on Saigon. Do's initial eleven-battalion assault force was primarily composed of local force units since they were most familiar with the routes to the capital. After capturing key points in the city during the night, these battalions—operating under 9th VC Division control—were to hold in place until joined by a second wave of main force units that would arrive at daybreak, brushing aside what remained of the ARVN and igniting the people to rise up with the liberation fighters. It would all be over very quickly, the capital under the Viet Cong banner before the U.S. could respond.

Many members of the C-10 Sapper Battalion worked in Saigon as taxi and pedicab drivers and led attacks on primary objectives like the Presidential Palace and the Joint General Staff HQ. The Embassy team, however, was from the C-10 headquarters near the Michelin Rubber Plantation north of Saigon. The VC arrived on buses packed with holiday travelers two days before Tet and went to safe houses. Their weapons, ammunition, and explosives had been smuggled in over the preceding three months in rented trucks loaded with rice, tomatoes, and firewood.

The sappers rendezvoused with their two team leaders after midnight on Tet at an automobile repair shop five blocks from the Embassy. The garage was owned by a female Viet Minh veteran. The weapons cached there—brand-new AK-47s and RPG launchers—were broken out, and the team departed for the Embassy in a taxicab and a small Peugeot truck. The sappers were dressed as civilians in slacks and shirts, the only thing uniform about them being their red armbands and red-and-blue checkered neckerchiefs. They were to breach the walled compound and seize the main building. There was no withdrawal plan.

Two military policemen were on duty at the side gate of the Embassy. The front gate in the southeast wall had been secured for the night, but the side gate in the northeast wall along Mac Dinh Chi Street remained open. The tree-shaded Embassy compound was situated at the intersection of Mac Dinh Chi and Thong Nhut Boulevard. The rectangular, six-storied Embassy Chancery fronted Thong Nhut. It had shatterproof Plexiglas windows and an outer facade of gleaming white, rocketproof concrete. The nine-foot wall around the compound, also made of white concrete, was hemmed in by buildings on two sides and paralleled by Mac Dinh Chi and Thong Nhut on the other two.

There was a South Vietnamese police station near the Embassy on Mac Dinh Chi, but the officer at the checkpoint there took no action when the taxi and truck rolled past with their lights off. As the taxi turned right onto Thong Nhut, one of the men inside fired his AK-47 back at the two MPs standing just outside the side gate. The vehicles stopped out of sight around the corner, and the sappers climbed out, hurriedly unloading RPGs and satchel charges.

The helmeted, flak-jacketed guards at the side gate—Specialist Four Charles L. Daniel and Private First Class William E. Sebast of the 527th MP Company, which was attached to the 716th MP Battalion—immediately rushed inside, slammed shut the steel-barred gate, and locked it with a heavy padlock and chain.

It was 0247 on January 31, 1968. Daniel grabbed the radio in their guard post. "Waco, Waco, this is the American Embassy!" he shouted, using the call sign for the PM Office, and then the brevity code for enemy attack: "Signal 300!"

In the next instant, the sappers blew a hole at the base of the southeast wall near the corner. It was just big enough to wriggle through. "They're comin' in, they're comin' in!" Daniel screamed on the radio. "Help me, help me . . .!"

Daniel and Sebast wheeled toward the hole, their backs to the wall of their post, and sprayed it with M16 fire. Leading the way, the two VC cadre were killed instantly. The others kept coming, some firing AK-47s through the hole while others vaulted the wall. Daniel was shot in the face and Sebast the chest, cut down in a flurry of cement dust as the wall behind them was blasted, too. The dead military policemen lay sprawled on their faces as the sappers spread out across the manicured lawn, heading for the Chancery. One leveled his RPG at the front door.

Though the Embassy buildings were guarded by United States Marines, exterior security for the compound was the responsibility of the Saigon police—the infamously corrupt Canh Sats. Four officers were assigned to the Embassy from the adjacent First Precinct station house. One manned a concrete kiosk on the northeast wall near the Mac Dinh Chi-Thong Nhut intersection; had this officer responded in concert with those stationed along the southeast wall where another kiosk was located, the sappers would have been caught in a crossfire as they emerged from their vehicles. The terrified officers did not fire a shot, however.

Two lightly armed Marine Security Guards (MSGs) were on night watch in the Chancery; a third was stationed on the roof this night because of the maximum alert.

When the sappers opened fire, Sergeant Ronald W. Harper, the senior Chancery guard, was pouring a cup of coffee in the guard post of the two MSGs assigned to the consulate offices in what was known as the Norodom compound. This rectangular complex occupied the southwest side of the Embassy grounds, and though within the security wall, it was separated from the main compound by an inner wall.

The shooting was followed by a jarring explosion. While

the Norodom MSGs took up positions to cover their gate on Thong Nhut, Harper ran to a gate at the far end of the wall between the two compounds, then raced across the parking lot behind the Chancery while one of the four Vietnamese drivers on night duty went by in the other direction, seeking refuge in the generator building along the back wall.

Sergeant Harper yanked at the side stairwell entrance of the Chancery. It was locked, as was the service entrance. Fearing that he was locked out—Corporal George B. Zahuranic on duty in the lobby would have secured the main entrance by now—he was surprised and relieved to find one of the front doors still open. Zahuranic was on the phone at the receptionist's desk, calling for help. The telephone at their adjacent guard desk was ringing. Zahuranic went to answer it while Harper bolted the three-inch teakwood double doors he had just rushed through. He then spun around and ran for the armory to secure a weapon with more punch than his revolver. The first RPG hit the front wall then. . . .

Sergeant Rudy A. Soto had helplessly watched the rocketeer take aim at the Chancery from his special rooftop post. Barely able to hear the firefight over the roaring air-conditioner motors on the roof, Soto had originally tried to fire his pump shotgun when the MPs at the side gate were silenced and two figures immediately crawled through the hole in the wall. The shotgun jammed.

The two sappers rushed to a circular concrete planter to the left front of the Chancery. There was a line of low, approximately twelve-foot-wide planters in the front lawn, a little tree sprouting from each. Putting aside his jammed shotgun, Soto drew his .38 and proceeded to fire the only five rounds he had been issued at the sappers behind the planter, one of whom had shouldered an RPG launcher.

From six stories up, Soto couldn't help but miss. The first rocket penetrated the granite slab bearing the seal of the United States by the front door and exploded over the receptionist's desk in the lobby. Harper was knocked to the floor, wounded in his leg. The next RPG punched through the front doors and sailed across the lobby to explode against the back wall. Harper secured a 9mm Beretta submachine gun, while Zahuranic—hit in the shoulder, arm, chest, and head, his right leg broken—dragged himself into the armory and grabbed a Beretta of his own. He was too badly injured to load it. Harper fired three test shots into the receptionist's desk, then got a handful of paper towels for Zahuranic to hold against his head wound, which was bleeding badly.

The attack could be heard five blocks away at the security guard billet, a converted hotel known as the Marine House. Because of the maximum alert, Captain Robert J. O'Brien, the Officer in Charge (OIC) of the MSGs, had secured all liberty, and those troops not on duty were on standby at the Marine House. Awakened by the duty NCO, O'Brien—sleeping in civvies on a sofa in the movie room, having returned earlier from a tour of the detachment's fifteen posts—raced to his radio-equipped sedan and immediately departed with one of his sergeants. Three more marines piled into a jeep and followed the sedan out the compound gate.

The MSGs had neither standard infantry weapons nor helmets and flak jackets. They wore Stateside utilities and covers. The reaction force stopped as it turned onto Mac Dinh Chi from Hong Thap Tu—the police station was at the corner—because a Canh Sat at the checkpoint was frantically pointing toward the Embassy and shouting, "VC, VC!"

Captain O'Brien and his four men—Sergeants Richard J. Frattarelli, Michael J. Patullo, Raymond E. Reed, and Corporal Timothy P. Inemer—hurried up the tree-lined street on foot. Reaching the locked side gate less than ten minutes after the initial distress call, O'Brien softly called out to the MPs stationed there, unaware that they were already dead. In response, a half-dozen sappers spun toward the marines.

Stunned by the abrupt face-to-face confrontation, no one moved for a second—then O'Brien, armed only with a pistol, shouted at Reed to open fire with his Beretta. The husky black sergeant jammed the muzzle of his submachine gun through the barred gate and pulled off a burst. One of the sappers fell. The rest returned fire, forcing the marines across the street, where they ducked behind trees and fired back at the gate, revolvers against automatic weapons.

Having scrambled aboard a truck, the second reaction force proceeded up Thong Nhut toward the front gate but encountered two MP jeeps a block from the Embassy. There had been three tarp-covered jeeps patrolling the area when the frantic call for help originally came from the Embassy. Sergeant Jonnie B. Thomas and Specialist Four Owen E. Mebust of the 527th MPs—in the first jeep to reach the scene—also roared right up Thong Nhut, disregarding battalion policy to dismount one block from an area of enemy activity and approach on foot to make ambush more difficult. Thomas was shot in the back as soon as they stopped across the street from the front gate and he emerged from the passenger side of the vehicle. Mebust rushed to him, grabbed the radio handset from the jeep—and took a burst of fire before he could use it, killed like the sergeant by a sniper in an eight-story apartment on their side of Thong Nhut Boulevard.

The MPs at the two-jeep roadblock told the marines to vacate the area, then said they'd be crazy to proceed when they explained that they were the Embassy MSGs. "I was getting mad and saw that time was wasting," wrote Staff Sergeant Leroy J. Banks, the second reaction force leader. "I ignored the MPs and ordered my men to get out of the vehicle, to form in two columns and spread out. Our job and orders were to get to the Embassy and save it. I had one column take and move down by cover of the trees lining the wide sidewalk and my column was to move along the wall. We took off with a dash . . ."

Upon reaching the Norodom gate, Banks left his five-man right column to provide cover fire while he proceeded toward the front gate with his other two marines. They passed a Canh Sat playing turtle in the kiosk between the two gates—then a grenade landed on the sidewalk, and automatic fire from the apartment across the street stitched the white wall against which the marines were silhouetted. Hitting the deck, they had no option but to withdraw.

Banks covered them, then fell back last.

The sappers lobbed another grenade over the wall. It hit Sergeant James W. Jimerson in the leg as he crouched behind a tree, but he kicked it into the gutter before it exploded.

The Norodom MSGs unlocked their gate, and the reaction force hurried inside. Several marines climbed atop the Office of the Special Assistant (OSA), which ran along the inner wall and overlooked the Embassy grounds. Two others rushed to the gate between the two compounds. "When we arrived, I saw a Vietnamese walking behind a blue sedan [in the Chancery parking lot]," wrote Corporal Richard L. Huss, who had drawn his .38, but held his fire, thinking the man might be an Embassy employee. "He continued walking into the light. When I finally noticed his rifle, I emptied my [pistol] at him, apparently hitting his lower body, because he fell and crawled behind another vehicle."

Covering the Chancery lobby from the doorway of the armory, Sergeant Harper could hear Vietnamese voices just outside the main doors, and he ducked when a grenade bounced in through a damaged window grill. Harper expected the enemy to burst through the doors any second. He braced himself to go down shooting. The two radios on the guard desk had been destroyed, but the telephones were intact. Harper was thus out of touch with Sergeant Soto—the guard on the roof had a radio, no phone—but he did have an open line with Mr. E. Allen Wendt, a USAID economics expert serving as Embassy night duty officer on the fourth floor of the Chancery. Wendt, in turn, was in touch with civilian and military officials in Saigon and Washington. There were also two Vietnamese employees trapped in the Chancery—a night watchman and a teletype operator on the ground floor—plus a code clerk, an army communications man, and the CIA night duty officer and two of his men on the fourth floor.

The only other friendlies in the compound were Colonel George D. Jacobson, U.S. Army (Retired), and Master Sergeant Robert L. Josephson, U.S. Army (Retired), who served as assistants to the ambassador. Jacobson's title was mission coordinator, and he lived in a French villa in the north corner of the compound behind the Chancery. Jacobson and Josephson, a houseguest on his last night in-country, were both unarmed, and in desperation, the old sergeant grabbed a coat hanger as a weapon.

When Harper told Wendt that they needed to get Zahuranic to the rooftop helipad for medevac, Private First Class Charles M. Fisher, the army communications man, came down. Harper had the GI cover him with his Beretta while he dragged Zahuranic into one of the two elevators in the lobby, both of which were exposed to fire from the front windows. Retrieving the submachine gun, Harper handed the unarmed soldier a revolver and shotgun, plus a box of shotgun shells for Soto on the roof.

Next, Sergeant Banks phoned from the Norodom guard post and instructed Harper to ensure that no VC had gotten inside the Chancery. Harper crawled out of the armory and was dashing to the service entrance when a Vietnamese suddenly popped his head out from the alcove. Harper almost blew the apparition away with his Beretta, but recognized that it was their elderly night watchman a second before he squeezed the trigger. The man had run inside from his post at the front doors when the attack began.

Harper frisked the watchman, then took him back to the armory, where he sat in a corner for the rest of the night. Meanwhile, Soto had locked the door to the roof, thinking the enemy was inside the building. When someone tried to open it, the unarmed Soto—not knowing that it was Fisher trying to get Zahuranic to the helipad—retreated to a secluded spot on the roof. Informed of the problem, Harper had the civilian code clerk come down for the passkey, which he tossed to the man along with a revolver. Before the code clerk went back up, Harper shouted at him to lock both elevators at the fourth floor so that the enemy would be unable to use them if they got inside the building. He then resumed his lone defense of the lobby.

At about the twenty-minute mark, the first military police reaction force was dispatched to the Embassy from the International Hotel in central Saigon. Lieutenant Colonel Rowe's 716th MP Battalion was headquartered in the hotel with three companies. The fourth company was at Tan Son

Nhut. "Our method of operation was quite simple," noted Lieutenant Colonel George. "There was a reaction force at the ready twenty-four hours a day. Vehicles were previously loaded with equipment, ammo, etc., and the men were in their alert gear. As soon as the first reaction force was committed, another predesignated force moved up. . . ."

First Lieutenant Frank Ribich led the first reaction force, a 527th MP Company squad that leapfrogged up Thong Nhut under sniper fire after detrucking at JFK Square.

The MPs reached the Norodom compound at 0330, and were taking up positions with the MSGs when Huss ran back to Sergeant Banks to report the open gate into the main Embassy compound. Banks grabbed two MPs with an M60 who had just arrived in a gun jeep, and hustled to the gate with six of his marines. Three more MSGs were already there, exchanging fire with VC crouched behind cars in the parking lot. Banks thought they could slip through one at a time, and Sergeant Jimerson elected to go first since he had a Beretta. Darting through the gate, he emptied his submachine gun at two sappers running across the parking lot. He hit one while the other dove for cover, then started backing up to escape all the return fire. A rocket-propelled grenade slammed into the wall with an ear-ringing blast, and he was knocked down in a daze, hit in the hand.

Jimerson was shot in the leg in the next instant, but the M60 team took the heat off him as he groped his way back through the gate. Banks and several MSGs were moving him toward the guard post—Banks had taken superficial arm wounds himself from the rocket—when another RPG sent them ducking for cover. Having been bandaged, Jimerson was lying on his back near the guard post when yet a third RPG was fired—and two flak-jacketed MPs instantly jumped on him to shield him from the blast, so that he only caught a small fragment in his arm.

Jimerson was trundled off in an ambulance at 0355. As the battle continued, Corporals James C. Marshall and Dennis L. Ryan lay on one side of the peaked OSA roof—Marshall had gotten there first, but armed with only a .38, had gladly pulled the Beretta-toting Ryan up with him—and engaged a group of sappers ensconced behind the decorative planters in front of the Chancery. Three of them tried to crawl along the front wall to get a good shot at the two marines, who were shielded by a tree, but jumped up to run when they were spotted and taken under fire.

Ryan dropped all three. Another sapper emerged from behind a planter, crawling forward with a grenade. "[Marshall] opened up with his pistol and blew his head off," wrote Ryan. "[W]hen he hit the lawn [the] grenade went off under him[,] blowing him about two feet into the air. . . ."

Ryan sprayed another sapper who popped up from behind a planter with an AK-47—then an RPG slammed into the roof. Badly injured and blown backward, Ryan rolled into the gutter. Marshall helped get him down to the ground, then ignoring his own injuries—he had been hit in the side of the head—he climbed right back onto the roof with another MSG and resumed firing with Ryan's Beretta.

Lieutenant Ribich dispatched two MPs to join the marines on the roof. Shortly thereafter, Ribich was checking the MPs he had stationed on Thong Nhut when a black sedan approached from the direction of the Embassy. Ribich ordered the driver to stop, but the man kept going, perhaps because others were shouting at him to get out of the area. He finally halted at the roadblock down the street.

The driver was either a panicked civilian or an enemy agent dispatched for the sapper team. He told the MP who approached the sedan that he was trying to get home, but when the MP leaned over to look in the backseat, he hit the gas, spun around, and roared back up the street. The MPs at the roadblock chased the sedan with machine-gun fire, and Ribich sprayed the driver's door, engine, and left front tire with his M16 as it came past. The troops on the OSA roof fired down at it, and in the confusion an MP across the street also cut loose, forcing Ribich to dive for cover as stray rounds splattered the front wall. The bullet-riddled sedan, its left-side windows shattered, veered to the right, coming to rest at the curb. The driver was dead at the wheel.

Ten or fifteen minutes into Captain O'Brien's firefight at the side gate, the OIC sent Sergeant Frattarelli back to the police checkpoint where they had left their radio-equipped sedan. O'Brien wanted Frattarelli to get more men and ammunition from Gunnery Sergeant Allen Morrison, the senior MSG at the Marine House. The Canh Sats opened up on Frattarelli as he approached, but ceased fire after he identified himself. Frattarelli was able to get through then to Morrison, an older black NCO who organized needed support throughout the battle and who served as a link between the forces converging on the Embassy, relaying information from Soto, for example, about the disposition of the enemy, and otherwise maintaining coordination between the MPs and Marine Security Guards.

Frattarelli was still on the radio when gray-haired Leo E. Crampsey, the senior Embassy security officer, drove up with Robert J. Furey, his deputy. Crampsey and Furey's house on nearby Pasteur Street served as Ambassador Ellsworth Bunker's predesignated emergency hideaway, and only moments after the security officers had scrambled to their car upon hearing the gunfire at the Embassy, the ambassador had arrived in an armored personnel carrier.

Sergeant Kenneth W. Ariola, the MSG in charge of the ambassador's security detail, had awakened Bunker with the startling news that Saigon was under attack. The location of Bunker's villa obviously being known to the enemy—it was four blocks from the Embassy—Ariola told the ambassador that there was no time to dress, that he should simply put a bathrobe on over his pajamas. As Ariola hurried Bunker out to the armored vehicle, the MSGs remaining behind to defend the villa were in the process of burning the secret documents in the ambassador's safe and briefcase.

Having joined up with O'Brien, Furey tried without success to shoot the lock off the side gate with his .357 Magnum. Frustrated and outgunned, O'Brien and Crampsey finally decided that they should cover all exits from the compound and resume the attack only after bringing up reinforcements. Ribich and Banks had come to the same conclusion. "[S]ince I felt that any attempt on our part to gain entry by scaling the walls would result in extremely heavy casualties, I ordered [Sergeant] Banks to team up with the Military Police and maintain a holding action until daybreak," wrote Gunny Morrison. "I believed that this was the most sound tactic, since the enemy was unable to either enter the Chancery or effect a breakout."

At this time, General Westmoreland was trapped in his Tran Quy Cap Street villa but was in uninterrupted phone contact with the MACV Operations Center at Tan Son Nhut. With a nationwide conflagration at hand, the theater commander was not overly concerned with a doomed VC squad in the Embassy compound. When the general's aide, Captain Charles W. Sampson, USMC, telephoned Harper in the Chancery to get a situation report, he was unimpressed with the urgency in the guard's voice. "What's the trouble, Sergeant?" Sampson barked.

"The VC are right outside the door, I tell you."

"You're not scared or anything, are you, Sergeant?" asked Sampson, suspecting Harper of exaggerating the situation.

"You bet your ass I am," Harper shot back.

The sappers had enough plastique to reduce the lobby doors to splinters, but instead of using it, they merely fired four more RPGs at the upper floors of the Chancery. With their two cadre killed in the first moments of the battle, the remaining VC—leaderless and unaware of the psychological impact of their attack on the U.S. Embassy, and how much greater it would have been had they seized any part of the Chancery—took up defensive positions and fought it out like the simple and dedicated soldiers they were.

Lieutenant Colonel George had no contact with the Embassy personnel. "I was operating under the worst case scenario, i.e, that the VC had gained entry to the [Chancery]," he wrote. George therefore planned to land MPs on the roof in coordination with an assault into the compound itself, but was unable to shake loose any helicopter support from the U.S. combat units base-camped around Saigon.

Urged by civilian officials to clear the Embassy posthaste to minimize the political damage, Westmoreland presently telephoned George to indicate "that the Embassy has first priority." George called the 101st Airborne Division (ABD) then, having been rebuffed by the unit when originally searching for helicopter support. He repeated his request, but this time added, "General Westmoreland says—"

The provost marshal was immediately interrupted by a suddenly receptive voice at the other end of the line: "Where do you want the choppers?"

As the counterattack was organized, the stalemate continued. From atop a two-story building overlooking the side wall, Furey used a borrowed M16 to shoot a guerrilla he spotted crawling towards the front of the Chancery. To block enemy escape over the rear wall, Captain O'Brien and Crampsey darted across the street to the agricultural school between the Embassy and the police station. Climbing a bamboo ladder to the top of a shed situated against the outside of the rear wall, O'Brien and Crampsey opened fire on two or three sappers in the driveway behind the mission coordinator's villa. It looked as if the security officer hit one—the man stumbled and fell behind a car.

Captain O'Brien sent Frattarelli back to their sedan again to request more ammunition. The Canh Sats shot at him in the dark, however, even as he crouched behind a tree, shouting that he was an American. With O'Brien cut off from his one and only radio, Banks sent several men to physically reestablish contact with him. Incredibly, the Canh Sats would not let the marines through their checkpoints.

At 0430, a fifty-man reaction force under Captain James T. Chester, CO of B/716th MP Battalion, was dispatched by truck from the International Hotel. The reinforcements arrived during a heavy flare-up in the action—a medevac was trying unsuccessfully to land on the Chancery—and as the MPs deployed across the street from the front wall, they scurried behind trees and lampposts and vehicles at each burst of automatic-weapons fire. They returned fire through the steel bars of the front gate.

Correspondents were gathering, and one asked if the enemy had taken the Chancery. "My God, yes," said Captain Chester. "We are taking fire from up there. Keep your head down!" The inaccurate press reports about VC in the Chancery all originated with troops on the scene. The MPs also did not know that most of the fire coming in their direction was actually stray stuff from the marines.

This confusion may have resulted in tragedy. At 0600, Corporal Marshall was firing his Beretta from atop the OSA when he was suddenly shot through the throat and killed. The MSG and two MPs with him scrambled off the roof, thinking the apartment sniper had them in his sights. The shot had definitely come from across the street, but there was speculation later that it was the keyed-up military policemen along Thong Nhut who were responsible.

Sergeant Banks did not think so. "We spotted the sniper and opened up on him with an M16. . . ."

Fifteen minutes later, Captain Thomas W. Hill, the medevac pilot previously forced away, tried again. Hill approached the rear of the Chancery with his lights off and landed on the helipad, which was marked by four corner lights that were turned on only at the last moment. The crew unloaded several cases of M16 ammo—they went unused, no one in the Embassy had an M16—then Soto and Fisher helped Zahuranic aboard, and the code clerk supervising the evacuation signaled the pilot to take off. Heavy fire was received as the Huey cleared the roof, and Soto saw a bullet tear through the floor seven inches from Zahuranic's head as he held the wounded man steady.

The Huey took multiple hits. Captain Hill was forced to set down in a rice paddy several miles south of the city—the helicopter was losing fuel from its riddled tanks—but another medevac had been alerted and immediately landed beside the first. Soto and Hill's medic sloshed through the waist-high water and mud to get Zahuranic to the second ship, which took off while Hill's crew chief climbed under their helicopter and stuffed the bullet holes in the fuel tanks with rags. They were airborne again in minutes.

Dawn was approaching when Captain O'Brien told Reed to make a try for the radio in their sedan. The light was such that the trigger-happy Canh Sats could clearly tell who Reed was. They held their fire, and the call for men and ammunition went through. With help on the way, O'Brien and Sergeant Patullo climbed the rear wall while Crampsey fired cover from atop the shed in the agricultural school grounds. As soon as they topped the wall Patullo was shot in the thigh. O'Brien and an MP got a tourniquet around his leg while Frattarelli ran back to their truck, which he and Inemer then used to evacuate Patullo.

The reinforcements arrived then. Gunny Morrison had called for volunteers from the Marine House guards, and Sergeants David R. Bothwell, Richard L. Johnson, and Joseph S. Wolff moved out in a truck. They scaled O'Brien's shed with extra ammo, enabling the OIC's group to keep the enemy around the mission coordinator's villa busy. Bothwell also leveled his revolver at two VC at the far corner of the Chancery, and both went down.

Meanwhile, Sergeants Reed, Johnson, and Wolff set out to find a firing position overlooking the parking lot. They moved across several closely packed buildings, using a bamboo pole to crawl under the concertina wire on the roofs, then jumped a five-foot gap to the generator building against the inside of the rear wall. Johnson crawled behind a ventilator, then ripped off some Beretta fire at three sappers across the parking lot. The surprised VC ducked behind the structural pillars around the first floor of the Chancery.

When Johnson paused to reload, one of the sappers stepped from behind his pillar to return fire—and instantly crumpled as Reed, who had just slid into position behind another ventilator, pumped a fifteen-round burst into him from his Beretta. Out of ammo, Reed called to Johnson to throw him a magazine. The other two VC edged around their cover to fire at Reed, and Johnson was able to bring the closest one down with several bursts. Johnson hit the other sapper with the last five rounds in his submachine gun, but the man managed to get back to his feet and slip around the side of the building. His escape was temporary—the MPs were about to bust through the front gate.

Daybreak on this overcast morning was at 0700. The attack to recapture the Embassy commenced fifteen minutes earlier to draw fire away from the heliborne assault force that had just arrived. Dodging and ducking, MPs made it to the locked front gate and tried to force entry as the six helicopters approached the Chancery. Major Hillel Schwartz, a division intelligence officer, and Captain John C. Speedy III, commander of C/1-502d Infantry, 101st Airborne Division—one of whose platoons had been selected for the combat assault on the Embassy—were in the lead Huey. The landing was unsuccessful, automatic fire hitting the right side of the command ship and the door gunner, whose blood splattered the passenger compartment ceiling.

The damaged Huey turned around for Long Binh, where

Schwartz and Speedy's command group scrambled aboard a new ship and immediately headed back for Saigon. Meanwhile, security officer Furey stumbled across the hole the VC had blown in the wall. He drew fire when he peered through, but apparently hit one of the sappers when he blasted back with his pistol. Borrowing an M16, Furey cautiously crawled through—and saw a wounded sapper preparing to throw a grenade at him. He shouldered his M16, but the sapper, too weak to throw the grenade, blew up in his sights before he could squeeze the trigger on him.

With the fire on the front gate suppressed, a lieutenant was able to shoot the padlock off. It still would not budge. The MPs rammed the gate with a jeep, forcing it open enough to allow them to enter one at a time—Private First Class Paul V. Healey, B/716th MP Battalion, was the first man through—and as the troops fanned out across the grounds, they were followed by a gaggle of reporters, photographers, and television crews. While crawling alongside the Chancery at this time, Furey was mistaken for a VC by the marines above the rear wall and fired upon. One round hit the granite facade by his head, stinging him with debris.

There was not much left of the sapper squad at this stage, and no fire on the second approach of the assault force from the 101st ABD. Upon landing, the paratroopers began to methodically clear the Chancery from the top floor down. Meanwhile, Healey made it to the front doors and told Harper to unlock them. "The MP hollered at his buddies not to shoot because there was a Marine inside," Harper wrote—but when he went past a window the MPs opened up, mistaking him for a VC. Healey, shouting at everyone to cease fire, suddenly had to use his M16 then. "I heard a movement to my left and turned and a VC threw a grenade at me," he told reporters. "I killed him—and I thought I was dead, too. But the grenade never went off . . ."

Earning a DSC, Healey got two more sappers with a grenade. Officially, nineteen VC were killed. The MPs and marines, who lost five dead and fifteen wounded, actually accounted for sixteen, to include a Vietnamese driver—a seventeen-year employee of the Embassy, and one-time chauffeur for the ambassador—who had a pistol jammed in his belt and an AK-47 beside his body. The other three Embassy drivers were also killed and counted as enemy, though all were unarmed. One was mowed down as he crouched behind a planter, frantically shouting and waving what turned out to be his employee identification card.

One blood-splattered sapper survived. His arms raised in surrender, he appeared on the cover of *Life,* flanked by Sergeant Robert Kuldas—an MP who helped capture him—and a younger GI. The Viet Cong was policed up after Kuldas and another MP noticed bloody footprints on the Embassy side of the Norodom wall, an injured VC having scaled the wall into the other compound. The Vietnamese watchman assigned to the Norodom compound had seen the guerrilla duck into the OSA building. He alerted an MSG, who joined the two MPs. Entering the OSA, they tried to open the door to the map room, but someone held it closed from the other side. They shouted at whoever was in there to surrender, and getting no response, opened fire on the door, blowing it open. The sapper stood there, unarmed and cornered.

The U.S. Embassy was secured around 0830, after an hour-long shoot-out with a wounded sapper who had holed up in Colonel Jacobson's two-story white stucco villa behind the Chancery. Jacobson had spent the night in the upstairs hall, clutching the only weapon he had—a grenade he had found in the desk in his bedroom. He had phone contact with the outside world, and when he noticed bloody spots on the rug at the bottom of the steps he was guarding, he whispered to a marine at another post in the city to notify the Embassy MSGs a sapper was inside his house.

It turned out to be one highly tenacious VC. When Furey led several MPs and MSGs in a rush on the back door, the sapper drove them back with AK-47 fire. The same thing happened at the front door. Again leading the way, Healey kicked open another door on the front porch and charged inside with Sergeant Bothwell, who was immediately shot through the thigh. Healey dragged the marine back out, then threw a grenade into the villa without visible effect on the enemy, though it stunned and deafened Jacobson who was lying quietly at the top of the staircase inside, ready to roll his own grenade down should the sapper appear.

Captain O'Brien ran in a crouch along the front porch, dashed up the steps, and started pulling Bothwell to safety. The sapper sent a grenade out the door at them, and O'Brien, dropping into a crouch over his sergeant, was peppered in his arm and side. Aided by an MP, O'Brien got Bothwell to cover, then slipped a gas mask over the sergeant's face because of the sudden sting of CS gas in the air. O'Brien also donned a gas mask.

Two tear gas grenades had been shoved through the barred first-floor window of the villa by an MP. Crampsey sprinted to the villa, meanwhile, and holding a Beretta over his head, fired it through the first-floor window, ducking when the sapper inside blasted back every now and then.

Colonel Jacobson appeared at his bedroom window, frantic to get his hands on a weapon because he knew the CS flooding the first floor would force the sapper upstairs to his hideaway. Healey stood exposed on the lawn to throw a .45 and gas mask up to him. The colonel masked up and crouched behind the corner of a thin plywood wall. The wounded Viet Cong came up the stairs and, as a precaution, began firing his AK-47 from left to right when he reached the top. The man was half blind from the tear gas. He stitched the wall right over Jacobson's head without hitting him, and as he shifted fire to the next wall the colonel leaped up, firing the .45 twice at point-blank range. The sapper spun and fell, and Jacobson, who instantly seized the dead man's AK-47, expecting more enemy to follow, was greeted moments later by the military policemen who had broken in through the back door.

The Embassy fight was over.

8

Banging Your Head
Against the Wall

The battle for the Embassy had just ended when General Westmoreland arrived, and it was there in front of the battle-scarred Chancery with begrimed MPs standing over dead sappers who were twisted about in bloody poses that COMUSMACV declared for the cameras that all was right with the war. "The enemy's well-laid plans went afoul," he said of the Embassy attack. "Some superficial damage was done to the building. All of the enemy that entered the compound so far as I can determine were killed. Nineteen bodies have been found on the premises—enemy bodies."

Westmoreland dismissed the wave of urban attacks as "diversionary" to the main communist effort still to come at Khe Sanh, and as foolhardy—"the enemy exposed himself by virtue of this strategy, and he suffered great casualties"—and he claimed that the VC had not even achieved tactical surprise. "As soon as President Thieu, with our agreement, called off the truce, American troops went on the offensive and pursued the enemy aggressively. . . ."

If one disregards the fact that Khe Sanh was the diversion, not Saigon, then Westmoreland's assessment was correct in a strictly military sense—enemy casualties were heavy, their grip on most cities quickly shaken off by U.S. firepower—but it is distressing that the theater commander was numb in both his contemporary remarks and in his memoirs to the political ramifications of the offensive, not only in America but in the hearts and minds of the South Vietnamese who watched as the U.S. Army and Air Force destroyed the towns the communists had seized in order to save them.

General Westmoreland had other blind spots. The press was dubious of COMUSMACV's declaration of victory, and Westmoreland would forever be bitterly convinced that Hanoi, unable to win on the battlefield, achieved a psychological victory on the American home front because of irresponsibly negative reporting of the Tet Offensive.

Westmoreland's assertion, however, that Tet was not a surprise made him appear incapable of admitting error and cast doubts on his assessment of the offensive. The general might have retained his credibility had he acknowledged that the Viet Cong regiments storming the cities of South Vietnam bore little resemblance to the worn-down enemy described in his we've-turned-the-corner-we're-winning-the-war briefings of November 1967. "Given what Westy had been saying before Tet, there was just no way that MACV could have been in the frame of mind to recognize what was coming," according to Chief Warrant Officer 2 James W. Creamer, who served two tours with the 179th Military Intelligence (MI) Detachment, 199th Light Infantry Brigade (LIB). "Even with intelligence that was as plain as the hand in front of their face, how could MACV buy into the idea of a massive enemy assault? It would have been contrary to the entire U.S. military-political line to stop and say that we were about to be hit by a whole lot of enemy units that the commander had just gotten through saying were whipped. MACV underestimated the enemy, a cardinal error in war. It was a matter of arrogance, arrogance beyond belief."

There had been many signs that the offensive was coming. Warrant Officer Creamer became involved in one portentous incident in mid-November 1967 when a platoon from D/17th Cavalry, 199th LIB, made contact in a hamlet some five kilometers west of Saigon. The platoon reported that it had a VC pinned in a bunker. Intending to collect a prisoner for intelligence purposes, Creamer loaded up a butt-pack full of CS grenades—in case the tear gas didn't drive the guerrilla out of the bunker, he also packed some lethal white phosphorus grenades—and hopped a helicopter out to the firefight. It was over before he got there, the cav having impatiently run a track over the bunker, crushing the diehard within. "They thought they had a VC unit in the village, so they surrounded it and started searching through it," remembered Creamer. "It was a pretty, orderly little village, and every house had a haystack beside it—and every haystack covered a pile of weapons or ammunition. It was staggering what was in that village. Mortar rounds, cases of small-arms ammunition, hand grenades galore, rocket-propelled grenade launchers—you name it."

It was too late in the day to lift all the supplies out by helicopter, and the cav platoon could not remain overnight in the ville, should there be a large enemy unit in the area. The decision was finally made to burn all the haystacks in the dry rice paddies surrounding the hamlet.

Creamer went up in his Huey. "We'd chug by, and I'd drop a grenade into each haystack," he said. "We set all the haystacks on fire within five thousand meters of this village. It looked like pictures of Russia during World War II with all these columns of smoke going up."

When Tet hit, the haystack incident clicked into full focus for Creamer. The hamlet had been a step in the supply chain leading to Saigon. Brought across the Cambodian border, then ferried to the hamlet by sampan—a canal passed by to the west—the enemy had probably intended to smuggle the weapons and ammunition into a cemetery at the edge of Saigon due east of the hamlet. "I suspect the VC placed two or three caches for every one they needed because they knew we were going to find a lot of them," said Creamer. "The most amazing thing about the whole story is that this was a village that you could see from a rooftop in Saigon. It had a population of some two thousand people and was in an area that was heavily patrolled by U.S. and ARVN units. It was full of government officials, government police, government schoolteachers. It was a safe, pacified village—and nobody said anything. The enemy moved in so much stuff that virtually every house was involved, but whether the people were sympathetic or not to the communists, nobody raised an alarm. We stumbled on it, just stumbled on it, and it was a real revelation to me about how the people felt about the government in Saigon."

Except for the Embassy attack, General Do concentrated on South Vietnamese facilities in Saigon during the Tet Offensive. The ARVN armor headquarters and part of the artillery school fell, as did the government radio station, which was seized by VC in riot police uniforms who drove right up to the front gate in a convoy of jeeps and civilian automobiles. The "lieutenant" in the lead jeep briskly informed the guard that the "reinforcements" had arrived —then drew his .45 and shot the confused guard, who had begun to protest that he knew nothing about such plans. Other guerrillas opened fire with a machine gun from the window of an adjacent apartment building, wiping out an ARVN airborne platoon that was sleeping on the station roof, having been positioned there that night in anticipation of a possible attack on this key installation.

The communists had planned to broadcast tapes from the radio station proclaiming the General Uprising and the liberation of Saigon. However, power to the station was shut off by prearranged signal as soon as the attack began.

Like the frustrated VC who found no tanks at the armor headquarters and only disabled howitzers at the artillery school, those at the radio station—unable to make use of their prize—hunkered in against counterattack. It took the ARVN six hours to clear the million-dollar installation, at which point it was a shambles. It would take four days and two battalions of elite Vietnamese Marines to dig the last of the invaders out of the armor and artillery compounds.

Most of the attacks were instant disasters, however. The twelve sappers who attacked the Vietnamese Navy headquarters—they planned to use captured ships as ferries for VC units standing ready across the Saigon River—were all killed or captured within five minutes of blowing a hole in the compound wall. The sapper team that hit the heavily defended Presidential Palace was repelled at a side gate, and then cornered and eliminated in an unfinished apartment building across the street.

To ensure secrecy, many units received their attack orders only two or three days before Tet, not enough time for proper reconnaissance. The battalion sent to liberate the main prison got lost and was shot to pieces in a cemetery. The ARVN captured the battalion commander and his political officer, plus several company commanders.

A more successful assault on the Joint General Staff compound a kilometer east of Tan Son Nhut began at 0300 when the main gate was opened for an ARVN general's car. Having waited for such an opportunity, a sapper squad rushed the gate under cover fire from a nearby pagoda.

At that moment, a U.S. MP jeep appeared and the sappers paused to fire on it, giving the ARVN time to slam the gate shut again. "[F]ate seemed to decree that the MPs would just happen to be wherever the VC were trying their luck," wrote Lieutenant Colonel George, the Saigon Provost Marshal. In fact, the number of mobile patrols had been nearly doubled because of the maximum alert. There were forty-one on the streets of the capital when Tet erupted.

Two more jeeps joined the one that had accidentally disrupted the JGS attack. The MPs did not know what they had by the tail. Their inaccurate report to the PM headquarters—"BOQ 3 under attack!"—was followed by a request for the local reaction force. Bachelor Officers Quarters 3, a billet for field-grade U.S. Air Force officers assigned to Tan Son Nhut, was on the south side of east-west Vo Tanh Street, directly across from a side wall of the JGS compound. The enemy fire in that direction was only in response to the MPs firing from behind the jeeps hurriedly parked on both sides of the street and to either side of the billet's front gate.

The VC were still trying to take the JGS compound.

The north gate was finally blown down with rocket-propelled grenades after daybreak, but the Viet Cong battalion that poured inside seized only the headquarters of a support company, mistaking it for the vital JGS HQ.

Backed up by tanks, it took ARVN paratroopers all day to dislodge the invaders. Meanwhile, within minutes of the initial attack, the requested reaction force mounted up under Lieutenant Waltman of Company C, 716th MP

Battalion, which was stationed at Tan Son Nhut. It left the air base under blackout conditions—Waltman and his driver in the lead jeep had their headlights off, the windshield lashed down, and everyone was wearing helmets and flak jackets—and sped along the deserted and dimly lit streets. The lead jeep was followed by a 2½-ton troop truck with three military policemen in the cab, and seventeen more packed on the two parallel benches in the tarp-covered bed. A three-man gun jeep brought up the rear.

The MPs knew this part of the city well. Lieutenant Waltman avoided the most direct route to the action—it was a straight shot down Vo Tanh from the main Tan Son Nhut gate to the front door of BOQ 3, but the street was blocked by fire—and instead jumped on Nguyen Minh Chieu, which ran parallel to, but a block south of, Vo Tanh.

From Nguyen Minh Chieu, the group turned left into an unnamed alley that cut due north to Vo Tanh Street, and straight across to a side gate in the JGS compound. BOQ 3 was less than a block east of the intersection. The reaction force never got out of the alley, however, because a Viet Cong unit—later estimated at company-size—occupied both sides of it. The guerrillas were in the buildings at the mouth of the alley, and they were behind the chest-high, tree-lined walls that extended the length of the passageway. The enemy, invisible in the dark, had either been on their way to hit the side gate of the JGS compound, or had already been waiting in ambush for whatever reinforcements might respond to the stymied sapper attack on the main gate.

They opened fire at a range of ten feet.

The enemy initiated the ambush with either claymore mines or rocket-propelled grenades. At that instant, Lieutenant Waltman's jeep was some twenty-five meters from the end of the two-hundred-meter-long alley, and his driver was slowing down so they could park and proceed on foot to the embattled officers quarters. The troop truck had just cleared the white stucco buildings at the mouth of the alley. The gun jeep was still between them.

The guerrillas hit the troop truck first. "Suddenly there were two loud explosions and bright flashes of light behind me," said Specialist Four John R. Van Wagner, the lead jeep driver. "Automatic weapons fire swept the alley . . ."

Putting the jeep into second gear, Van Wagner roared out of the kill zone—and right into a hail of friendly fire from the ARVN at the side gate of the JGS compound. The MP in the sandbagged, tin-roofed concrete kiosk in front of BOQ 3 joined in, as did a gun jeep across the street.

Waltman and Van Wagner scrambled under their jeep, then dove into a ditch that ran up the side of the street to BOQ 3. "The ditch was full of concertina wire, but I crawled right through it, and when my gas mask got hung up, I threw that damn thing away," said Van Wagner, who was followed by Waltman. "Tracer rounds were coming right at us from the MP in the kiosk. We kept crawling, and I kept hollering and screaming at him to stop shooting. I trained my M16 on him several times, thinking it was him or me. I could see him, I could see the MP letters on his helmet liner, but I couldn't bring myself to pull the trigger."

The MP finally heard the frantic calls to cease fire. Upon reaching the guard kiosk, Lieutenant Waltman grabbed the radio inside and tried to make sense of what had happened. It turned out that the gun jeep at the rear of the column had been able to back out of the alley unscathed. The troop truck had taken the brunt of the ambush, brought to a halt by the first explosions—the front tires were blown off their rims—its canvas tarp immediately riddled then by guerrillas firing down into it from the buildings to either side. Every one of the twenty military policemen on board was hit in a matter of seconds. Some were killed outright, others succumbed to their wounds as subsequent efforts to reach them bogged down in the face of heavy resistance.

In all, sixteen MPs died in that truck.

They never had a chance. "[T]his patrol should have dismounted a block or two from the firefight and approached on foot," wrote Lieutenant Colonel George, citing the 716th MP Battalion's established procedure to minimize the chances of ambush. "These men may have failed to comply with their instructions because of the intense excitement [and confusion] of the moment . . ."

There was another reason for haste. The various billets and installations in the capital were virtually defenseless. At best, each had one MP on duty in the front kiosk. Many had only Vietnamese guards because "some 'brain' at USARV [United States Army, Vietnam] decided we could reduce the number of MPs in Saigon by using VN civilian guards," wrote George. "[M]any of these civilian guards didn't show up or deserted their posts as soon as things started to happen, forcing us to scramble to cover their posts with MPs we needed for reaction forces."

Unauthorized to carry weapons, the residents themselves had only a few privately owned handguns. None of the billets had an armory in case of emergency. "It was our job to get between the attackers and the virtually unarmed officers in BOQ 3," explained Lieutenant Waltman. "We went as fast as we could. . . ."

The tragic irony was that the billet was not actually under attack. Specialist Van Wagner rushed to the roof of BOQ 3, a French villa set back from the street in a walled compound, and fired down into the trees along the alley. "After about 20 minutes I went through the BOQ checking the conditions of the occupants . . . Many of the occupants were still sleeping, unaware as to what was happening, and were quite annoyed when I woke them," he wrote in his after-action report, leaving out the fact that some of the air force majors and colonels were irritable when he banged on their doors because they were hung over. "The air conditioners in those rooms drowned out most of the noise outside," he later said. "Even those who could hear the firefight just assumed it was more of the fireworks that had been going off all day and night for Tet. . . ."

Several officers rushed out the front door to see if they could help, but Lieutenant Waltman herded them back inside lest a sniper take notice of all that rank. "It was just me and Van Wagner—and a whole bunch of people shooting at us," remembered Waltman. Another reaction force was being mobilized, but it would take over an hour to arrive. Meanwhile, Waltman and Van Wagner—both of whom were awarded Silver Stars—made repeated attempts to reach the disabled truck in the alley. They used their jeep as cover and dodged behind the palm trees lining the darkened passageway. "We got pretty close a couple times, but we just took too much fire to do it by ourselves,"

Waltman said. "We would see muzzle flashes up in the buildings overlooking the alley, and we'd fire up at them. We finally ran out of ammunition and had to back out of there to get more from the gun jeeps."

The stalemate was agonizing. Cries echoed up the alley from wounded MPs in the back of the troop truck.

"Somebody get down here!"

"Help me! . . ."

"They were piled on each other and shot up and screaming," said Waltman. "We tried to get them to hold the noise down. The idea was to give the VC the impression they were all dead so they would stop shooting."

Three wounded MPs managed to crawl out of the alley. Finally, it seemed that the only one still alive was a man who had rolled underneath the truck. He had been shot six times in his hip and groin. "He would let out a little moan every once in a while, and you could see his leg move. We kept trying to get down to him, but the VC fired at every movement, every sound," remembered Van Wagner. "I would run up on the roof, trying to get a shot at them, then I'd rush back down and we'd try to get into that alley again. We'd get stopped, so I'd run back to the roof again and lay down some more fire, then run back around to the front of that alley—but every time you thought you had everybody dead in one of those damn buildings, you'd start down there and it would all blow loose again. . . ."

Many things were happening at the same time. Flares hung over the air base to the west, and the sounds of that battle were continuously in the background of Lieutenant Waltman's lonely little war in the alley. He was using the radio in the guard kiosk—there was excited and confused chatter on the MP tactical net from the Embassy and other firefights all over the city—when the second reaction force out of Tan Son Nhut notified him that it had reached the traffic signal at Vo Tanh and Cach Mang one block west of the top of the alley. From Vo Tanh, Cach Mang ran in a diagonal line to Nguyen Minh Chieu, coming out at a point immediately west of the mouth of the alley.

First Lieutenant Joseph Cisneros, the second reaction force leader, intended to seal off the bottom of the alley and hit the enemy from that direction. "I'm going to proceed slowly down Cach Mang, okay?" Cisneros radioed Waltman.

Waltman agreed. "Cover your ass," he told Cisneros, the transmission being recorded by a senior officer.

It was about 0440. "Waco, [this is Car] 6-0," came a call from one of the jeeps in front of BOQ 3. (Waco was radioese for the net control at the PM Office.) "We got a survivor just snuck through from the alert force. He's pretty bad off. We need to get him out of here in a hurry. . . ."

"6-0, I copy. What are the chances of getting an ambulance in there, or near there, and taking out injured by foot?"

"We can try it."

"10-2-4, we'll get some ambulances there."

"Waco, [this is] 6-0. If you can get some flares dropped on this area, maybe we can see what's going on."

Waco reported that two gunships with flares were already en route from U.S. Navy headquarters in downtown Saigon. Meanwhile, Lieutenant Cisneros was just moving out when he was joined by an ambulance from the 3d Field Hospital on Vo Tanh. "[Charlie Company Alert Officer] Number 1, [this is] Number 2," Cisneros reported to Waltman. "I've got an ambulance here. Could you use 'im up there?"

"We need him very bad," Waltman answered. "We need him at the main gate at this BOQ 3, but I don't know how you're going to get him in here without him getting hit."

"Okay, I'm taking him up [Vo Tanh]. We're going to see how far we can get up there without being fired upon. He's willing to go. Over."

"Be extremely careful. . . ."

Fearing another ambush, progress was slow and Waltman finally got back on the horn with Cisneros to speed things up. "We need that ambulance bad."

"That's a 10-2-4. We'll try to get her into you."

"10-2-4. Tango Yankee," Waltman said—thank you.

The first helicopter arrived then, but its flares were off target. The ambulance approached BOQ 3 on Vo Tanh. *"Get that vehicle out of here,"* someone suddenly shouted on the radio. *"They're throwing grenades!"*

The ambulance withdrew. Lieutenant Cisneros, however, was able to slip down Cach Mang at this time and get into position at the mouth of the alley with the bulk of his reaction force. "Be advised—Victor Charlie [is] in the trees," Waltman radioed from the other end of the embattled passageway. "They're on the rooftops. They're shootin' down on you. They're not on ground level. . . ."

There was a lull in the action, but when Cisneros sent a squad into the alley, it suddenly reverberated with more fire. "Number 1, this is Number 2," Cisneros said, catching his breath. He was on the verge of tears. "We tried to get down the alley. They blew up a claymore on us, and there was small-arms and automatic fire. We're going to hold tight right here. It's about the best we can do. Over."

"10-2-4. I know you can't help it," Waltman said reassuringly. "Just keep trying. Do the best you can. . . ."

"Number 2, are any of your people hit?"

"No, thank God. They got out," Cisneros answered. "We're down here at the corner of the alley, we're just holding tight. We got sniper fire, and we're putting fire to the rooftop whenever we see 'em firing. Over."

"10-2-4. Keep your fire high," said Waltman. ". . . We got 'em boxed in. We just got to try to get to 'em. . . ."

The effort continued. The flares presently being dropped by the navy choppers were right on target, and in their light Lieutenant Cisneros put his machine-gun team in action while getting four MPs into an advantageous firing position on an adjacent rooftop. It did no good. The well-ensconced guerrillas continued to defy the fire splattering the buildings they were in, and several MPs were wounded by a group of grenade-throwing enemy soldiers who were in a small walled cemetery next to one of the buildings.

Lieutenant Cisneros had ammunition brought up by jeep and his casualties evacuated in ambulances—Nguyen Minh Chieu was open to the 3d Field Hospital—but the continuing enemy fire kept the ambulances standing by at Vo Tanh and Cach Mang from reaching the three badly wounded MPs who had made it out of the alley to the BOQ 3 compound.

Discouraged and out of options, Waltman finally radioed Cisneros. "We just got to wait 'em out."

Waltman and Cisneros imagined that the VC would withdraw before dawn—an hour and a half away—and that they could then move in and recover survivors from the troop truck. It did not work that way. It was still a good thirty minutes before daybreak when Waltman angrily radioed Cisneros. "Our alert truck got hit by grenades again. I've still got some guys in it. I've *got* to do something to get 'em out of there. Can you give me an M79?"

Cisneros sighed. "That's a 10-2-3 [negative]," he said. "I've got some fragmentation grenades down here. Over."

"10-2-4. We've got a machine gun down here [in the small cemetery]. If I can get rid of it, we can get in there."

Using side streets, it was possible to reach BOQ 3 from the east. "I'll send a jeep with some grenades down to your location," Cisneros radioed Waltman.

"10-2-4. Tell 'em to use caution."

"10-2-4. . . ."

"Alert Officer 2, this is Alert Officer 1."

"Go ahead, 1."

"Be advised, I received the grenades. . . ."

The grenades did not dislodge the enemy.

It was almost dawn. Two of Lieutenant Cisneros's men were wounded and pinned down in the alley. "I'm bringing a deuce-and-a-half up there," he told Waltman, referring to the second reaction force's 2½-ton truck. "I'm going to back it in because it's the only way I can get these people out," he said, requesting that Waltman's people "hold their fire until they see the deuce-and-a-half go out of the alley. Over."

"10-2-4. Hold one. I'll notify them," Waltman said. ". . . We'll cover you as best we can. . . ."

Cisneros went into the alley with the truck.

"This is Number 1. Are you having any luck?"

"The lieutenant's trying now, sir," the second reaction force's radioman answered.

"10-2-4. Keep me informed. . . ."

When Cisneros finally got back on the net, Waltman asked if he had recovered his casualties. "That's 10-2-4," Cisneros answered with great relief. "Got 'em both out! . . ."

* * *

A little later, Cisneros radioed Waltman: ". . . they're in that little graveyard, and they're lobbing hand grenades . . . They just injured another one of my men . . ."

The enemy did not melt away at dawn. The battle lasted well into the afternoon because the military police lacked the firepower to blow the VC out of the houses they had occupied. "Hell, all we had was machine-gun jeeps, and as we kept trying to get to our dead and wounded in that alley, we just kept getting clobbered," said Lieutenant Colonel George, who controlled the action from the PM Office. In the absence of U.S. combat units, he requested that CMD dispatch an ARVN armored force to BOQ 3. The request was not acted upon. "To have the lives of the Americans in Saigon depend on the whims of the ARVN at CMD who couldn't or wouldn't react most certainly is not the solution," George wrote to a fellow officer at the time. "As usual the National Police and ARVNs were conspicuous by their absence," he added. "[T]his last episode has made me extremely bitter towards our Vietnamese 'allies.' At each of the locations where we took losses they had the capability of helping but didn't . . . At BOQ #3 the ARVN had 2 tanks just inside the JGS Compound gate within 40 yards of the battle that wouldn't come to our aid or even give fire support. I feel certain we could have saved the lives of some wounded if we could have reached them in time. Armored vehicles were all that was needed."

The pleas for help and the sounds of fire echoing over the radio were nightmarish. "To put our kids in these situations and then not be able to help them when they need it most is more than I can stomach," Lieutenant Colonel George wrote. "As the day progressed, I became almost physically ill. I have never felt so helpless in my life. . . ."

Dawn was an overcast, luminescent gray. By then, Lieutenant Waltman had finally been able to evacuate the three MPs who had escaped the alley, enemy fire having petered out on Vo Tanh Street between BOQ 3 and the 3d Field Hospital. In addition, more MPs had arrived, as had Captain Drolla, the headquarters detachment commander for HAC, the U.S. support command in Saigon. Drolla's platoon-size alert force—consisting of HAC troops suited up in their helmets and flak jackets never before worn, and armed mostly with M14 rifles—assumed positions behind the wall that ran along the street on either side of the top of the alley. Equipped also with machine guns and invaluable grenade launchers, the alert force sent a thunderous storm of fire into the housing to either side of the alley.

The fire seemed to push all the enemy back into the pair of white two-story buildings that dominated the mouth of the alley, one to either side of it. "We started going into adjacent houses and firing from courtyards and second floors," said Waltman. "We were just blowing the hell out of the place, but the VC were absolutely invisible. We were firing and ducking. You pop up, you fire, you drop back down—and you really don't know if you hit anybody. . . ."

"It was just a throw-a-whole-lot-of-stuff-at-'em-and-hope-it-hits-some-of-'em scenario," Waltman added.

Drolla and Waltman were joined by Major Eugene J. Conner, Operations Officer of MACV Advisory Team 100, who brought forward two ARVN V-100s—low-profile, armor-plated security vehicles with four doughnutlike tires and twin .30-caliber machine guns in a little turret.

Major Conner, the senior officer on the scene, organized an attack on the last two enemy-held buildings. While one of the V-100s laid down suppressive fire from behind the wall at the top of the alley, the other was to move down it to the disabled truck, followed by eleven troops who were to load the casualties into the second V-100. To secure the area during the evacuation process, Conner and Waltman would take twenty-five MPs down the left side of the alley and destroy or drive out the enemy in the building on that side, while Drolla and his thirty-man HAC alert force proceeded down the right side to the other enemy strong point.

"We had a lot of trouble with the ARVN. They didn't want to get involved, and weren't too enamored with the idea of going down that alley," remembered Waltman. "We basically told them they could go down the alley and fight the VC or they could stay there and fight us."

The assault groups moved quickly down the tree-lined alley, hemmed in by the wall running down either side of it. Reaching the truck, Lieutenant Waltman was stunned to find that the MP who had been shot six times and had rolled under the deuce-and-a-half was still alive. The blown-up, shot-to-hell troop truck was otherwise stacked with flak-jacketed bodies, with several more sprawled stiffly beside it, upturned helmets scattered in the roadway.

The sole survivor was loaded into the V-100, which had just enough room in the narrow alley to squeeze past the driver's side of the truck. "[A]fter we had gone a short distance past the rear of the 2½ ton vehicle," read Specialist Van Wagner's after-action report, "the two ARVN V-100s began letting up on their fire coverage and then the Viet Cong seemed to pour everything they had at us. . . ."

The result was bedlam. The driver of the V-100 in the alley immediately threw it in reverse, reportedly backing up over an MP in his haste to vacate the area. Captain Drolla's group double-timed it back down the fire-swept lane, too, as did the rear half of the MP force on the other side.

Major Conner, Lieutenant Waltman, and nine of their lead troops scrambled for the nearest cover—a little one-story house adjoining the two-story building the enemy held on the left side of the alley. "The Major stood at the door checking to see that all of the men were safely inside," noted one after-action report, referring to a little room in the house that faced the alley. "Once he was assured that all were safely inside, he took one last look for sure and took a direct hit in his chest from a rocket, killing him instantly."

Major Conner was blown in half.

Lieutenant Waltman was blasted across the room, peppered with fragments in his left shoulder, left arm, and up the left side of his face. Momentarily dazed, Waltman blindly called out for help—the explosion had filled the little room with smoke—and Van Wagner quickly bandaged the lieutenant's bloody face, not realizing in the confusion that he himself had taken a chunk of metal in his left forearm.

Private First Class Jerome A. Jefferson, a black MP, caught a fragment in the hollow just above his left eye, resulting in permanent blindness in that eye. Having bandaged Waltman, Van Wagner turned next to the advisory team E7 who had been standing behind Conner when the RPG shrieked in. "He was sitting there with his left arm blown off at the shoulder," Van Wagner remembered. "He had a chunk of bone sticking out of the wound. I can still see the wound—smoking, black, charred. He was in shock. He kept wanting me to straighten out the fingers on his left hand, but he didn't have a left hand anymore. . . ."

There was a hole in the roof. Van Wagner looked up through it—right at two Viet Cong who were at an open window frame in the adjoining two-story building. The guerrillas were so close that he could see their faces and their red and blue armbands as they fired their AK-47s down the alley toward Vo Tanh Street.

Moving slowly, Van Wagner put his M16 sights on the window, then whispered to Waltman, "Gerry, do you want me to take these two gooks out?"

"No, no, *don't shoot at 'em.*"

The lieutenant's thinking was obvious. Even if they hit the VC in the window, the fire would reveal their hideaway to other guerrillas who could easily finish them off with more rocket-propelled grenades.

Everyone got quiet and pressed against the wall between their room and the enemy-occupied building, hoping to stay out of sight while Waltman explained the situation by radio to Captain Drolla. Meanwhile, the one-armed sergeant was mumbling incoherently. "I was trying to shut him up because I sure as hell didn't want the enemy to look down through that hole in the roof," said Van Wagner. From the door, the MP could see his dead buddies in and around the troop truck. Many had had their faces blown off. "I remember huddling up, bringing my knees to my chest, pushing my helmet down forward over my forehead, and wrapping my arms around my knees. I wanted to keep my helmet over my face because I wanted them to recognize me when they recovered *my* body."

Help arrived in the form of rocket-firing gunships, one of which scored a direct hit on the window from which the two VC were firing. "When they fired those rockets, smoke and dust and just total chaos broke out," said Waltman. "The rockets went right past us. If we had stepped out in the alley, we could have read the serial numbers on them."

The gunships gave the VC considerable pause. "We knew

they were going to fire the rockets," noted Waltman. "The goal was to get up and get out of there once they created enough confusion—and that's what we did. We flat out ran back up the alley."

There was an ambulance standing by on Vo Tanh, along with numerous correspondents. Photographs of the BOQ 3 battle published in *Time* magazine included a shot of Jefferson sinking to his knees upon escaping the alley and looking up at the ambulance with one eye from under the thick bandage wrapped around his head. The next shot was of Lieutenant Waltman, his own bandage hanging loose from his face, going to the aid of Jefferson, who had collapsed in shock along the side of the street.

The ambulance roared off with the wounded.

The battle continued, and in addition to the dead major, some two dozen other advisors, MPs, and HAC GIs were wounded in various unsuccessful attacks down the alley.

Lieutenant Colonel George had been correct. It took armor to finally drive the enemy out of their positions. The records do not indicate which unit came to the rescue, as it was on its way to another objective and only made a hasty, on-the-spot diversion to BOQ 3. "Around 1400, I got a call from an armored cavalry unit north of Saigon, coming south," George recounted. "The commander of the unit, a lieutenant colonel, told me that he had to pass through Saigon for a mission south of the city, and he requested an escort through town. I had one of my patrols meet them at the highway bridge north of Saigon."

The unit in question may have been Troop A, 1st Squadron, 4th Cavalry, of the 1st Infantry Division. The squadron had been tasked to send one troop into the capital that first afternoon of Tet, though it did not pass on to the south as George remembers it. Troop A instead secured five BEQs in downtown Saigon. "I had my MP patrol keep me informed of the unit's progress through town, and when they got as close as they were going to get to that BOQ 3 abortion, I told them to halt the convoy and to put the unit commander on the radio. I talked to the lieutenant colonel again, and told him my problem. I said, 'Can you help us?' He said, 'Hell, yeah,' and twenty minutes later it was all over. They went in there and shot hell out of the buildings along the alley. They just blew the place apart."

The guerrillas pulled out under the onslaught. The area was secured at five that evening, sixteen hours after the battle had begun. Trees along the alley had been uprooted by main gun fire, and the white stucco buildings were speckled with thousands of little holes from canister rounds. Tin roofing sheets littered the alley. The enemy left few bodies amid the debris. In contrast, the BOQ 3 battle was the single costliest incident for the U.S. forces in Saigon, and there was a full-color photo in *Time* of the last sorry act of the debacle. It showed an APC evacuating some of the bodies recovered from the troop truck. There were at least six dead MPs stacked grotesquely atop each other on the lowered back ramp of the armored personnel carrier, their faces blackened, their legs hanging stiffly over one side of the ramp.

9

Hold, Reinforce, Counterattack

Though the enemy appeared to be everywhere in the shock of the moment, there were actually glaring holes in the communist plan to take Saigon. "Their first objective should have been the Provost Marshall Office, and their second objective the 716th MP Battalion headquarters, where my reaction forces were coming from," said Lieutenant Colonel George, who kept waiting for the hammer to fall, stunned that it never did. The PM Office was the de facto operations center for the defense of the capital. "The whole command called us to find out what was going on. If the VC had hit us, the confusion would have been terrible," George noted. The 716th MP's HQ at the International Hotel remained untouched, too, even as supply choppers landed and reaction forces assembled in jeeps and trucks on the street out front. "If the VC had disrupted that operation, all of our installations could have been theirs for the taking and casualties would have been astronomical."

That these oversights doomed the communists to failure was not at all clear at the time. "Everyone it seemed was under fire, everyone was under attack," said Brigadier General Irzyk, the HAC commander, noting that the 716th MPs responded not only to the Embassy but to reports of fire at installations all over the city. "The MPs were going in dozens of directions at the same time. That battalion was like a rubber band that was stretched to its limit . . ."

Saigon seemed to hang in the balance.

Pajama-clad patients at the 3d Field Hospital were issued weapons and took up defensive positions. Personnel in some BOQs and BEQs shot at anything that moved. "In one instance [an] MP vehicle was dispatched to a billet to stop the firing and the [MPs] came under fire from the occupants," George dryly noted in his after-action report.

A jeep moving past the Korean Embassy was blasted by a recoilless rifle or RPG. Both MPs were wounded, and two more were killed when a gun jeep speeding to the scene ran into a hail of automatic-weapons fire.

The VC removed the M60 from the jeep, and fired it from a hotel roof. Shortly thereafter, at about 0540, another jeep patrol, Car 9-5, accidentally drove into another enemy force. *"Get off the damn radio!"* a member of the three-man crew shouted, cutting into the net. "Waco, this is Niner-5. We're on Plantation Road. The jeep's been hit. The driver's wounded . . . We need assistance *immediately!"*

"10-2-4. Whereabouts on Plantation Road are you?"

"By the racetrack. Over . . ."

The Phu Tho Racetrack was at the northwest corner of north-south Plantation Road (also known as Nguyen Van Thoai) and east-west Tran Quoc Toan in Cholon, the area in southwest Saigon populated mostly by ethnic Chinese. "The jeep's got two flat tires, gas tank's been hit, the window's all shot up," the MP continued, having taken cover behind the wreck. "The driver's got it right through the guts . . ."

Waco immediately dispatched an HAC reaction force. "Sir, this is Niner-5 . . . [static] . . . tell 'em to be careful at that first circle before you get to the racetrack."

There was a pause in the transmissions, then the MP jumped back on the net. *"This is Niner-5! Get out here, get out here now!"* he screamed hysterically. ". . . them motherfuckers got *RPGs!"*

"Niner-5, keep calm, there's someone in route now."

"Where the hell are they?!"

Coming north on Plantation Road, the HAC force

detrucked two and a half blocks from the racetrack and moved forward on foot. The GIs were unable to reach Car 9-5 before coming under fire from an ARVN compound and from Viet Cong on both sides of the tree-lined street. Up ahead, the jeep they had come to rescue was by then burning fiercely in the predawn darkness, its crew sprawled around it. The driver and the NCOIC had been killed. The MP who had been on the radio, however, was only playing dead and would eventually be recovered alive.

The MP had a long wait. The area was crawling with guerrillas. "We are caught between a grenade launcher and heavy automatic weapons [from] the rooftops," the HAC reaction force reported shortly after daybreak.

"Charlie 5-2 is in route at this time," Waco replied, referring to a reaction force from a security guard company, C/52d Infantry, attached to the 716th MP Battalion.

This second reaction force was led by First Lieutenant Stephen L. Braddock, who radioed ahead for directions. "Make a right at the ARVN compound coming down Hong Bang. We're up about two blocks," the HAC force answered. "Most of us are down here behind a white water barrel. You'll see our deuce-and-a-half parked in the road. From there you'll have to walk up. They're starting to zero in with this grenade launcher on us now. We need help fast. Over."

"Charlie 5-2, roger . . ."

"We just had a grenade dropped about fifteen meters from us. We think it got a couple of MPs. *Hurry up! Over.*"

"Charlie 5-2. On our way! Out."

The second reaction force never made it. Viet Cong had slipped in behind the pinned-down HAC troops, and Lieutenant Braddock was killed about two blocks short of the firefight he was rushing toward when his truck was suddenly riddled by a .51-caliber machine gun, then set ablaze in the street by an explosion. Another officer and two NCOs were wounded trying to rescue Braddock.

A third reaction force from A/716th MP Battalion rushed in, but it too got nowhere fast. "[The VC] have about a block section of this street sealed off. We can't go either way," the HAC force radioed in. "They're at both ends, and it's pretty much of a stalemate . . ."

The situation kept getting worse. "Waco, [this is] Charlie 5. We're getting mortared over here . . ."

In all, five MPs were killed and twelve wounded on the road to the Phu Tho Racetrack. It was later determined that the MPs had bumped into two Viet Cong battalions assigned to seize the racetrack, an excellent observation point just within 82mm mortar range of Tan Son Nhut Air Base.

The chance encounter bogged the enemy down and kept them from their objective. They were pushed back during the afternoon by an infantry-cavalry task force from the 199th Light Infantry Brigade, the first of many combat units rushed into Saigon during Tet. "We delayed their plans long enough to upset their mission," said Lieutenant Colonel Rowe, commander of the 716th MP Battalion, precisely summing up the cumulative effect of all the confused and scattered actions in the capital. Twenty-seven MPs were killed and forty-four wounded, but by responding without hesitation to each crisis they had bought time.

The military police thus saved Saigon, for the VC, having failed to secure their objectives during the night, had no chance against the combat units that piled on during the day. "Colonel Rowe should be bursting his buttons," General Irzyk said in a staff meeting after the battle. Irzyk went on to say that George, his provost marshal, had performed more like a "field marshal" as he juggled radios and telephones in the PM Office. "He is the one who got the thousands of requests, each one critical and high priority, and he was the one who unraveled them. I don't know how he did it, but he kept his composure, his patience, his cool, and he did it for hours on end. He performed magnificently."

Lieutenant Colonel George won a BSM in addition to his end-of-tour Legion of Merit, and the Saigon MPs earned the Presidential Unit Citation. There was, however, a discordant note to the victory. "I constantly bumped heads with Rowe during Tet," George said. Though the PM exercised operational control of the 716th MP Battalion on paper, Rowe was actually a few months senior to George in date of rank. "That created a fuzzy area, and after about the first hour of Tet, Rowe became more and more reluctant to provide the reaction forces necessary to handle new situations as they arose," according to George. "We argued repeatedly. He kept saying, 'We're taking too many casualties, we're taking too many casualties,' and we were, God help us, we were—but I couldn't just sit there and not respond to these installations that were under attack. We had to try, and he'd finally back off when I said, 'Let's go to the general and let him decide.'"

Rowe's side of this is not known. George was of the opinion that Rowe was "positioning himself. No one knew how our [response to the enemy attacks] was going to be perceived when the emergency was over. We were either going to be heroes or the goats. If it went against us, he could say that he fought my decisions . . ."

Perhaps Rowe was concerned about being spread too thinly, given that the 716th MP Battalion was the only unit capable of organized resistance in Saigon. If a few more VC battalions had marched in, the dispersion of the MPs at nonvital BOQs and BEQs could have been disastrous. George does not buy this argument. "Rowe's only objection was casualties," he notes. "Lieutenant Colonel Rowe was as much of an ass as Richard George relates," wrote Master Sergeant Robert J. Woods, the Operations NCO at the PM Office. "One time I spoke with Rowe and requested he dispatch a V-100 armored car to a location where we had men trapped. Rowe stated that he had signed for those vehicles from Group (89th MP Group, his next higher headquarters), and he wasn't going to send them back full of holes. This man had no concept of what was going on in Vietnam."

In retrospect, George was able to pluck a light moment out of that first grim morning. "Two MPs came into the station with a Viet Cong between them. One had a .45 to his head," George recalled. The MPs explained that they had been in the downtown area when they turned a corner and found themselves face-to-face with three guerrillas. Firing first, the MPs dropped the VC to either side of the one in the middle who promptly shit himself and raised his hands. "He was stinking up the station something awful. I had to get rid of this guy, and immediately thought of a lieutenant colonel acquaintance who was the intelligence advisor at

CMD. It's standard procedure to turn over prisoners to intelligence interrogators, so I told my men to deliver the prisoner to the ARVN and specifically to turn him over to my friend. About thirty minutes later, I received a phone call from the lieutenant colonel, and the first words he uttered were, 'George, you son of a bitch!'"

The battle had almost been lost before it began. General Westmoreland turned over full responsibility for the defense of Saigon to the ARVN on December 15, 1967. As the theater commander saw it, the U.S. units around Saigon had worked themselves out of a job. The communists had been pushed back toward Cambodia, and Westmoreland planned to use the U.S. units released from the Saigon area to reinforce the massive search-and-destroy operations scheduled to begin along the border in early 1968.

"It's a great plan, but it won't work," said Lieutenant General Fred C. Weyand, commander of II Field Force, Vietnam, when briefed by a colonel from MACV in the fall of 1967.

An informal man of much humor, wisdom, and courage, Weyand, with an ROTC commission from the University of California at Berkeley, had served as an intelligence specialist in the China-Burma-India Theater during WWII, and had brilliantly led a 3d Division rifle battalion in the Korean War. As CG of the 25th Division at Cu Chi in 1966–67, Weyand—one of the great commanders of the war, and a future Army Chief of Staff—had quickly learned that the key to the war was in providing security to the villages and towns of Vietnam. He did not believe in fighting a war of attrition in the hinterlands while leaving pacification in the indifferent hands of the ARVN.

General Weyand was thus at odds with Westmoreland at the most fundamental level. At II FFV, Weyand had forty-three mostly U.S. combat battalions—there were also Australian, New Zealand, and Thai units—in III Corps, the eleven provinces around Saigon. Three fourths of the population of III Corps lived in a forty-five kilometer circle around the capital. According to the MACV plan, by the time of Tet only thirteen battalions would remain in that circle, the rest having been shifted toward Cambodia to hit the enemy's base camps and infiltration routes. This re-alignment would leave only one quarter of Weyand's forces in the area containing three quarters of the people.

Neither Weyand nor his deputy for pacification, the legendary John Paul Vann, shared the conceit upon which the border offensive was based. The main and local force Viet Cong battalions had been punished but were not incapable of sustained campaigning in the interior of III Corps as Westmoreland believed. In addition, Weyand and Vann thought that MACV had seriously underestimated the power of the next layer of guerrilla forces—the hamlet squads, village platoons, and district companies—and feared that when the U.S. units moved to the border, the VC battalions would slip into the vacuum, join with the local guerrillas, and roll back the pacification projects that were the cornerstone of any real hope of allied victory.

On January 10, 1968, Weyand spoke with General West-moreland at MACV HQ and laid out intelligence that indicated that even as U.S. operations began on the Cambo-dian border, the enemy's force was infiltrating into the populated heart of III Corps. "I don't know what they've got in mind, but there's an attack coming," Weyand said.

General Weyand won the battle for Saigon at that meeting when he asked that the border offensive be postponed and certain U.S. units returned to their positions in the popu-lated areas. Westmoreland agreed, and by the time Tet broke, twenty-seven U.S. combat battalions were back in-side the Saigon Circle. If not for the ready availability of these units, the security forces at Tan Son Nhut and Saigon would have cracked before reinforcements could have made it in from the border, and the enemy would have been able to dig in for a house-to-house battle that would have dragged on for weeks and demolished major portions of Saigon.

Three days after the pivotal meeting between corps com-mander and theater commander, the unit that would be the first to reach the capital when needed, Lieutenant Colonel John K. Gibler's 3d Battalion, 7th Infantry, 199th LIB, helicoptered into positions immediately southwest of Sai-gon. It was familiar ground. The entire 199th Light Infantry

Brigade had previously operated in the area with the 5th ARVN Ranger Group. "Each of our battalions was totally integrated with a Vietnamese battalion—double squads, double platoons, double companies," explained Lieutenant Colonel William S. Schroeder, another battalion commander in the 199th LIB. It was a small-unit, grass-roots war designed to secure the population in this flat expanse of rice paddies. "We basically lived in villages," said one GI. "We developed a pretty good rapport with the Vietnamese. It got to the point that they would tell us if there was a VC tax collector around."

The security mission was phased out during the realignment for the border offensive. "The integration of units was a wonderful concept, and it was a mistake to stop it," said Schroeder. "Our generals didn't understand the Vietnamese, and they didn't understand the impact we were having in the integrated mode. I think they ended the program simply so they could have all-American units out there fighting the war with the flags and guidons flying."

The area changed after the 199th LIB departed.

The trust of the villagers was lost. It is likely that the Viet Cong executed many for their previous cooperation with the wrong side. "We knew something was up," said Lieutenant Colonel Gibler, who established his new 3-7th Infantry firebase a klick west of Binh Chanh district headquarters, which was approximately ten kilometers southwest of Saigon in Gia Dinh Province. "We had several contacts in the last few days before Tet, but none of the enemy wanted to join battle. You'd see 'em, you'd go after 'em, and they'd fade—and that wasn't like the enemy we knew. When you had a small U.S. unit, a larger enemy concentration would usually set up an ambush and attempt to take you on."

Gibler was uneasy, and on January 30, he decided to circle the wagons. "Call the companies," he told Major James F. MacGill, his S3. "Get 'em on their way back to the firebase."

"Why?" the major asked.

"I don't know, but I want 'em on their way back in."

Using the secure radio, Gibler called Bill Schroeder, who was then up at II FFV. "What's going on?" asked Gibler.

"We don't know," Schroeder said. "But *be ready.*"

Gibler's company commanders helicoptered into the fire-base for a briefing. The companies themselves would not close until the next morning. "I kept looking at Saigon on the map," remembered Gibler, suspecting that the VC had avoided contact so as to infiltrate the capital for some type of attack. "I asked the company commanders, 'When's the last time any of you ever did any instruction in your units about Combat in Cities?' They never had, so I said, 'Well, get in the footlockers and get the manuals out—we're going to have classes tonight on Combat in Cities.'"

Gibler's best company commander, Captain Antonio V. "Tony" Smaldone of A/3-7th Infantry, was pulling firebase security at the time. "Smaldone and company were using the backs of C ration cartons as chalkboards," said Gibler. "They were really getting into it, because they knew that if we had to move out they'd be the first to go."

The world went crazy that night, and in the morning they could see the smoke boiling out of Saigon. Gibler soon received a call from CMD, to which the 3-7th Infantry was opcon, to secure the Phu Tho Racetrack in Cholon and rescue the pinned-down MPs in the area. MacGill cranked up an H23 to shepherd Smaldone's company—it was a straight shot up Highway 4 from the Binh Chanh district headquarters to the southwestern side of Saigon—and in short order the infantry was packed aboard several troop trucks with convoy security provided by eight armored personnel carriers positioned to the front and rear of the column as well as between the deuce-and-a-halfs.

First Lieutenant Richard W. Harper, the cavalry platoon leader—he rode in the lead APC—was attached from D/17th Cavalry, 199th LIB. The infantry-cavalry task force got rolling at about 0800, January 31, 1968. It was an hour trip up Highway 4, the column pausing at PF outposts along the way while concertina-wire barriers were pulled aside. "As we got into the outskirts of Saigon, we started passing bodies along the road," said Specialist Four Al Schlenker, a track gunner. "You'd see a smashed moped, and a Vietnamese would be laying there shot up. They might have been civilians, or ARVN who were returning to their units—or running away."

There were more bodies in the city, to include those of

several U.S. Army and Air Force officers who had been caught unawares by the Viet Cong. "They were in khakis and had obviously been going into Tan Son Nhut or another duty station from the BOQs in Cholon. They had just been slaughtered in their jeeps," said Major MacGill, who was guiding the column from his command ship.

The column continued on until taking fire from a rooftop up ahead. Smaldone immediately detrucked his troops while Lieutenant Harper silenced the enemy with a 106mm recoilless rifle mounted on one of his APCs. The task force turned north on a side street and advanced to within a klick of its objective—at which point Harper was killed, along with his track commander and driver, when an RPG suddenly slammed into the lead APC, and automatic-weapons fire raked the vehicle and the street.

Captain Smaldone spread his force out east for several blocks to north-south Plantation Road, then began moving north through the densely packed buildings. (MacGill and Smaldone had previously served advisory tours with the ARVN. "Both of us had chugged all over Cholon during our first tours," said MacGill, "so we used bars and whore-houses as points of reference during the battle.")

The advance was slow and methodical. Smaldone used two APCs with 106mm recoilless rifles to blast enemy strong points—the task force had to hold fire on several occasions as fleeing civilians ran past—and instead of trying to go around corners or down the streets themselves, the troops went house to house, blowing holes in the walls with plastic explosives to give themselves room to maneuver.

Gunships added to the destruction, and by 1300, Captain Smaldone and A/3-7th Infantry—which had one KIA and several wounded during the battle—had pushed to within a block of the racetrack. The attack then stalled in the face of heavy machine-gun fire from a building at the northwest corner of Plantation Road and east-west Hoa Hao Street.

From the command ship, Major MacGill could see two MPs firing down into the strong point from the roof of a building at the southeast corner of Plantation Road and Hoa Hao. "We were running out of fuel, so I said, 'Hell, set me down there,'" recalled MacGill, who jumped onto the roof from the hovering H23, along with his Arty LNO, the only other passenger. "Those MPs were so happy to see us, you couldn't believe it, especially since the H23 had skid-mounted machine guns and they had an M60 up there but had run out of ammunition. We took all the ammo off the helicopter, and then the pilot took off to re-gas."

There were also two Canh Sats there, firing down the stairwell that led to the roof. "It turned out we had the roof, but the VC had the rest of the building," said MacGill.

Figures darted between the houses as the MPs blasted away with the M60. Major MacGill spotted a lone VC who attempted to rejoin his comrades by stashing his AK-47, removing his red armband, and crossing the street with his arms up like a civilian. MacGill cut him down. Meanwhile, Smaldone had worked one of the 106 tracks up toward the VC strong point. Leaving the APC behind cover, he brought the driver and gunner forward on foot and pointed out the target so that they knew the area and when the infantry laid down a base of fire would be able to roll up, stop, and shoot before the enemy could sight in with an RPG.

Having refueled, the command ship presently returned. "It landed on the roof to pick me up, and we were just taking off when they fired the recoilless rifle," MacGill said. The 106 crew scored a direct hit, the explosion touching off mortar shells cached inside the strong point. "Debris from the building went about a hundred feet in the air right in front of the chopper. It scared the shit out of us. The secondary explosions started a horrendous fire, and I got on the radio with CMD, requesting that they call the fire department. I was worried about burning down all of Cholon!"

During the night, General Weyand's headquarters at Long Binh, twenty kilometers northeast of the capital, had been rocketed and hit by a major ground assault. The fight was still raging in the morning when Weyand instructed Major General Keith L. Ware, deputy commander of II Field Force, Vietnam—and a Medal of Honor winner from the Battle of the Bulge—to helicopter into Saigon with a small task force command group so as to assume operational control of all U.S. units fighting in the capital, and to then

Maj. Carl A. Bender and Capt. Carl B. DeNisio of the 377th SPS won Silver Stars for leading the defense of Tan Son Nhut Air Base during the 1968 Tet Offensive. (Courtesy Carl Bender)

The 051 Bunker was temporarily captured by the enemy during the Battle of Tan Son Nhut, January 31, 1968. (Courtesy Mel Grover)

Capt. Leo B. Virant, commander of C/3-4th Cavalry, which slammed into the enemy regiment attacking Tan Son Nhut. (Courtesy Leo Virant)

Dead VC and NVA at the west end of Tan Son Nhut. (Courtesy Richard George)

Pfc. Frank Cuff (left, holding 90mm shell) and Sp5 Dwight W. Birdwell of C/3-4th Cavalry. (Courtesy Frank Cuff and Dwight Birdwell, respectively)

MPs taking up positions outside the embattled U.S. Embassy in Saigon, January 31, 1968. (Courtesy Richard George)

Brig. Gen. Albin F. Irzyk decorates Lt. Col. Richard E. George, the Saigon Provost Marshal, with a Legion of Merit and Bronze Star. (Courtesy Richard George)

A rescue team follows a V-100 security vehicle toward a troop truck in which sixteen MPs were killed during the Battle of BOQ 3, Saigon, January 31, 1968. (Courtesy Richard George)

Lt. Col. Kenton D. Miller, commander of the 3d SPS (right, with camouflaged helmet), and Capt. Reginald V. Maisey, his operations officer, at Bien Hoa Air Base. (Courtesy Kent Miller)

Bunker Hill 10 lay directly in the path of the enemy that penetrated Bien Hoa Air Base on January 31, 1968. Note RPG hits. (Courtesy Kent Miller)

Capt. Donald W. Derrah, commander of L/3-11 Armored Cavalry Regiment, led the clearing of Bien Hoa City. (Courtesy Don Derrah)

Capt. Robert L. Tonsetic, commander of C/4-12th Infantry (199th LIB), receives the Distinguished Service Cross. (Courtesy Bob Tonsetic)

Lt. Col. Neal Creighton, commander of 3-11 ACR, snaps off a salute in the III Corps HQ, Bien Hoa. Maj. John H. Getgood is behind Creighton. (Courtesy Neal Creighton)

A Phantom jet conducts an air strike near an M48 tank from M/3-11 ACR. (Courtesy Neal Creighton)

clear the city of enemy forces and defend against further attack in coordination with the Capital Military District.

"General Ware was a very impressive individual," said Lieutenant Colonel Schroeder, the hastily appointed G3 of Task Force Ware (also known as Hurricane Forward for the nickname of II FFV). "He never got excited, never raised his voice, never wore his rank on his sleeve like so many of them did. He was just a good, soft-spoken soldier, and his calm demeanor instilled a lot of confidence."

Ware, Schroeder, and the general's aide flew directly from Long Binh to the CMD compound on Le Van Duyet Street in central Saigon. "During the approach we could see groups of Viet Cong running right down Le Van Duyet," noted Schroeder. The Huey landed on a helipad adjacent to the CMD compound, and Ware and Schroeder—wearing backpack radios—hastily disembarked with the aide, and piled into a waiting jeep. "There was an overweight U.S. Air Force master sergeant at the wheel. He was sweating blood, and shouting, 'Let's get the hell out of here!'" Schroeder said. "It was a little hairy. We were taking small-arms fire from the roofs of the apartment-type buildings around the compound as we barreled inside. We made a mad dash around the barrels they had emplaced to protect the entranceway from a suicide attack in an automobile—and through it all the general was as cool as a cucumber."

Task Force Ware was operational as of 1100. Five and a half hours later, Major MacGill reported that A/3-7th Infantry had secured the Phu Tho Racetrack. When the fire started by the secondary explosions forced the VC to retreat, an APC had rammed the southeast corner of the racetrack wall, knocking a hole in it through which the troops poured to take up commanding positions in the grandstands.

Enemy snipers pestered them, and one round hit MacGill's H23, blowing out a piece of the bubble at the feet of the Arty LNO. The captain's radio and CAR15 disappeared through the hole. Meanwhile, Lieutenant Colonel Gibler choppered into the racetrack with B and C/3-7th Infantry, having been relieved at Binh Chanh by the 5-60th Mechanized Infantry of the 9th Division. "There were still a dozen little Vietnamese horses in the stables, and as soon as our troops found them, they were out there riding them around. We had to get them off before they got shot!" remembered Gibler, who set up his CP in the racetrack director's office. "There was a huge television set in there, and during the course of the operation we could literally watch ourselves on the U.S. Armed Forces News."

The racetrack was vital as the only sizable landing zone in Saigon, and on February 1, Ware reinforced Gibler with B and C/5-60th Mech. Gibler immediately mounted a mech-infantry sweep to clean out enemy forces regrouping some blocks west of the racetrack. A major landmark, the race-track had turned into a rallying point for VC from units all over the city. Moving down a narrow street, B/5-60th Mech—having neglected to deploy dismounted security to its front and flanks as ordered—was ambushed a klick from the racetrack. The VC were entrenched in a cemetery on the company's right flank and occupied the buildings on the left. The lead APC was disabled by RPG fire, as were the last three, one of which burst into flames.

"The company was firing like hell with the .50-cals and M60s, but they couldn't get out of there," said MacGill, who was overhead with Gibler. "They were totally blocked in. I thought we were going to lose the whole company."

Three GIs were killed, and the B/5-60th Mech command-er was among the sixteen wounded. "We could not get any artillery or close air support in there," Gibler recalled bitterly, noting the restrictions placed on U.S. units in Saigon to minimize civilian casualties and property damage.

Huey gunships were made available instead, and after an hour of nonstop gun runs on the cemetery, the VC broke. The 3-7th Infantry swept the area for the next two days, reinforced by tracked M42 "Dusters" with twin, rapid-firing 40mm cannons in an open turret. "The twin-40s were a lifesaver," said MacGill. "Whenever we ran into resist-ance in a building, the company commander in contact would pull a Duster up and point out which room was giving him trouble, then they would wheel up there and pop four or five rounds through the window real quick. The shrapnel effect on the inside of the room just cleared 'em right out."

On February 3, TF Ware was deployed thusly:

The 2-27th Infantry and 3-4 Cavalry (25th Division) were securing the Tan Son Nhut area.

The 3-7th Infantry (199th Light Infantry Brigade) was securing the Phu Tho Racetrack area.

The 2-16th Infantry and A/1-4th Cavalry (1st Division) were securing the Binh Loi Bridge in northern Saigon.

The 1-18th Infantry (1st Division) was securing the power plant and water filtration plant east of Saigon.

The 2-327th Infantry (101st Airborne Division) was securing the POL storage area southeast of Saigon.

The 5-60th Mech Infantry (9th Division) at Binh Chanh, and the 1-27th Infantry (25th Division) at Hoc Mon, were screening the southern and western approaches to Saigon.

The main force VC battalions that were to have reinforced the initial attack never arrived, COSVN unwilling to reinforce defeat. Between February 4 and 5, General Ware shifted all U.S. units out of the capital at the request of the ARVN, which wanted the honor of clearing Saigon.

What happened in the capital happened throughout the country. The people did not rise up. The ARVN did not collapse. During Tet, the communists not only executed government officials and officers but murdered their families as well. It was fight or die. The ARVN fought. The enemy did not apply sufficient force to any one objective and were defeated piecemeal. In Saigon, fifteen battalions of crack ARVN rangers and paratroopers, and Vietnamese Marines, ground down the isolated VC units in a series of chaotic street fights. By day four, the fighting was mostly confined to Cholon, and there were spectacular fires and great palls of smoke over the area as VNAF Skyraiders bombed those neighborhoods where the guerrillas held out like termites amid the densely packed houses.

Fighting in Cholon continued into March. The outcome of the battle inevitable, General Ware's task force was actually disestablished on February 18. (Ware assumed command of the 1st Infantry Division in March, and this great soldier's general was killed in a helicopter crash near the Cambodian border on September 13, 1968.)

Though life soon returned to normal for the U.S. support troops in Saigon, things had been touch and go for the first few days. Many air force personnel billeted in the city, for example, had found themselves stranded as Viet Cong with bush hats and AK-47s took up positions just outside their windows. "We ran numerous convoys to evacuate those people," noted Staff Sergeant Robert L. Ruth of the 377th Security Police Squadron. In one case, Ruth's team took two jeeps and a bus to a BEQ whose occupants had only three weapons between them. "We sent word that when we arrived they were to wait for a signal before coming out to give us a chance to secure the area first. They were to bring minimum gear with them," Ruth said. "We stopped the bus in front of the hotel, and one sergeant had big tears running down his cheeks as he hugged my neck and thanked us for getting there. In the meantime, I was just trying to get him on the bus because I wanted to get out of there before we started receiving fire."

On day two, Sergeant Ruth led two jeeps and ten trucks on a hair-raising trip through the city to secure a food resupply for Tan Son Nhut from the warehouses on the Saigon waterfront. Along the way, they drove right into a firefight, ARVN to the left, VC to the right, and barricades blocking the street dead ahead. "By the time we realized what was happening, there was no way we could get out. The trucks were too big to turn around on those streets," said Ruth, whose column was obliged to gas it and hope for the best. "The only thing that saved us was that a Skyraider was making a bomb run at that moment. When it came in, both sides ceased fire and took cover, they were that close together. We went through the middle of it, ran over the barricades, and just as we came out the other side, the bombs exploded and the gunfire started back up."

Pulling into one warehouse area, the first truck had no sooner backed up to a loading dock when automatic weapons fire erupted outside the compound. "One of the guys had thrown a box of lettuce into the truck. That's all we had, but an MP sergeant shouted, 'Hey, flyboys, you better get out of here because here they come!'" said Ruth. "When we came out the gate, the enemy was probably a hundred yards away. The MPs were engaging them as they came across a bridge, and the only two MPs that were still outside the compound were running towards it as we got out of there."

The harried column sped to another warehouse, which turned out to be locked up and guarded by a single petrified GI who had neither keys nor a telephone. "We had no access to the building, so we turned around and made our way back to Tan Son Nhut. The sergeant in charge of the mess halls was highly perturbed that we only had a box of lettuce. We felt very fortunate to have gotten back at all, and our reply was, 'If you want it that bad, you go get it.'"

On February 9, Gibler's 3–7th Infantry redeployed to the racetrack to release the ARVN units securing the complex for the ongoing Cholon battle. Bill Schroeder helicoptered in the next day with a mission from TF Ware. "You sonofabitch, I just heated up a can of Cs," Gibler joked.

"Well, John, put 'em down because this is a biggie!"

Schroeder broke open his map and put his finger on the Phu Lam pagoda three klicks west of the racetrack in the rice-paddy fringe of Saigon. ARVN intelligence indicated that General Do's command post—which controlled the entire Saigon operation—was entrenched in tunnels and bunkers in an adjacent cemetery. "The ARVN want to go in and wipe 'em out if you'll block for 'em," Schroeder said.

"Bullshit!" Gibler rejoined. "I've got armor here, buddy. *I'm* going after 'em . . ."

The attack was launched on February 11. Gibler commanded the operation from the ground, turning his C&C over for use in medevacking B and D/3–7th Infantry's six killed and fourteen wounded as they ran into heavy contact while surrounding the enemy headquarters. With the VC boxed in, the Dusters chewed the bunkers up with their twin-40s. The body count was forty-nine, and four prisoners were taken, along with radios, documents, etc. General Do, however, was nowhere to be found.

Part 3

Bien Hoa

"I got my attack order from the division commander. We were standing on the patio by the general's mess, and he was pointing right at the VC. It was an unreal situation."
—Lt. Col. David E. Grange
Commanding Officer, 2d Battalion,
506th Infantry, 3d Brigade,
101st Airborne Division

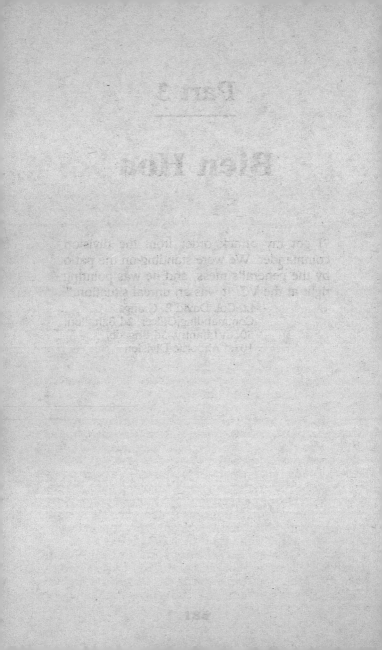

10

Itching for a Fight

Bien Hoa Air Base, the busiest air facility in the world, was located twenty kilometers northeast of Saigon in what was by air force standards a hot area. "We probably had a firefight out on the perimeter every third week with small teams of would-be saboteurs," said Lieutenant Colonel Kenton D. "Kent" Miller, CO of the 3d Security Police Squadron at Bien Hoa. The enemy usually came in from the north and east. These were the most accessible routes, given the army compound flush against the east half of the air base's northern perimeter and the fact that the southern perimeter faced the city of Bien Hoa, the province capital, while the western perimeter almost touched the Dong Nai River.

Lieutenant Colonel Miller took over the 3d SPS in February 1967, his predecessor having been hastily transferred after a penetration of the ammo dump on the north side of Bien Hoa. The sappers slipped in and out without detection in the middle of the night, and when the charges they had planted suddenly detonated, 2,600 napalm canisters went up like a scene from Dante's *Inferno*.

The sapper raid was the first enemy action at Bien Hoa in months. The security police had grown lax. They needed to wake up. Under the command of the 3d Tactical Fighter Wing, Bien Hoa was home to aviation units of all kinds, to include gunships, flareships, transports, the only VNAF jet squadron, and the defoliation aircraft of Operation Ranch Hand. "We had an aircraft take off or land every thirty seconds," remembered Miller, a fatherly, coachlike officer with a Texas accent whose efforts to reenergize the base's security squadron coincided with an attention-grabbing upswing in enemy activity. On their toes now, the SPs caught every additional sabotage attempt at the perimeter fence. They even captured one sapper. It was a lopsided encounter. "The SAT team must have fired 50,000 rounds at whatever was out there in the dark," Miller said, referring to a jeep-mounted Security Alert Team. "Finally, this poor little Viet Cong, dressed only in a loincloth, with a pistol hanging from a cord around his neck, stood up with his hands in the air. He had been hit in the leg and arm."

The right mood having been established, it was time to refine technique. "Saigon complained about all the ammunition we were using because I conducted weapons training every single night," said Captain Martin E. Strones, the new commander of the night shift. "The troops had a lot to learn, and the training was also sort of a psychological battle I was playing with the VC. We knew they were observing us, and I wanted them to be aware that we had a lot of firepower and were always alert."

The enemy began mortaring Bien Hoa on a weekly basis that summer, and one night in May, 122mm rockets also shrieked in. One hit a 3d SPS barracks, killing six men. "According to 7th Air Force doctrine, the SPs were responsible for the base and the army for everything outside the perimeter. But there was no army out there," said Miller. "The Army believes its job is to seek and destroy the enemy in the field and will not consistently keep a force around an air base just for the purpose of defending the air base," he explained in his end-of-tour report. "Air Force ground defense forces must be prepared to defend air bases as far out as the 'mortar belt.'"

In September, Lieutenant Colonel Miller and forty volunteers attended the five-day 173d Airborne Brigade Jungle School at the adjacent army compound. The graduation exercise was the "the only SP helicopter assault into enemy territory [during the Vietnam War]," Miller wrote. Led by the training NCOs, he added, the air force troops went in as infantry, complete with green faces and leafy twigs in their helmet covers. "Army helicopters dropped us just at dusk and we organized a perimeter defense for the night, and at dawn conducted a search patrol through the jungle about 25 klicks back to the base."

Thereafter the 3d SPS ran unauthorized sweeps and ambushes outside Bien Hoa. "Morale was excellent. The troops were itching for a fight," Miller said. Two or three nights before Tet, Captain Strones organized a cookout, complete with a Korean band and an Australian stripper. "The troops were doing a real good job, and I thought it was time to let our hair down," he said. When it was over, the captain had to take a truck into Bien Hoa City to round up SPs who had gone off limits to continue the celebration. "It was one hell of a party, and it really put the guys in the right frame of mind," Strones concluded. "They were up, they were trained, they were confident. How you feel about yourself has a lot to do with how successful you are, and the troops had the attitude that nobody could mess with us."

Like Tan Son Nhut, Bien Hoa went to security condition red on the eve of Tet by order of the 7th Air Force. "We prepositioned SATs and Quick Reaction Forces throughout the base, and we put out extra listening posts," said Miller, who was particularly concerned with the east side of the base, having been warned by some old soldiers in the 173d Airborne that if an attack ever came, it would come from that direction. "I always thought it would come from the northwest, so the VC wouldn't have to move past Long Binh to the east to get to us, but they said the enemy would never take the chance of crossing the river up there." There was much tall, concealing elephant grass on the east perimeter, but "we could never get permission to burn it because the smoke would hinder the vision of the pilots who were constantly taking off and landing. We took advantage of the truce, however, when the aircraft were down, and burned off considerable amounts of the vegetation."

Ammunition carriers were also strategically placed, "so if

we did have a big firefight and the troops ran out of ammo," Miller added with a touch of humor, "more could be rushed up in that great military vehicle known as a Ford pickup."

Unlike their Tan Son Nhut counterparts, however, the Bien Hoa SPs anticipated a quiet night, such was their experience with 7th Air Force intelligence. "I thought, I'm not buying any of this, it's just another damn report, and I went to bed early," remembered Miller, who as a squadron commander rated one half of an air-conditioned trailer.

The intelligence proved correct when 122mm rockets began slamming into Bien Hoa AB at 0300 on January 31, 1968. "We were used to being hit by mortars and rockets, usually biweekly by that time," said Miller, "so when the incoming started, I thought it was just another raid, and I simply rolled off my bunk onto the trailer floor."

Four hours before the barrage began, a 199th LIB patrol out of Long Binh had spotted the rocketeers as they set up nine klicks northeast of Bien Hoa. When the rockets began flashing in the dark, gunships already on station proceeded to saturate the launch sites with minigun fire.

Though quickly snuffed out, it was an intense barrage with forty-five 122mm rockets landing like earth-shaking comets in the built-up part of the base south of the main east-west runway. "We usually received five to twenty-five rounds. This barrage was so heavy that it finally dawned on me that 'this isn't a normal raid, this is cover for a ground attack,'" recalled Lieutenant Colonel Miller, who quickly donned his fatigues and pistol belt, grabbed his steel pot, jumped in his jeep, and sped to the alternate Central Security Control, the power in the primary command post having been knocked out. Three USAF personnel had been killed and sixteen wounded in the bombardment, the roof had been blown off the control tower, and vehicles, trailers, warehouses, and barracks throughout the base had been damaged or demolished. Numerous parked aircraft had been peppered with fragments, flames roared skyward from a damaged POL tank, and more fires blazed in the night as a VNAF Skyraider and a USAF F100 Super Saber burned down to charred metal skeletons inside their concrete revetments, the latter taking a fuel truck with it.

Lieutenant Colonel Miller had no sooner reached CSC than a K-9 patrol on the east perimeter radioed in, the dog handler explaining that his German shepherd was having a heavy alert. Miller instructed the airman to fire a flare.

When the flare went off, the dog handler blurted on his handheld radio, "Oh my God, they're everywhere!"

The enemy was already inside the perimeter, streaming through the dark toward the interior of the base. The dog handler released his German shepherd on the invaders but was wounded an instant later. The attack dog was shot and killed as it lunged at the closest Viet Cong.

The battle was thus joined at 0320. It was later determined that when the rocketing began, the enemy assault force—two battalions from the 274th VC Regiment, over half of whose soldiers were NVA fillers—had just completed a nine-hour march from assembly areas twenty-nine kilometers due east of Bien Hoa. While the 274th overran the air base, another communist regiment was to hit the II FFV and 199th LIB headquarters compounds at nearby Long Binh. The entire operation was controlled by the 5th VC Division, normally headquartered to the north in War Zone D.

The enemy was confident. Many had their best baggy green dress uniforms in their packs in anticipation of a victory parade through Bien Hoa City. The penetration of the air base was indeed flawless. Staging in Dong Lach, a hamlet only two hundred meters east of Bien Hoa AB, the lead elements of the 274th moved out under cover of the rocket attack, slipped through an old French minefield without incident, and cut four gaps in the perimeter fence. Filing in and fanning out, the assault troops proceeded across the grasslands leading to the east end of the runways, ready to place their satchel charges on the jets along the flight line and blow them up in their revetments.

Two VNAF security police, or Quan Canhs (QCs), manned a bunker between the perimeter fence and the parallel outer perimeter road. "The QCs were famous for sleeping on post, and after the attack we found those two with their throats slit," noted Miller. They must have been the victims of sappers who crept in ahead of the barrage to neutralize the outpost. Awakened by the rockets, the QC squad in another position at the very eastern tip of the base managed to escape before being overrun in the main attack.

The perimeter road cut west at the second position. Running straight down it, the QCs headed for Bunker Hill 10, which was manned by Sergeants Marshall Gott and Neal Tuggle, 3d SPS, and Airman First Class Neil Behnke, an augmentee from one of the base support units used to beef up the line during red alerts. Bunker Hill 10—a six-sided, French-built concrete strong point with ground-level firing slits and ten layers of sandbags in a ring on the flat roof where an M60 was set up under the overhead cover of a circular concrete slab—sat on the south side of an access road that continued west while the perimeter road turned south again. The southern end of the north-south road at the east end of the runway met the access road immediately west of Bunker Hill 10.

The sentries who had their throats cut were stationed on the fence line between the hastily evacuated QC guard position and Bunker Hill 10. A creek meandered along the southern edge of the connecting leg of the perimeter road, and there were a set of bridgelike concrete culverts a stone's throw southeast of Bunker Hill 10 so the creek could run under the perimeter road where it turned south again.

The K-9 patrol encountered the point of the attack in this marshy area. Gott, Tuggle, and Behnke immediately popped flares over Bunker Hill 10 and opened up with a machine gun and grenade launcher. Meanwhile, the SPs on listening post duty just inside the wire could only pray that they would go unnoticed. "Most of them were in one-man foxholes in the elephant grass, and they were totally cut off from each other," said Captain Strones, who had climbed the water tower in the center of the base to get a commanding view of the action. "The LPs had radioed in warnings of enemy movement during the rocket attack, but the power had been knocked out in CSC and I couldn't get through to the alternate CSC. They hadn't picked up the command yet. The LPs got caught in the middle of the enemy advance, and they were really distraught. They were never discovered, but I never got any more volunteers for the LPs."

The eruption of fire to the east had puckered everyone,

but "Lieutenant Colonel Miller simply said, 'If you see any VC, make them 10-7 [out of service],'" recalled Airman First Class David C. Chunn, an SP on the north perimeter. "He sounded so cool on the radio, everyone calmed down . . ."

Miller ordered a three-man SAT and a nine-man QRF to Bunker Hill 10. "We didn't know if the action on the east perimeter was the main attack or a feint to cover infiltration at other points," he later said, noting that fire was also coming from a hamlet to the northwest and from Bien Hoa City itself. "The base perimeter covered ten miles. Our present-for-duty strength was 350, not including about 75 augmentees. Enemy strength was later estimated at 1,500."

To get a better picture of the situation, Miller dispatched Captain Reginald V. Maisey, the quiet, highly regarded 3d SPS operations officer, to Bunker Hill 10. Speeding through no-man's-land in the dark, Maisey reached the strong point by jeep. "They needed flares. CSC called the east resupply team, but they were pinned down at the checkpoint between our base and the army compound," noted Staff Sergeant William "Pete" Piazza, leader of the north resupply team (the army compound was then occupied by the headquarters of the 101st Airborne Division). Sergeant Richard E. Lee ran the east resupply team—each team had an NCOIC, an SP, three augmentees, and a truck stacked with flares and ammo—and Piazza linked up with him at that point. Lee's team and the checkpoint MPs, armed with M14s, were exchanging fire with the overrun QC position at the east end of the base. After deploying his team, Piazza "checked with CSC to see if the south resupply team could go to Bunker Hill 10. They were busy in their own sector, so I told Lee to turn his augmentees over to the other SP on his team and to come with me. We climbed aboard my truck, and I got behind the wheel for the run to Bunker Hill 10."

To avoid the enemy fire, they took a circuitous route to reach the strong point from the rear. "I told CSC which way I was going so as not to get shot up by friendly fire," noted Piazza, a stocky, bespectacled career SP on the second of three Vietnam tours who would subsequently be awarded the Silver Star for his role at Bunker Hill 10. "I originally made Piazza a supply team leader because he had a real outgoing personality," said Strones, the night guard commander. "We put a big coffeepot on his truck, and he'd travel from position to position, cheering the guys up on those lonely nights on the line. He was great for morale, and during the big attack he turned out to be a real hero, too. . . ."

Coming down an access road that cut to Bunker Hill 10 from the east end of the runway, Piazza was halted by an SP that Captain Maisey had posted about a hundred meters to the rear of the strong point to prevent additional vehicles from piling up around it. Maisey's jeep was already there, along with a firetruck and the SAT and QRF vehicles. Leaving the truck, Piazza's team hustled forward with cases of flares, whereupon the troops bunched up behind the bunker hurriedly dividing up the flares.

The first RPG hit the sandbag ring on Bunker Hill 10 at that moment, blowing Sergeant Tuggle's M60 overboard. The next one was at least twenty feet too high and shrieked by harmlessly with a rooster tail of sparks. "It was like looking up and seeing Superman," remembered Piazza. "We all watched this RPG go over us, go past us, and land in the elephant grass behind us. Holy shit!"

The third RPG blew up the firetruck parked beside the bunker. "Take cover," Captain Maisey shouted at the dumbstruck troops. "Everybody take cover!"

Sergeant Piazza ended up on the right side of the bunker with an army captain who served as the liaison officer between the 3d SPS and the 145th Aviation Battalion, which was headquartered at Bien Hoa AB. The liaison officer had come up with Maisey, and packed an XM148, an M16 with a tubelike 40mm grenade launcher mounted under the barrel. "He didn't know how to use it, he didn't know what to do. He was just scared shitless, so I gave him my M16 and took the '148 and his ammo bandolier," said Piazza, who didn't notice that the captain was wounded moments later. He was too focused on finding the source of the fire. It turned out that the RPG team was in the overrun QC guard bunker about a hundred meters to the left front on the other side of the creek and the culvert bridge. "I saw the flash of their rocket launcher, and we started playing one-on-one," Piazza said. "I'd fire one, duck back, and they'd fire another one while I reloaded the grenade launcher. I'd wait for the explosion, then come around the corner of the bunker again and lob another round out there into the dark."

Four RPGs hit the concrete face of Bunker Hill 10, and a dozen more exploded around the strong point before Piazza's thirteenth shot dropped right into the open-topped QC bunker, igniting the RPG team's pile of rockets. "There was a big explosion, and two or three VC went flying into the air," he said. "We all yelled and cheered, but then some small-arms fire started and we took cover again. . . ."

Someone put up another slap-flare. Trailing smoke, it floated down into the elephant grass southwest of Bunker Hill 10, silhouetting a line of ten or twelve figures moving quickly across the field. Piazza got on the radio to ask CSC if there were any SPs in that area. The answer was no, and he blurted, "Well, we got somebody out there now!"

The enemy was bypassing the strong point, intent on reaching the runway three hundred meters behind it. The thirty or so SPs and QCs in and around Bunker Hill 10 were surrounded, "but then all of a sudden here came the choppers," exulted Piazza, who ended up diving into the bunker when the much-appreciated gunship fire ripped in a little too close for comfort. Piazza realized there was a dead man laying on the bunker floor, unidentifiable in the dark. He and Tuggle dragged the body up the steps and laid it outside. "Back in the bunker, we fired if we spotted a target," Piazza said, "but we were in a pitch-black box, trying to look out slits maybe two by ten inches, and all we could really see were flares and tracers. I thought, 'This ain't workin'! We can't do anything in here, we can't see nothing, we gotta get outside because all they gotta do is walk up behind us and lob a grenade in and we're dead meat!'"

Captain Maisey had disappeared in the confusion, presumably called to another hot spot, so it was Piazza, the ranking NCO at Bunker Hill 10, who led several troops up onto the roof to protect the position. "The main body went past us. They wanted the aircraft, so we weren't under heavy fire," he said. "We returned what fire we received, but mostly we were illuminating the area and keeping CSC informed of enemy movement so they could feed directions to the gunships and flareships and reaction teams."

Piazza realized only at dawn that the dead man he had dragged out of the bunker was Captain Maisey. Helmeted and armed with a CAR15, Maisey—posthumously awarded the Air Force Cross—had been wounded by one of the first RPGs fired at Bunker Hill 10. Talking to CSC at the time, he grunted, "I'm hit!" but after a brief pause was back on the horn. Maisey calmly directed and encouraged the troops as they returned fire, then dropped into the bunker so he could make himself heard as he got back on the radio to explain the situation to CSC. He was standing beside the rear door and the ladder that led to the roof, his back to the front firing slit, when one of the last RPGs impacted against that slit, spraying the interior of the bunker. Maisey caught the blast squarely in the back and was killed instantly.

Maisey's reports to the command post were pivotal in trying to assess the enemy's plan. "It looked like the main thrust was coming in from the east, and Miller told me to organize the counterattack force," said Captain Strones, who had been called to CSC from the water tower. "By the time I got to our assembly area at the armory, the enemy owned the east end of the runway. No one could take off, but when they tried to come across the taxiway ramp to reach the aircraft revetments they ran into a machine-gun bunker we had between the taxiway and the runway. That blocked their forward progress, that really screwed them up."

Flareships were up, lighting the way for the AH1G Cobra gunships of the 334th Assault Helicopter Company out of Bien Hoa AB. The newest weapon of the war, the sleek, shark-bodied Cobras had nose-mounted, two-thousand-rounds-a-minute miniguns, and a solid stream of red tracers connected ship to ground like a laser when they fired.

"Without the gunships it is doubtful if the security police could have stopped the enemy from overrunning the base," Lieutenant Colonel Miller wrote in his report.

The SPs lost direct contact with their aviation support when the army liaison officer was wounded at Bunker Hill 10. "We placed an enlisted man, Carl Smith, into one of the gunships and he had an SP radio and relayed our requests to the pilot," noted Second Lieutenant John A. Novak, 3d SPS. "Smith directed the helicopter support to where it was needed. The gunships were key, but so was the controlling info."

The battle looked like a Fourth of July celebration as Captain Strone's forty-man force moved into the median between the runway and the taxiway, and low-crawled past the machine-gun bunker that had stopped the enemy. "I had a Quick Reaction Force north of the runway on my left flank, and another group down to my right, so I felt reasonably secure," said Strones, who intended to launch a frontal assault across the concrete ramp that connected the east end of the runway and taxiway. "Unfortunately, we were spotted while still moving into position. We had tracers snap past, and the dirt was being bounced up around us from near misses. We kept going, keeping low."

The counterattack force made it to an earthen berm pushed up on the west side of the ramp during recent construction in the area. "There it was, right where we needed it," said Strones, whose line sheltered behind it, returning fire. Most of the enemy fire was coming from the arming shack on the southeast side of the ramp, a little, yellow, wood-framed building with screened windows and a corrugated tin roof. Two USAF or VNAF armorers were stationed in the shack at any given time, their job being to arm the bombs on the jets as they pulled up from the aircraft revetments on the way to the runway. "The two U.S. airman on duty that night took cover in the bunker next to the shack, and stayed there all during the fight," noted Miller. "The VC never discovered them, which was lucky because neither was armed. Except for the security police, the whole base, in fact, was basically unarmed because of previous raids at other bases in which sabotage teams had gotten in and the mechanics and cooks and clerk-typists had ended up shooting at each other all night."

Playing it safe, the 7th Air Force had put the support units' weapons under lock and key. "All the troops had an assigned bunker in case of incoming, and the senior NCO at each bunker was the only one with a weapon," said Miller, describing a fear shared by the Tan Son Nhut SPs during

Tet. "I could just see the headlines if the enemy had gotten past us and made their way through the base, clearing out all these unarmed airmen inside the bunkers. . . ."

Captain Strones cursed the fact that the security police themselves had only light weapons as his force blasted the arming shack with M16 and M60 fire to little effect. The SPs didn't even have LAWs, so Miller contacted his QC counterpart, who dispatched a 57mm recoilless rifle team. Taking up a position with Strones at the berm, the QCs used a loudspeaker to call to the VC/NVA in the arming shack to surrender. The plea was ignored, and the recoilless rifle put several rounds through the walls. The enemy vacated the shack and started running back the way they had come in, even as gunships roared in only a few feet off the deck, chopping figures down in the elephant grass.

It was dawn now. "Are you getting any more fire from that shack," the calm, laconic Miller asked Strones.

"Negative."

"Are you getting any fire from any place?"

"Negative."

"Well, let's go then. . . ."

Strones had his machine-gun teams on either flank fire down the east side of the taxiway, then went in after his M79 men laid down a barrage of tear gas canisters. The SPs fired from the hip during their mad dash across the concrete ramp, including Strones who had a CAR15. "The frontal assault worked, but it could have been a total disaster," recalled Captain Strones, who received the Silver Star. "There were still VC and NVA scattered in the elephant grass on the other side, but they were so focused on the M60 fire from the flanks that they didn't even see us start in— and then once you have forty people with M16s and grenade launchers running towards you, you're not going to have the presence of mind to respond. You're either turning and running, or you're hugging the ground."

The line rolled right over the enemy until hitting a jet-engine test cell, where several VC made a stand among the fuel trucks and dismantled engines, protected on two sides by prefabricated metal walls. An augmentee was killed by a grenade as he came around the corner of one of the walls. "My team was ordered to the scene, and we drove in aboard a flatbed truck, not knowing what to expect," recalled Master Sergeant Robert A. Knox, who was originally posted to the west side of the base. The action at the test cell was a real melee. "Bullets were flying everywhere when we pulled up," Knox continued. "They were hiding among some fifty-five-gallon drums behind the cell, and one of them fired an RPG at a Huey gunship as it passed almost directly overhead, firing at some other group of enemy. I thought that chopper was a goner, but the rocket tail started gyrating about halfway up to it and petered out about twenty-five feet short. The rocket turned around and came straight back down."

Knox was firing at the test cell when he saw movement under the arming shack. "It was only a small flash of daylight, but I knew someone was hiding under there, and I squeezed off an M16 burst at the space under the shack. I saw my tracers go in there." When Knox's team took up a position about ten feet from the shack, a VC or NVA "pulled himself towards me on his elbows, looking me square in the eye. He came from under the shack and had a head wound, was very bloody, and apparently had a spinal or leg problem. He was in very bad shape, but I couldn't help him at that time. Besides, he might have been booby-trapped."

The enemy was grenaded out of the test cell. Captain Strones now had about seventy-five SPs and QCs, and he stopped to reorganize while trucks pulled up with an ammunition resupply. "The ammo was still boxed, and I angrily told CSC that there were a lot of people sitting on their ass back on the base who could have loaded the ammo into magazines," said Strones. "We reloaded our magazines, and then we got our breath and moved out again to push the enemy off the rest of the base. . . ."

Most had already slipped back through the perimeter fence at the east end of the base, and as Strone's line plunged into the elephant grass on the other side of Bunker Hill 10, they policed up the stragglers. Some raised their AK-47s and died. Others hid, and Knox had one dust-covered, fifteen-year-old guerrilla, naked except for a loin cloth and a small bag tied by a string to his waist, pop from a crater in front of him. "He stood with his hands up, bowing and smiling," Knox said. "He took a couple steps towards me, and not knowing what he had in that bag I almost shot him, but someone came up behind him and tied him up. It turned out he had rice and a toothbrush in the bag."

Captain Strones pumped a few shots into each body that he passed, but almost eyeball-deep in elephant grass, he missed one guerrilla who was still alive and who raised his SKS carbine on his back. The SP behind Strones dispatched the diehard with an M16 burst. "We took considerable sniper fire as we neared the perimeter fence, but we couldn't figure out where it was coming from," said Strones. A low-flying Cobra roared in then from the rear. "I was concerned that the pilot thought we were VC, so when he passed over I had everybody hold up their M16," remembered Strones, who had neither communication with the gunships nor smoke grenades to mark his unit. SPs were not issued smoke grenades. "The gunship circled around and came straight at us again," said Strones, one of whose augmentees, a seven-striper, was in a panic. "He was going to make a run for it. Everyone was tense, and if a senior NCO bolted, then all my airmen would probably start running, too—and if the pilot saw people running through the grass, there was no doubt in my mind that he would open up on them. I told the sergeant, 'If you make a run for it and route my whole line, I'm going to be the guy that shoots you!'"

The Cobra flashed over, unleashing its rockets not into the SPs but into one of several hootches on stilts a couple hundred meters off the east end of the base. "We hadn't seen any fire come from the shack, but the gunship pilot had somehow spotted the snipers inside who were firing at us," said Strones, who realized that the pilot's first pass had been a signal for the SPs to get down before he made his firing run. "The gunship blew the shack to smithereens. We encounted only very light resistance after that and quickly reached the perimeter fence, thus securing the base."

11

The Screaming Eagles

During the afternoon, the security police set fire to the elephant grass on the east perimeter, flushing several guerrillas. "We were still finding stragglers out in the grass two or three days later," noted Lieutenant Colonel Miller. Having lost two killed and ten wounded, the 3d SPS rounded up twenty-five prisoners in all and counted 153 VC/NVA bodies inside the east end of the base. "In one incident, a mechanic stopped one of our SPs and asked to borrow his M16 for a minute," Miller said of the battle's aftermath. "He trained the weapon under a culvert, and a Viet Cong who had been under there for two days came out with his hands up. They were just scared and hiding."

The unit which would pursue the enemy who hit the air base, Major General Olinto M. Barsanti's 101st Airborne Division, had only arrived in-country on December 13, 1967, from Fort Campbell, Kentucky. Westmoreland had greeted Barsanti as he disembarked from a C141 transport with the division color guard at Bien Hoa AB. "It was like Mutt and Jeff," mused Captain George William Lanahan, the division commander's aide-de-camp. Westmoreland was a broad-chested, heroically chiseled general. Wiry little Barsanti didn't look the part with his black-frame glasses. He had assumed command of the 101st five months earlier at Campbell. "Barsanti was airborne qualified, but, alas, a 'cherry jumper' who had never had an airborne assignment," wrote a staff officer. "'Legs' and 'cherry jumpers' just didn't command airborne line units," he added, speculating that Barsanti had been placed in command over the objections of senior Airborne Club members in the Department of the Army. "The rumor mill said that Barsanti's gift of the prized 101st was a DOD [Department of Defense] payoff for the general's saving of multiple millions of dollars in a previous tour of duty. Senior leaders in airborne units usually worked their way up or had enough airborne assignments to understand the mission, the people, and the needs of both. Barsanti entered this semi-closed society, knowing nothing about the remarkable people he was about to encounter."

Lanahan had the head of the division jumpmaster school coach Barsanti back through the process. "He was very excited the first time we went to jump. I offered to go out the door first, but he said, 'No, I'm the CG,' and out he went. When we landed, he said, 'Let's go do it again.'"

Barsanti was an energetic, hot-tempered man from a tough Nevada mining town who had won an ROTC commission in 1940. A battalion commander from Omaha Beach to V-E Day, and a regimental commander in Korea—he was with the 2d Division in both wars—he held the DSC, three Silver Stars, and five Purple Hearts. His angry explosions were as eye-opening as his awards. "Barsanti was a madman. I loved him dearly, but he was a hard man to work for," said Lanahan. "He'd change moods in a heartbeat and blow up over things that often seemed trivial. If you could ever get one-on-one with him in a quiet moment, though, you would find a kind, gentle side of him that only those of us who worked closely with him ever saw."

"Barsanti had a very abrasive personality, and he did a lot of shouting and stomping and steaming," said Colonel William P. Tallon, chief of staff of the 101st ABD. "He would chew ass with 'ruffles and flourishes,' but afterwards he would make it clear that it was over—new page, go on. He would say, 'Goddamnit,' but never, 'Goddamn *you*.'"

Other senior officers took a much dimmer view of the

general's leadership style. "It was a reign of terror under Barsanti," said one, speaking for many. Barsanti's command would eventually come to an end amid much controversy. Meanwhile, the division base camp was itself caught up in the Tet Offensive. "We had a fifty-yard-line seat for the assault on Bien Hoa Air Base," noted Lieutenant Colonel Ran L. Phillips, division surgeon and commander of the 326th Medical Battalion, which occupied a sector of the perimeter berm. "I was in one of the operating room tents when a runner from one of our berm listening posts burst in with 'Cunnel, you gotta git yoo ass out thar quick! All hell's breaken loose! They's fucking gooks everwhar!'"

Two or three mortar rounds landed in the base camp, and small-arms fire was taken along the southern berm as the enemy assault force swept past at a distance of two hundred meters while moving west to hit Bien Hoa Air Base. "It was an idiot stunt," opined Tallon, surprised that the enemy did not launch a secondary attack to protect their right flank. Actually, the maneuver would not have seemed foolhardy had the penetration of the air base not been so quickly blunted by the defense forces, leaving many enemy out in the open on the wrong side of the wire. They were exposed by flares and mercilessly flayed by gunships as they kept trying to work their way into their objective.

Security for the division headquarters was being provided by Captain Speedy's C/1-502d Infantry. "Neutralizing the Cobras was crucial for the VC/NVA, and they concentrated their fire on the aircraft," wrote Speedy, noting that the streams of green tracers further pinpointed the enemy. Speedy had his M60s open fire from the berm. "Now the attackers faced direct frontal fire from the Air Force security police, plunging fire from the Cobras and flanking fire from a previously unknown company-size unit."

The enemy muzzle flashes were quickly winked out, noted Speedy. "A night of glorious dreams for the foe had degenerated into the horror of his own butchery. . . ."

At dawn, Phillips realized that his medical tents had been riddled by hot ejected brass from the Cobras. "Our equipment was a shambles, and most of us had sore heads and shoulders from falling debris [despite our helmets and flak jackets]," he wrote. The surgeon was no fan of Barsanti. "We couldn't go to bunkers. We had not been able to construct them, due to a loudly proclaimed lack of building supplies. This lack was not evident at division headquarters down the road where the commanding general had a well-fortified command bunker and quarters."

When Speedy departed for the Embassy, Colonel Tallon took charge of the MPs and support troops guarding the gates in the berm through which the two east roads exited. The enemy was still firing. The MPs returned the fire, as did medical and finance detachment personnel who were on the berm or up on the slopes of roofs overlooking the gates.

Tallon braced for a frontal attack. It never happened. Nonetheless, several troops became casualties during the exchange, including of all people General Barsanti's enlisted aide, Sergeant First Class James L. Wages, a popular, easygoing family man whose duties were mostly administrative. "I was in D-TOC with Barsanti when the general's driver rushed in wide-eyed and shouted to me, 'Sir, Jim's been hit!'" remembered Captain Lanahan, the aide-de-camp. "It didn't make any sense. It didn't register. How the hell could Jim be hit, I thought, he's in the office, for Christ's sake!" Lanahan ran to the adjacent headquarters building and found Wages sprawled near his desk in the anteroom outside the CG's office. The senior NCOs huddled around Wages explained that he'd caught a stray round that came through the wooden wall with a resounding crack. "They had already used his belt buckle to pry his teeth apart because he was gagging on saliva and his own tongue," said Lanahan, who took over for a sergeant trying to revive Wages. "He had slipped into shock by then, and was almost comatose. He was laying perfectly still on his back with his eyes glazed, but there was no blood, no nothing. . . ."

Confused and agitated, Lanahan shouted, "Where the hell is he hit?" and someone pulled Wages's shirt up to expose the bloodless bullet hole in his stomach, the wound having sealed in on itself. There was no exit wound. Realizing that Wages had internal bleeding, Lanahan and the general's driver loaded him into a jeep and—with fire snapping overhead—sped down the perimeter road that followed the inside of the southern berm to the aid station. More fire cracked over the open-walled medical tent as division surgeon Phillips started cardiopulmonary resuscitation. "I could tell by the look in his eyes that it wasn't good," remembered Lanahan. "The medics were treating a couple lightly wounded troops, and they told me that a staff sergeant, a cook from the division support command, had taken a round right through the center of his forehead. He was in the next tent with a poncho over him."

Lanahan brought in the Huey that landed for Sergeant Wages. "Later that day, we found out that he never regained consciousness. The round had ripped up his intestines and he died from internal bleeding," said Lanahan, who insisted that the round be checked, fearing his friend had been killed by a wild M16 shot. "It turned out to be from an AK-47."

The battalion that General Barsanti had ordered to push the enemy back from the berm was presently landing inside the headquarters compound, and after a quick meeting with the battalion commander, the CG went aloft in his C&C with his aide and the division sergeant major. The famous 101st Screaming Eagle insignia was painted on the nose of the Huey. The battle below centered on Dong Lach, the hamlet off the east end of the air base, and as the infantry advanced on it under heavy fire from those Viet Cong hunkered among the foliage-shrouded hootches, other enemy soldiers withdrew at full speed across the grassy fields. The door gunners stopped several in their tracks, walking long bursts into them even as return fire snapped up at the pursuing Huey.

The adrenaline was pumping. "That's one for Bold Eagle!" Barsanti exulted on the radio to D-TOC, using his call sign. "Two . . . Three . . . Make it four for Bold Eagle!"

Barsanti subsequently decorated everyone aboard the command ship with Air Medals for Valor. "I hate to admit it, but the general got one, too, thanks to the division G1 who wrote up the citation," Lanahan observed.

Barsanti had a generous awards policy as demonstrated during Tet and in the months that followed as the bulk of the 101st ABD moved north to I Corps and saw heavy combat in the Hue AO and the A Shau Valley. "Barsanti would helicopter in after an action and present impact awards on the spot. I carried two briefcases full of medals for him when we went out to the units," noted Lanahan. The CG also dropped into the division aid station to be briefed on actions by the casualties themselves. In one instance, he questioned a wounded company commander while the captain was still in triage. It transpired that during a patrol off the Street Without Joy near Hue, a trooper was wounded by a booby trap when he opened the gate to a Buddhist shrine. The man who went to his aid was wounded by another booby trap. The company commander rushed to the rescue next but was injured by yet a third booby trap.

"Captain, you're a dumb sonofabitch going in there like that," Barsanti rebuked the company commander. "I ought to court-martial you. That's not your job."

Barsanti then thumped a Silver Star on the captain with the comment, "But you're also a brave sonofabitch."

Lanahan ended up with a Silver Star himself for another action outside Bien Hoa during Tet. "I didn't do anything special. Barsanti just gave it to me," the aide-de-camp later said. "The general must have sensed my discomfort because he shared his philosophy with me. 'You know, Lanahan,' he said, 'you may not have deserved the medal at that moment, but sometime while you were here, you did.' He looked at it that way with the troops because those kids put up with a lot of shit out there, they really did . . ."

General Barsanti could be genuinely warm and paternal. He displayed an informal jocularity when he visited units, occasionally arm-wrestling with some surprised trooper. That was one side of Barsanti. There was another. "He would erupt like a Vesuvius three or four times a day, and it was almost inhuman the way he treated people when he exploded," said Brigadier General Frank B. Clay, an assistant division commander (ADC) in the 101st ABD. Barsanti would literally froth at the mouth as he took apart people of all ranks—from Clay on down to hapless grunts—like a drill sergeant. Barsanti had been an ass-chewing, hard-charging, Patton-style leader in WWII and Korea. In Vietnam, the big heart that he'd also been known for seemed to be missing. "Rather than fearing and loving General Barsanti [like Patton], the troops feared and despised him," wrote Phillips, who would always remember the encounter one of his medics had with Bold Eagle. "He was an excellent soldier and General Barsanti took a liking to him, making him his driver," wrote Phillips. Promoted from private first class to sergeant, the medic-turned-driver subsequently displeased Barsanti in some way, and was reduced to E1 and sent to the infantry. Phillips was unaware of his former medic's plight until he saw him by accident several months later when visiting a medical company in a remote area. "He was filling sandbags for a bunker in an adjacent infantry area. I was appalled at his condition. His spirit had been broken, and not by combat fatigue. His depression was akin to one seen in a consistently badly abused teenager. Whereas before he had been full of piss and vinegar, now he was defeated, an emotionless and bewildered lad. He was nonfunctional and could only do manual labor."

The division staff lived in a state of nervous anticipation. Meals at the general's mess were eaten in silence for fear that an innocent comment would bring down the wrath of Barsanti. "Although the food was excellent, the mood was gloomy, dispiriting, and grotesque," wrote Lieutenant Colonel Phillips. "Meals usually ended up as a good case of literal and figurative heartburn."

In one incident, noted a senior officer, an enraged silence "swept the mess while Barsanti berated some poor spec five who had starched his fatigues too much or something."

The scene was so humiliating that Lieutenant Colonel Charles "Chargin' Charlie" Beckwith, the division G2—and future leader of the Iran hostage mission—rose from his seat with blood in his eye, apparently intending to thrash Barsanti.

General Clay threw a shoulderblock into Beckwith and barked, "Back off, buddy. We'll settle this later."

Colonel Tallon stumbled upon a key to understanding the CG's vicious rages the day Barsanti was out in the field and the chief of staff needed something from his desk. As he had permission to do, Tallon opened Barsanti's desk, and was startled to find one big drawer filled with bottles of amphogel, a Pepto Bismol-type medicine. Tallon called the division surgeon. "What the hell is this stuff for?"

"You don't want to know," Phillips sighed.

"I've *got* to know. Sometimes the general borders on the irrational when he really gets going."

"He has stomach cancer," Phillips said. "The amphogel neutralizes the acid, and let's him function."

Tallon was stunned. Part of Barsanti's stomach had already been removed, but he was so tight-lipped about it that only Phillips and Lanahan were aware of his condition when the division deployed to Vietnam. General Barsanti—in terrible pain and always irritable—didn't even have to be in Vietnam, given his condition. He had only five years left to live. "Knowing now that he had cancer, I'd swear the guy had a death wish in Vietnam," mused an attached cavalry commander, citing Bold Eagle's casual use of his own C&C Huey as a recon ship on the road to the A Shau. "He had it way down on the deck, and we could see these bastards firing down at us from the jungled slopes to either side . . ."

Lieutenant Colonel Phillips thought that Barsanti's cancer was contributory to but not the cause of the general's quirks and temper tantrums. "Senior staff and commanders at multiple levels knew that General Barsanti was mentally ill. It was only the classification that eluded us," he wrote. Phillips was of the opinion that the CG was manic-depressive, which would explain his "wide mood swings" as well as "his hyperactivity and recklessness, followed by his periods of profound dissatisfaction with any and everything. Conversation on the subject was lively but confined among the closest and most trusted of comrades."

At one point, Phillips approached Clay, the ADC, about Barsanti, and said, "You must not let any decision that this man makes be issued without your reviewing it." Meanwhile, the division surgeon was himself approached "by a group of high-ranking officers and asked to go through medical channels to have General Barsanti committed involuntarily for psychiatric evaluation." Phillips thought that such an attempt to unseat the CG would be "an exercise in frustration and futility, given General Barsanti's supporters at DOD. I counseled that the best course of action would be to trust in the wisdom of General Westmoreland, who had been making seemingly overfrequent visits to the division. I was sure he understood the situation and would remedy it when he could."

That is exactly what happened. Westmoreland found Barsanti "too hotheaded for a division command," and "asked the Army Chief of Staff to move him to some other post outside my command." Barsanti was replaced with honor and ceremony in July 1968, having served a normal one-year tour with the division at that point. The unit had been in Vietnam only seven months, however, and Westy's intentions were clear. "Barsanti commanded the division with great skill," said the ever-loyal Tallon. "That he may have dented a few personalities in the process I don't think makes a big damn because he won every fight we were in. He made sure that casualties were minimized and that things happened on time, aggressively and professionally. But some feared him, and we didn't need that."

Others thought the battles had been won in spite of not because of Barsanti. Bold Eagle was replaced by polished, professional Major General Melvin Zais, a longtime paratrooper who "loosened the whole thing up and got people working together as a team again," as one senior officer put it.

Before the change in command, Brigadier General Clay's role had been pivotal. "Clay was loved in the division," noted Tallon. Barsanti did not want any assistant division commanders, however, being of the mind that he needed only a chief of staff to implement his orders, and his treatment of Clay was rude and humiliating. The gentlemanly Clay soldiered on. "Clay was the CG's alter ego," said First Lieutenant Paul Robblee, aide-de-camp to the ADC. "I remember making some kind of comment like, 'You know, sir, you're the last of the great democratic generals, you're really holding this division together.' Clay got upset at that and said, 'I'm probably the worst autocrat you'll ever meet,'" Robblee remembered. "I never saw that side of him. It wasn't his style to chew people out. He tried to energize people, and he felt he needed to be accessible to the subordinate commanders because there was the need for that buffer between them and Barsanti. Clay knew all the brigade and battalion commanders, and even many of the company commanders and platoon leaders, because any time there was a firefight he'd be over it in his helicopter or down on the ground trying to help."

The counterattack against the enemy who hit the air base was launched by elements of the division ready force, Lieutenant Colonel Grange's 2-506th Infantry, which saddled up in the dark of night at Phuoc Vinh base camp in War Zone D. "I will never forget being awakened in my tent, and told, 'Grab your gear—there's a fight going on down in Bien Hoa,'" said First Lieutenant J. Keith Kellogg, the reconnaissance platoon leader. "My first reaction was, wait a second, I thought the annual Tet truce was in effect, and then I scratched my head because division headquarters was at Bien Hoa. I kept saying to myself, 'What are they doing taking on *division?*'"

Companies A and B also moved out. "As I watched the troops file by to the airfield to be lifted into Bien Hoa by helicopter, I had my transistor radio turned to Armed Forces Radio," wrote First Lieutenant Richard L. St. John, XO, B/2-506th Infantry. "It was full of reports of attacks. Hue hit! Saigon hit! Bien Hoa hit! It seemed like the whole country was on fire . . ." Adding to the drama, the battalion's Catholic chaplain blessed the troops as they passed in the dark. Grange thought the old-for-his-rank captain was a wonderful chaplain with a great feel for the men, having served himself as an enlisted paratrooper with the battalion at Bastogne. "Everyone was nervous as we saddled up, however," noted St. John, "and the chaplain's blessing wasn't helping. The colonel finally told him to stand behind a nearby tree and bless everyone from out of sight."

Lieutenant Colonel Grange helicoptered into division headquarters at first light ahead of his companies and was briefed by the CG. "Barsanti was a real combat soldier. I've never been chewed out by anybody as ferociously, but I knew he respected me and I always felt very warmly towards him," said Grange. The briefing was almost surreal. From the patio outside the general's mess, Barsanti could point directly at the objective, Dong Lach, where retreating enemy soldiers were visible as black dots in the grass. Cobras were rolling in on them. Meanwhile, the battalion minus was being shuttled onto the chopper pad adjacent to the mess. Barsanti and Grange joined Tallon's ad hoc force at the east gate, and the assault commenced. "Barsanti stood by the gate and saw us off with words of encouragement," noted Grange, whose command group accompanied the lead platoon through the perimeter berm and down the road that cut through the minefield and wire barriers. "We picked up two 12.7mm machine-gun teams right away. They had been waiting to fire on planes taking off from the air base," said Grange. "They were all camouflaged, painted up green, and were hiding behind the mounds of a graveyard near the edge of the wire. Because of the minefield, no one had been in there grooming it, so the grass was thigh-high and they were hard to see. They were afraid to take us on, so we got the drop on them and eliminated them on the spot."

Pushing on south across the open ground, Grange and the lead company, First Lieutenant Ronald H. Darnell's A/2-506th Infantry, came under heavy fire from the north side of Dong Lach. "We spread out and started working our way in by fire team and squad rushes," said Grange, who won the Silver Star for Tet. "When we were in a fight, Grange was there with us," observed Kellogg, the recon platoon leader. "That's why we loved the guy. We knew he wouldn't be orbiting in a helicopter at three thousand feet like most battalion commanders, saying, 'Do this, do that . . .'"

Grange was a standout in a division full of superstars, and would retire a lieutenant general. The son of a New York City longshoreman, he had fought across Europe as a private in the 517th Parachute Regiment. After OCS, he led a rifle platoon and company during two tours in the Korean War. He pulled three tours in Vietnam, first as an advisor, then as a battalion and brigade commander in the 101st Airborne. "Dave Grange was an outstanding soldier in every respect," Clay said of this cool, charismatic, hard-as-nails infantryman. "He used to strap a radio on his back and go walk with his company commanders to get a feel for how they were doing and what their problems were."

While the lead company made its frontal assault from the north, Lieutenant Colonel Grange ordered his recon platoon into a blocking position west of Dong Lach. "We started moving, but hadn't even gotten out of the perimeter wire when rounds came over so close that me and my platoon sergeant dropped flat on our faces. He looked at me and said, 'This is going to be an interesting day,'" remembered Lieutenant Kellogg. Cutting across the east end of the air base, the recon troops passed a dozen dead VC/NVA strewn along the gully they were using for cover. The platoon came under heavy fire when it emerged from the gully, presumably from both the enemy and the Air Force SPs presently sweeping through the elephant grass, then established its blocking position on a small, grass-carpeted rise just inside the perimeter fence. "A few VC at a time would break contact, and try to get out of the village where the main firefight was raging," said Kellogg, who had a panoramic view. "It wasn't a turkey shoot, but we were able to take them by surprise, and my troops definitely had enemy soldiers go down in their sights. We would take fire occasionally when they realized where we were."

General Barsanti's command ship was strafing other guerrillas pulling out to the south and east. Meanwhile, Captain Freddy D. Rankin and B/2-506th Infantry had assumed blocking positions south of Dong Lach. The line included two platoons from Captain Ralph B. Garretson's A/3-5th Cavalry, 9th Division, which had been securing an artillery battery at FSB Apple on Highway 1 thirty kilometers east of Bien Hoa. Dispatched to the air base shortly before dawn, Garretson—a smart, sharp West Pointer—left one platoon at Apple and proceeded down the highway at top speed with the other two. It was a wild ride. The column was fired upon from almost all the hamlets along the way, but roared through unscathed, machine guns leveled and blazing at the roadside hootches. The lead tank crossed a little concrete bridge just before unseen enemy detonated the charges fixed under it, dropping the span into the stream below. The other tanks in the column were stranded on the wrong side of the demolished bridge, too heavy to ford the muddy stream bed, but the lighter tracks made it across and jumped back on the highway to continue the race to Bien Hoa.

Lieutenant Colonel Hugh J. Bartley, the squadron commander, shadowed the column in his H23. Another first-rate West Pointer, he too had a wild ride. Having taken off from his headquarters at Camp Blackhorse, Bartley was passing over Long Binh—down below, A/3-5th Cav was streaking right past the battle in the village hugging the north side of the sprawling base—when sappers blew up part of the ammunition storage area. Bartley's little scout ship was hurled some two hundred feet up by the titanic explosion, then dropped some five hundred feet in the ensuing vacuum before the pilot could regain control. After determining that he was still alive, Bartley stared in awe at the giant mushroom cloud sprouting from the base, and blurted on the radio to his squadron headquarters, "My God, you ought to see this!"

Captain Garretson's column took the highway into the east side of Bien Hoa City, the lead tank not even slowing down as it forced a crowd in the market square to make way. The lead platoon was in the midst of the crowd before the GIs realized it was not civilians they had bulled aside but openmouthed VC and NVA. Recovering quickly, the enemy disabled two tracks with RPGs. The wrecks were pushed out of the way by the second platoon in line, which came through the square in a blaze of fire and picked up the crews that had lost their mounts. The column swung north on a side road leading to Dong Lach, and Bartley, swooping in ahead to recon the route, spotted enemy soldiers lying in ambush in the ditches along both sides of the road. They opened up on the helicopter. Bartley tried to suppress the fire with his CAR15 as his pilot pulled away hard, but a lucky hit severed a fuel line and forced them to find a landing area in the nearest relatively safe place.

As the helicopter skimmed away, Bartley warned Garretson of the ambush, and Troop A turned off the road and drove parallel to it, tank and tracks raking the enemy positions from the rear as they passed. The troop then linked up with B/2-506th Infantry below Dong Lach. At that time Lieutenant Colonel Bartley was swapping H23s at a bridge on Highway 1 between Long Binh and FSB Apple, a replacement ship having flown up from Troop D at Bear Cat. After the pilot of the shot-up H23 departed, Bartley had yet to go airborne in the new bird when a five-ton supply truck loaded with tires appeared on the highway, heading east. The driver was from the 11th Armored Cavalry Regiment (ACR), whose support elements were located at Camp Blackhorse. The lone GI was on his way back from the supply depots in Long Binh or Saigon, but the return trip wasn't as quiet a ride as the driver had had in the other direction the day before, and he stopped and shouted to Bartley, "Hey, sir, what the hell's happening?"

"The goddamn war's started up again!" Bartley exclaimed. "Look, pull in to Fire Support Base Apple. Go down the road about a mile, and stay there until things settle down."

The kid grimaced. "Jesus, sir, Sergeant Smith—the motor sergeant for the 11th Cav—he wants these fuckin' tires."

Bartley tried to tell the driver that the motor sergeant would have to wait under the circumstances, but the kid said, "Sir, you don't know Sergeant Smith—I'm not getting off this goddamn road till I get these tires to Blackhorse!"

Bartley checked later to see if the driver made it. He had. Meanwhile, Captain Garretson and A/3-5th Cav were engaged in a ferocious firefight with the enemy in Dong Lach. Two of the eight remaining tracks were disabled and the lone tank hit by so many RPGs that the crew was twice replaced. Three troops were KIA and twenty-four WIA. (General Barsanti was so impressed with Garretson's tenacious stand alongside his paratroopers that he awarded him a Silver Star across division channels that very night. Tasked to detach a troop to support the 101st's push toward the A Shau two and a half months later, Bartley naturally sent Troop A. Barsanti's face lit up when Garretson was introduced at the operation briefing as the attached cavalry commander. "Garretson, get your ass up here!" he said. The embarrassed captain did so, trying to avoid the smoldering stares of the assembled brigade and battalion commanders as Barsanti grabbed him by the cheek Italian-style and boomed, "Garretson, it's good to see you. You and me—we'll show these fuckin' shoe clerks how to fight a war!")

Two of Captain Rankin's paratroopers were killed on the south side of Dong Lach. The roar of fire was constant on the north side, too. "We were shooting, they were shooting, all those tracks were shooting, and we were really hugging the ground as we closed on that damn town. The only cover we had were little paddy dikes a foot or two high," noted Lieutenant Colonel Grange, whose assault company, A/2-506th Infantry, was under fire not only from the enemy but also from the blocking force on the other side of the hamlet. Most of the trouble was coming from the guerrillas hunkered down in and around several hootches at the northern fringe of Dong Lach, but a two-tour career sergeant in the lead platoon leapfrogged close enough to eliminate thirteen of them with grenades and his M16.

The sergeant was himself killed, but the platoon leader, Second Lieutenant Sam H. Galloway, led a charge into the hootch area then, winning the DSC. The award was posthumous because "as I understand it, Galloway started into this one hut, and there was a Viet Cong hiding in the little pit under the sleeping platform," said Grange. "The civilians all had bunkers under their beds that they could roll into. The VC in this one shot Galloway as soon as he came in the door."

Lieutenant Colonel Grange pulled his forward elements back, four paratroopers having been killed and a dozen wounded on the north side of Dong Lach. Grange was joined at this time by his brigade commander, Colonel Lawrence L. Mowery, another three-war pro, who disembarked from his C&C Huey and crawled up to the grave mound shielding the battalion command group at the forward edge of the battle line. Grange wanted an air strike. "No, we need to use artillery," Mowery countered. "You're pretty close to have air come in here between two companies with the enemy in the middle." Grange was out of range of his normal direct support battery, however, and was reluctant to use the II FFV artillery unit that had been made available. Air operations had resumed at Bien Hoa, and Grange trusted the F100s to put their high-drag bombs right in the slot between his two elements. "The discussion went on and on. The artillery outfit that could range us from Long Binh didn't have forward observers with us and was very reluctant to fire," said Grange. "They weren't sure about our instructions, but they finally fired—and the first damn round landed about twenty feet in front of me and the brigade commander. It was a dud, thank God."

Grange turned to Mowery and asked wryly if the colonel now agreed that they should use air. Mowery gave the green light, and Grange threw smoke grenades to mark his position as four F100s flashed in low and fast in the light of the setting sun. "They used bombs and napalm, and they were right on the money. It was only a little town, and it was obliterated when the napalm set fire to the thatch roofs," said the battalion commander. Most of the villagers had already vacated the area. The paratroopers swept the rubble, and came up with sixteen prisoners and a body count of one hundred and six before pulling into a night perimeter near the smoldering, smoke-shrouded hamlet. The battle dribbled on under illumination rounds. One bypassed VC in a little wall-enclosed burial plot opened fire with an AK-47 on a resupply party moving down the road through the perimeter minefield. He was silenced with a grenade. To the west, Kellogg held his hillock with one squad while the other two set up ambushes along a narrow stream that snaked off the east end of the air base. Ensconced in the elephant grass, the paratroopers caught small groups of guerrillas as they tried to slip away by following the stream. There were flare-ups of automatic fire every twenty or thirty minutes, followed by whispered reports over the radio that, "We got another one," or "We got two more. . . ."

12

Urban Renewal

In the morning, Lieutenant Kellogg's platoon, having killed about twenty stragglers during the night, was under fire from one last little group holed up in a little clump of hootches about three hundred meters southeast of the air base. "It wasn't a constant drumbeat, but if you put your head up, you were going to get shot. We had to operate from the prone," remembered Kellogg, whose troops fired M60s from their hillock and lobbed M79 rounds into the distant hootches. By the time two Cobras were made available to Kellogg, the enemy fire had started to peter out. He nonetheless instructed the pilots to make their gun runs. "I'm getting tired of this crap," Kellogg said. "Let's take out the front row of that ville. Let's just finish this off."

The gunships orbited behind the hillock and made their runs right over the heads of the recon troops. The Cobra conducting the third or fourth pass punched off a rocket directly at Kellogg's platoon, and Kellogg—who had turned to watch the gunship come in, and who would never know if the rocket had malfunctioned or if the pilot had gotten disoriented—screamed at his men to hit the deck even as he spun around and literally dove for cover. He scooped up his radio along the way, and just seconds after the errant rocket impacted about fifteen meters to his right in a shower of dirt clods, he was screaming at the pilot about the screw-up.

"God, can I do anything?" the pilot asked, sounding sick.

"No, it's too late, the damage is done," snapped Kellogg, breaking off the mission then and there.

One recon trooper was in shock, mumbling to the medic that he couldn't see. Sergeant Philip M. Germain had been killed by the friendly fire, as had Private First Class Norton Z. King, a black kid who had only joined them the week before. Germain was the last of Kellogg's original three squad leaders, one having been killed and another losing an eye in the platoon's first contact in War Zone D. "The fight was suddenly over after the gun runs, and we got the word to move back to division headquarters," said Kellogg, who looked at his troops as they tramped up the road between the two bases and realized that they had all changed. "We had seen friends die, twice now in two weeks. We were different people," he remembered. "Our Catholic chaplain held an impromptu service when we got back. I happen to be Catholic. My platoon was clearly not all Catholics, and I didn't require the guys to go to the service, but the entire platoon took communion that day. We'd come back as a platoon, and we went to the service as a platoon. We had just become very bonded."

The air base having been secured, the clearing of Bien Hoa City fell to Lieutenant Colonel Neal Creighton's 3d Squadron, 11th Armored Cavalry Regiment. The counterattack began after an extraordinary example of U.S. mobility, for when Tet erupted, Creighton was opcon to the 1st Division and headquartered at Loc Ninh on Highway 13 in the rubber plantation country 110 kilometers due north of Saigon. Operations in the area were abruptly broken off at midmorning when Creighton received an ambiguous and dramatic order from regiment to "move toward Saigon as fast as possible." With one troop detached and a second left to secure the logistical elements at Loc Ninh, 3-11 ACR was rolling down Highway 13 as of 1300. The column passed through light sniper fire below An Loc, and soon thereafter the rest of the regiment fell in behind it, having hastily pulled out of War Zone C on the Cambodian border. Creighton and his operations officer, Major John H. Getgood, rendezvoused at Lai Khe at that point so they could refuel their H23s and "talk the situation over and see if [we] couldn't find out something from the 1st Infantry [Division] about what was going on," Creighton wrote in an informal after-action report. Getgood noted, however, that "we no sooner met on the chopper pad than mortars started walking down the runway, and we dove into a slit trench under a culvert. The fire was sporadic, a dozen rounds or so, but my pilot looked over our helicopter real carefully afterwards because the bubble had a hole and a few cracks in it."

Colonel Jack MacFarlane, the regimental commander, assembled his squadron commanders for a quick briefing along Highway 13 below Lai Khe: 1-11 and 2-11 ACR were to proceed to Long Binh, 3-11 ACR to the ARVN III Corps HQ in Bien Hoa. "The VC, I was told, had attacked the Corps Headquarters during the night, but had been repulsed at the walls. The place was still under siege and I was to get there and see that it didn't fall to the VC," wrote Creighton, a consummate West Point professional and future major general. The attacking force was later identified as the 238th VC Local Force Company. "[I]t was all very unreal," Creighton continued, noting that Bien Hoa was "where I came into the country; where I rode an unarmed bus from the Airfield across the town to the Replacement Center. I couldn't really visualize the VC fighting in a place like that. The only VC or NVA I had ever seen had been jungle rats and did their fighting in hit and run tactics."

Lieutenant Colonel Creighton helicoptered into the corps headquarters at dusk. Several tracks from A/3-5th Cav were parked in the main quadrangle. "Obviously tired troops were leaning against them or sleeping in the grass not far away. Even my chopper landing did not seem to awaken them," he noted. Creighton was ushered into the ARVN command post—the advisors and their counterparts were "a pretty tired and worried group"—and was joined just at dark by Getgood, who reported that all was going well. As planned, a guide from the corps advisory team had joined the lead troop, L/3-11 ACR, after it reached Saigon and turned northeast on Highway 1 to cross the Dong Nai into Bien Hoa. Creighton worried that since the guide "would be on the lead vehicle, what would we do if something happened to him while he was moving down the road in the dark? I could visualize his vehicle taking a hit from an RPG or a mine and the column not having the faintest idea of where to go from there. My [H23] wasn't much use at night. It had no instruments for night flying. So, if we lost our one guide, we could well blow the whole plan . . ."

Highway 1 ran past the front gate of the corps headquarters, and the column began arriving without incident at 2100. The armored cavalry assault vehicles (ACAVs) of L/3-11 ACR were in the lead, and as they "drove in one after the other, the whole damn place seemed to erupt in cheers," wrote Creighton. "Both the Vietnamese and Americans jumped around and hit each other on the back. When the M48 tanks of 'M' Company arrived, the people in the place shouted all the louder, waving and shouting to the somewhat bewildered crews."

The rear of the corps headquarters abutted the air base. Enemy soldiers in buildings on the other three sides kept the compound under AK-47 and RPG fire during the night. There were no casualties, but it did get a little personal at times. "I was checking positions at about one in the morning when somebody sniped at me," remembered Major Getgood. "The round hit the wall right above my head. I was standing there, and all of a sudden I had cement chips hitting my helmet. The bullet fell at my feet."

Creighton and Getgood were sleeping on the ground beside their command vehicles about an hour later when a mortar round crashed in nearby. "It gave us a start, but we were so tired, we went right back to sleep," said Creighton. Two Cobras came in at dawn. "The pilots spotted a sniper on a water tower in town," noted Specialist Four Anthony N. Stanfa of M/3-11 ACR. "The sniper would have had a clear shot at us, but the choppers opened up on him with rockets or machine guns or both. I watched him fall. . . ."

Lieutenant Colonel Creighton radioed MacFarlane for instructions on the morning of February 1, 1968, but regiment was still getting established at Long Binh. "They didn't know anything about III Corps Headquarters nor the situation there. Basically, I was told by Regiment to figure out what should be done and do it," he wrote. Informed by the advisors that the 101st ABD had begun clearing operations in the vicinity of Bien Hoa, the squadron commander hopped over to the division headquarters and was briefed by Generals Barsanti and Clay. Creighton was teamed with Grange, who joined the huddle in the D-TOC. "It didn't take Dave Grange and I long to come to a meeting of the minds," noted Creighton, who sent two Troop L platoons and one tank platoon from Company M down the highway to the east to pick up B/2-506th Infantry. The grunts rode in aboard the tracks, then dismounted and began fanning out through Bien Hoa City. "Contact was light until the Armor-Infantry team approached the area immediately to the front of III Corps Headquarters and here they ran into very heavy fire," Creighton wrote. "The VC apparently had decided to make a stand. It was a poor decision, but it might have been their only choice as the only path of retreat for them was blocked by two ARVN battalions placed along roads to the south and west of III Corps."

Captain Donald W. Derrah, the Troop L commander, had his ACAVs put .50-caliber fire down alleys and into certain buildings at the direction of Company B. "We did what we could, but the streets were so narrow we could barely get our vehicles turned toward the enemy," said Derrah, who felt especially vulnerable when he received reports of return fire coming from second- and third-floor balconies. Derrah requested permission to use his attached tank platoon. Creighton agreed, given that "we had been announcing in Vietnamese all morning by [helicopter] loudspeaker that all civilians should clear the area, and indeed large numbers of them had done so. Those who had come out indicated that the VC did not try to stop them and that there were very few, if any, innocent civilians left in the area."

Creighton was overheard in his H23 as five tanks lined up on the highway in front of III Corps HQ, their 90mm guns trained on the houses across the road. "They fired canister rounds, which are packed with little steel balls like grapeshot," Creighton said later. "They'd fire one at the first floor of a building, and the entire building would go *crump*, right straight down! We were absolutely amazed. We'd never fired canister at a building before."

The tanks fired for five thunderous minutes, completely

leveling the first block of back-to-back, densely packed homes and shops opposite the corps headquarters. "[S]ome buildings caught on fire because the VC had so much ammunition stored in them. Many VC fled from the houses only to be gunned down in the streets," wrote Creighton, noting that when the tanks ceased fire "there was no return fire, only silence and burning buildings."

Though the main guns were devastating, Creighton was concerned enough about the political ramifications of the destruction that he didn't use them again during the rest of the battle. With his H23 taking fire every time it passed over a particular part of town, Creighton finally received a call from Captain Donald R. Robison, CO, M/3-11 ACR, who had pinpointed a church as the source of the fire. "Robison was in his tank ready to blast the church down. He had it in his sights, and he kept requesting permission to fire," remembered Creighton, who frustrated Robison by never giving the order. "The fight was almost over and the only people being threatened from the church were me and my pilot, so I backed off. I had the impression the Vietnamese might be forgiving of a few blown-down houses, but it's a little different when you blow down a church. It wasn't good policy for the U.S. Army. I could see the headlines, 'American troops blow up church.'"

The original tank fire had been a reflex action, Creighton and Derrah responding as they would have to an enemy encountered in the field. That buildings had been leveled instead of thatch hootches only prompted jokes that 3-11 ACR had gone into the business of urban renewal.

There were repercussions. Lieutenant Colonel Creighton was sitting on a tank at dusk when approached by Wilbur "Coal Bin Willie" Wilson, a tough old retired paratrooper colonel serving with Civilian Operations and Revolutionary Development Support (CORDS). "Wilson was irate about the use of tanks earlier in the day. He went on about all that CORDS was trying to accomplish to raise the Vietnamese economy and that we were destroying any progress they had made," Creighton recalled. Wilson was quite agitated, and Creighton, bristling a bit himself after the long day, replied that he had put his tanks in action "to save American lives, which, in this case, I considered the more important priority. Wilson left in pretty much of a huff."

It was a clash of missions typical of Vietnam. Creighton was there to destroy the enemy at the least cost to his own troops. Wilson was trying to win the hearts and minds of the people who Saigon needed to beat the VC. Creighton was directed to report to General Weyand the next day, Weyand having been alerted to the destruction by an angry John Vann, the pacification chief for II FFV. "Both the Vietnamese III Corps commander and the senior advisor were strong supporters of what we had done, and the senior advisor told me not to worry and that he would immediately go and talk to Weyand," wrote Creighton, who found both his champions in the general's office when he arrived. "Weyand heard them out, then told me I was doing a good job and that I should get back to the fight as soon as I could," Creighton noted. "Later, however, an order did come down from II Field Force that no more tank guns were to be used inside the city. At the time, our tanks were supporting Grange's battalion sweeping east. I had to withdraw the tanks. This was toward the end of the fighting in the built-up area, but it had to be somewhat demoralizing for the men in Dave's battalion. I was thankful that he didn't blame me or think that I had anything to do with withdrawing the tanks."

The battle did not end with the canister volley. When the tanks ceased fire, Captain Derrah pulled back inside the corps headquarters to make room for the gunships dispatched to further soften up the area before the ground attack resumed. The lead Cobra came in from the south, then banked to the east as it dove in to make a firing run through the shattered buildings. "Unfortunately, the pilot opened up too soon, and we got a spray of minigun fire before he completed his turn and came on line with the highway," noted Derrah, who watched in horror as the wild burst hit among his line of ACAVs inside the front wall of the headquarters compound. One of his track commanders took a round in his forehead and was killed instantly as he stood behind his shielded .50-cal MG. "That was the only loss I had during the retaking of Bien Hoa, and it was very difficult to live with the way that young soldier died. It was my responsibility to notify the next of kin, but I couldn't bring myself to provide them the real story. I didn't think the specifics would be very comforting, so I merely wrote that he died during a heavy contact in the Tet Offensive."

After the gunship prep, Captain Rankin and B/2-506th Infantry began a methodical alley-to-alley, house-to-house sweep through Bien Hoa. "I dismounted the majority of my force as well to help clear the area," said Derrah, a smart, tough, super-aggressive combat commander who left only a driver and .50-cal gunner on each of his supporting ACAVs. The paratroopers and cavalrymen worked in small teams. "There were probably five of us in the group I joined with my first sergeant," noted Derrah, who was suited up in helmet and flak jacket and slung with ammo belts for the M60 machine gun he carried. "It was the type of thing you see in the movies. We'd fire an M79 into a building, then the lead man would kick the door in and go in shooting."

Most of the houses were empty, most of the surviving guerrillas in the labyrinthine maze interested only in escape. "Once you found a pocket of them, your first kill would scatter the rest," Derrah said. "They would move out on us as quick as they could, but in a couple instances when they were trying to run away between the houses I did see some of them fall as I opened up with the M60 . . ."

Captain Derrah received a Silver Star from the 101st ABD, cited for personally eliminating seven VC/NVA. "There were some bitter little battles. We didn't always surprise them, and they didn't always get up and run . . ."

Thirty-six enemy were killed. There was a certain pathos in some of their deaths. Derrah's group was taking a respite in the courtyard of a rubbled house when a platoon sergeant stepped onto a little dirt mound and suddenly tore off an M16 burst right at his feet. "We stared in shock, wondering what the hell he was doing, but when he kicked the dirt away, there was an enemy soldier laying there," Derrah recounted. The sergeant had felt something move under his feet and fired instinctively. The young guerrilla, who had been breathing through a reed as he hid in his clawed-out burrow, had a massive sucking chest wound. "He was coherent, but we couldn't speak the language, and he didn't say anything. There was a lot of blood, and the medic tried to get him to sit up so he wouldn't choke to death. The medic would prop him up, but as soon as he let go, the man would sink back as if he wanted to die. He was very passive. He might have nodded, he might have gestured to us, and then he just faded out as he lay there."

Several guerrillas surrendered. The prisoners being hustled back to the corps headquarters included at least one wounded enemy soldier on a stretcher and several who had discarded their weapons and stripped down to shorts and undershirts in an attempt to slip away as civilians. "We also detained a lot of patients from a local mental hospital that the VC had released to confuse the situation," said Lieutenant St. John, the XO of B/2-506th Infantry. The asylum was run by an order of French-speaking Vietnamese priests, and the hapless inmates wandering the embattled city streets were of both sexes and all ages. "Word was that a gunship had rolled in on some of the patients, mistaking them for the enemy. The ones we found were almost hysterical. We couldn't understand Vietnamese to begin with, and now we had *crazy* Vietnamese talking real fast at us. Our *chieu hoi* scouts said that they weren't making any sense. They were just completely out of it."

There were other bizarre aspects to the battle. Tet was payday, and though St. John had drawn the company payroll the night before, it was five days before events slowed down long enough for him to pay the troops. "It was a strange feeling to carry $32,000 in military payment certificates in my rucksack during the battle of Bien Hoa," he wrote. "I was more afraid of losing the cash than I was of being hit. All I could think was, how would I ever pay back $32,000 to the army on the $220 a month pay of a lieutenant?"

Because of this problem, the battalion executive officer had ordered all the company executive officers to remain behind when the 2-506th Infantry originally deployed from Phuoc Vinh to Bien Hoa. "We were furious, just absolutely beside ourselves," remembered St. John. Being young, hard-charging airborne lieutenants, the execs got together during the second day of the battle and defied orders by taking a resupply Huey into Bien Hoa. "We thought it was a big deal, but with everything else that was going on, nobody ever chewed us out about it," said St. John, a BSMv winner this day. After dealing with the prisoners and mental patients, the exec joined a group of paratroopers pinned down by heavy fire from a particular building. "We couldn't get tac air, arty or mortars, so noticing a tank down the road I ran to it and asked the TC if he would help. A few well-placed main gun rounds solved the problem."

The company had not received a water resupply, and the troops were parched given the blast-oven heat of the burning buildings. One paratrooper emerged with a case of Coke from a little abandoned grocery store to which the flames had just spread. "He was going to share the bottles with his buddies, but the first sergeant saw this and jumped all over him for 'looting,'" noted St. John. "He ordered the trooper to put the Cokes back, but by now the store was fully engulfed. I still have a vivid memory of the soldier running back into the store, framed in the doorway with flames all around, and heaving the Cokes into the fire."

Company B was pulling back to the corps headquarters before dusk when the platoon bringing up the rear came under fire among some hollowed-out, pock-walled houses just across from the front wall. The company had taken no casualties during the afternoon of street fighting, but one paratrooper was killed now at the far end of an alley. Three others were wounded, including a platoon sergeant with a bullet in his guts. "They were pinned down and couldn't crawl out of there. I was with the last squad at the top of the alley, and it was like shooting down a tunnel as we tried to suppress the enemy fire," said St. John. The paratroopers sprayed the windows overlooking the alley so furiously that St. John and two or three enlisted men were able to sprint down it and frantically drag the casualties back by their web gear. "We loaded them inside the last ACAV in the line that was moving back," said St. John. "There was no room left inside, so I climbed up on top with the .50 gunner who was firing away as we roared down the street. The thing was going as fast as it could, and I was laying on my back, firing up with my M16 on full automatic at the NVA shooting down on us from the rooftops along the street."

The last of the enemy slipped away during the night. The area was again secure. "When we rode on top of the tanks and ACAVs into Bien Hoa Air Base, it was like we were liberating Paris," noted St. John. "All the USAF personnel were out on the streets cheering us. One airman ran up alongside the track I was sitting on and handed me an ice cold can of Budweiser. It tasted great!"

Part 4

Long Binh

"This time they've accommodated us. They're attacking us for a change."
—Col. Frederic E. Davison
Acting Commander,
199th Light Infantry Brigade

Long Ball

13

The Surprise Attack That Wasn't

From Bien Hoa Air Base new troops were shuttled to the replacement center in Long Binh aboard the olive-drab buses with the screen-covered windows described in all the memoirs. On the afternoon before Tet, Private First Class Thomas A. Tadsen of the 552d MP Company, II FFV, was stationed at a two-man checkpoint along the bus route in downtown Bien Hoa City. Deciding to have some fun with the new guys, Tadsen and his partner gathered up spent casings from ammunition fired off into the night sky the previous evening by ARVN celebrating the lunar new year a little early. Piling the brass around their gun jeep as if they had been engaged in furious battle, the MPs grimly manned their pedestal-mounted M60 when the buses rolled past. Their jaws were set, their helmets buckled, their flak jackets zipped up to their chins. The replacements looked petrified as they passed through this make-believe ambush alley.

"They thought they were in for some deep shit," remembered Tadsen. "Later on we found out the joke was on us because we were all in for some deep shit. . . ."

A primary enemy objective during Tet, the command and logistical complex at Long Binh sprawled across thirty square kilometers of cleared rubber trees southeast of Bien Hoa. The joke was also on the VC because General Weyand,

CG, II Field Force, Vietnam, suspected that they were coming. To deny the enemy cover and concealment along the approach routes, engineer units equipped with Rome Plow bulldozers had spent the previous three weeks leveling the remaining rubber plantations between Bien Hoa and Long Binh.

It was a major undertaking. The felled trees were even hauled out lest the guerrillas find shelter among them. The premature attacks up north validated the precautions, and Weyand placed a mechanized battalion in ready positions immediately south of Long Binh before nightfall on January 30. Meanwhile, II FFV staff officers "formed a betting pool as to precisely when the Viet Cong would strike. The bettor had a choice of fifteen-minute intervals beginning with darkness on the 30th. All the money was being laid on intervals between midnight and 5:00 A.M."

Extra perimeter bunkers had already been built, and the security forces were bolstered that night with support troops armed with M14s. On the other side of the line was the 275th Regiment, 5th VC Division. Fifteen hundred strong, the 275th planned to attack from two directions; while one battalion launched across Route 316 into the II FFV compound on the northwest perimeter, two more were to hit the 199th LIB base camp, which extended partway down the northeast perimeter from the northern tip and faced a thin hamlet strung out along both sides of Highway 1.

In addition, the U-1 VC LF Battalion was to harass the eastern side of the base with fire to cover a sapper penetration of the Long Binh Ammunition Depot.

The northern tip of the base was formed by the juncture of Highway 1 and Route 316, which branched southwest from the east-west MSR. The five kilometer northeast perimeter fell away at an angle from Highway 1; the northwest perimeter hugged Route 316 for nine kilometers to where it crossed the Dong Nai River on the way to Saigon.

Bien Hoa and Long Binh were connected not only by Highway 1, but also by Route 15—it was a four-kilometer trip—which passed through Long Binh from northwest to southeast, splitting the giant base in half. Long Binh Post, as the southwest side was designated, enclosed the USARV

HQ and a labyrinth of support facilities, to include the infamous Long Binh Jail, better known as the LBJ Ranch.

The compound which included Weyand's headquarters was nicknamed the Plantation. Captain Shockley D. "Hap" Gardner, CO, 552d MP Company, which provided security for the II FFV HQ, called a company formation the night of Tet. "We'd never had a formation like this before," noted Tadsen. "The captain stated that between one and three that night, the II Field Force compound would come under attack by an enemy battalion composed of NVA reinforced by local VC. He added that the attack would begin with prep fires from 122mm rockets and 82mm mortars, followed by a ground attack from the northwest utilizing rocket-propelled grenades, light and heavy machine guns, and automatic weapons. We were all a little unnerved . . ."

The enemy performed on cue. Anticipating that the attack would begin at three, Weyand, unable to sleep, had gone to his Quonset hut TOC an hour earlier. Colonel Marvin D. Fuller, the G3, had set the alarm in his trailer for 0300, and when it went off, he telephoned the TOC duty officer for a status report. Before the major could answer, the first rocket slammed in. The explosion caved part of Fuller's trailer in as it blew the phone out of his hand. "What happened?" he asked upon retrieving it. "We've had a direct hit!" the major shouted, the fluorescent lights in the unprotected, above-ground TOC having crashed down, plunging the Quonset hut into darkness. Fuller told the duty officer to calm down, that a direct hit would have killed everyone inside, and as emergency gasoline lanterns were lit, the major confirmed that, "No, we're all right . . ."

The barrage lasted only ten minutes, thanks to the prewarned gunships that homed in on the launch sites. The ninety rockets that boomed into the Plantation caused only minimal damage. After a twenty-minute lull, machine-gun fire began cracking past the TOC. The thin-skinned Quonset hut reportedly took a number of hits. Thinking it was stray stuff from a U.S. unit, Weyand dispatched his G1 in an MP jeep to get the firing under control. The MPs returned in short order with a shot-up jeep, and the G1 colonel exclaimed, "The VC are right across the street."

The enemy were in a hamlet on the northwest side of Route 316 known as Widows Village because the wives and children of ARVN KIAs lived there on small government pensions. The perimeter bunkers returning fire across the paved, two-lane road were manned by personnel from several units headquartered in the Plantation, most notably the 79th Engineer Group, 12th Aviation Group, and the 219th Military Intelligence Detachment.

Early in the action, Sergeant First Class William Kerr's gun jeep from the 552d MP Company pulled onto Route 316 via the south gate and headed for Gate 6—the north gate of the Plantation—which had reported heavy fire. "When we reached the area in front of II Field Force Headquarters, there was a heavy firefight. There wasn't anything to do but keep going," noted Specialist Four Jerry D. Hill, the driver. Sergeant Peter D. Hoffman manned the M60. "Hoffman was pinning the VC down on our left side, and Sergeant Kerr was leaning over the hood of the jeep with a Thompson. The guys on our perimeter were cutting their fire off about thirty meters ahead of us as we drove by. They picked up their rate of fire as we passed. We had our radiator shot up a bit, a headlight shot, and two spare tires shot . . ."

Private First Class Tadsen was at a distinct disadvantage when the attack began. He was, in fact, virtually naked and unarmed. The explanation was simple. Following Captain Gardner's briefing, the MPs had received several replacements who arrived sans weapons and gear. The supply room, however, was bare. "My platoon sergeant ordered a number of us to lend them our rifles, helmets, and flak vests," Tadsen said. "We bitched up a storm, but it didn't do any good. This left me with my 'trusty' .45 and three ammo magazines—and the clothes on my back."

The platoon sergeant was being logical. The disarmed MPs had no assignments that night, but the replacements were pulling guard duty at the II FFV TOC. That was small comfort when the 122s started shrieking in. Jolted awake, Tadsen grabbed his pistol belt and fatigue shirt—he had been sleeping in his boots and trousers—and flew out the front door of his barracks. Running to the MP station, he offered his help, but the desk sergeant told him to take cover until the shelling stopped. Fire was snapping in from across the highway by then. Tadsen waited for a lull, then sprinted toward a perimeter bunker. "The firing started again. I seemed to be the target, silhouetted a bit by lights behind me in the company area which hadn't been turned off yet," he said. Blindly crossing paths with a drainage ditch in the dark, he somersaulted forward, hitting his head, spraining an ankle, and wrenching his back. "I was apparently knocked out but came to quickly and heard the guys in the bunker yelling to me. They thought I had been hit. I yelled back that I was okay, and as soon as the firing stopped, I jumped up and ran as well as I could the rest of the way to the bunker. I was still seeing stars, but some of the guys came out and gave me a hand getting inside the bunker."

Most of the rockets landed around the II FFV TOC in the center of the Plantation. The 552d MP Company area was at the southwest end but was hit by mortar fire from Widows Village. The shelling stunned the combat-green MPs in Tadsen's bunker. "Even after the mortars let up, I realized that all the guys were still under cover. They weren't guarding their sector," he recalled. In a letter home he described how his buddies were "lower than the lowest gun port. I got pissed off, told them that they were a bunch of cowardly assholes, and vacated that sorry place . . ."

Tadsen had no sooner emerged from the bunker than two shots rang out nearby: a new MP in a sandbagged emplacement behind the main firing line had mistaken another MP crawling through the grass toward a perimeter bunker for a sapper and had nailed him with his M14.

Luckily, though the other MP was hit behind his ear, the round shattered without penetrating the skull. Meanwhile, Tadsen hustled to the company orderly room, hell-bent on securing a rifle. The motor pool lieutenant turned over his own M14 and ammo to this trooper in need, but as soon as Tadsen went back out the door he stepped right into the grazing fire coming across the highway and had to eat dirt as tracers passed by on either side at knee level.

Tadsen found a steel pot in an empty barracks and returned to the MP station just as Sergeant James McDaniels—a tough, husky, cool-headed black MP—

wheeled up in a gun jeep to pick up ammo for the embattled troops at Gate 6.

Tadsen asked the sergeant if he needed any help. "Damn, right," McDaniels replied. "Get on the '60!"

McDaniels jumped back behind the wheel. The MP station and Gate 6 were at opposite ends of the three-kilometer-long compound. "We hauled holy ass," Tadsen wrote. The closer to the gate, the heavier the enemy fire. Unloading the ammo at the Gate 6 guard bunker, Tadsen begged a flak jacket off one of the senior NCOs hunkered inside, then went out through the gate with two other MPs to grab a firing position in the drainage ditch running along Route 316. Tadsen got into a one-on-one firefight with a guerrilla who was in a ditch of his own at the edge of Widows Village. Tadsen finally shouted to a nearby MP lieutenant with an M79 and "asked him if he could drop one on my friend over there. He didn't believe anyone was shooting at me, however, because he couldn't see any tracers. The VC wasn't using any. I told the lieutenant to come over and see for himself. As he crawled over to us, the VC made him a believer. The lieutenant put two rounds right on top of the gook—and the firing stopped."

The frontal attack on the Plantation completely bogged down. Meanwhile, Staff Sergeant David A. Jared, an intelligence analyst with the 12th Aviation Group, was on the compound's back perimeter, which faced an uncleared mass of vegetation between the Plantation and the ammo dump. The barrage caught Jared as he was out checking his little sandbagged, horseshoe-shape firing points, and as he dove back for the one he had just exited, a rocket exploded behind him. Slammed to the ground, he crawled on into the firing point, unaware in the shock of the moment that his back had been splattered with dozens of small fragments.

Jared counted twenty-seven rockets in his area, one so close that it bounced him off the ground. "It had missed us by three feet," he said. "We were lucky because the rocket motor had a tendency to drive the warhead into the ground before it exploded, thus minimizing the effect of the blast. There were holes in the ground with an aluminum tube sticking up out of each like a stovepipe."

Crawling into his machine-gun bunker, Sergeant Jared found that the line to his field phone had been cut by a rocket. Next, long rounds began zipping overhead from the enemy firing on the main bunker line from Widows Village. There was more firing in the dark as VC sappers slipped through the ammo dump to attack the 12th Aviation chopper pad. "My guys were clerk-typists, and one of them decided that we were being fired on, too," Jared said. "I don't know where it started, but everybody up and down the line opened up into that jungled area on the other side of our concertina wire. We were really turning it to salad in there, but I finally realized that there was nothing coming from the other direction, and I hollered to cease fire."

The scene in General Weyand's operations center was dramatic during the first hours of Tet. The corps commander wore a helmet and flak jacket in the lantern-lit Quonset hut. The teletypes were clacking, the phones ringing. As the staff plotted the seemingly endless reports of enemy attacks on a map, Weyand was reminded of a pinball machine lighting up. Moving units to counterattack, the general later compared himself to a fire chief who was afraid he was going to run out of engine companies. Thanks to his own foresight in prepositioning units, he did not. "When Weyand analyzed the battle later, he saw that the assault on [the] Saigon [Circle] was actually a large number of relatively small independent actions, with each unit assigned to its own job and its own area of operations," wrote one reporter. "Despite the large number of Communist troops committed, insufficient force was applied in any one area to take and hold the objective. Some of the attacks were intended to divert U.S. troops from more important actions, and other attacks seemed peripheral to the main battles. The assault had been launched piecemeal, and it was repulsed piecemeal in a series of relatively small battles."

By dawn, Weyand had no more readily available units with which to block the enemy and was relieved when his G2 reported that every major VC/NVA unit known to be in III Corps had been identified in the battles. Weyand's great fear—that units had infiltrated from North Vietnam without being detected—did not materialize, and the late-night arrival of the 11th Armored Cavalry Regiment extinguished all communist hopes in the Saigon Circle.

Lieutenant Colonel Edward C. Peter of the II FFV staff wrote that "Weyand later said he would not have prepared differently—except to have the 11th ACR more centrally located, rather than north of the Iron Triangle."

While Weyand was saving Saigon, his TOC was only removed by some hundreds of meters from the ongoing Widows Village engagement. "The battle was right outside, but, hell, it could have been twenty-five miles away as far as we were concerned," said Peter. "We were working the telephones. We couldn't see the actual fighting."

Another firefight raged in the ammo dump. The compound was ringed with towers, but when the pre-attack barrage drove the guards into the bunkers underneath, sappers easily penetrated the perimeter wire with bangalore torpedoes. Three MPs, including a sentry dog handler, were killed. An element from the prepositioned reaction force, B/2-47th Mechanized Infantry, 9th Division, roared to the scene in APCs. While part of the company engaged the enemy, dismounted troopers ran from ammo bunker to ammo bunker, collecting satchel charges that the sappers had planted. It was a heroic effort, but it was still unfinished when a time charge exploded in a pallet of 175mm propellant charge. Three more pallets were instantly consumed, and a titanic blast rocked the base like an earthquake, a mushroom cloud rising from the epicenter.

The detonation occurred at about 0730. "We could see the shock wave coming through the foliage. Everybody ducked as it passed over, stirring up a tremendous amount of dust in its wake," remembered Sergeant Jared, who was in a sandbagged position on the rear Plantation perimeter. "When I went back to our S2 shop, the fluorescent lights were smashed on the floor, and the wall facing the explosion was bowed in from the concussion."

Lieutenant Colonel Peter was in the G3 office attached to the II FFV TOC when the shock wave blew him backward out of his chair. "The ammo dump kept exploding all day and into the night," he noted. "There were fires burning out of control in there, setting other stuff off. It was like watching a fireworks display that night . . ."

The battle in Widows Village also continued that first morning, though the enemy troops facing the Plantation seemed possessed of some strange inertia. They never rushed the bunker line, and by daylight were under not only frontal fire but heavy flanking fire from an old French blockhouse designated as Tower 4. "There were about nine of us up there, and we had a better view of the village than the guys on the ground. We could really pick our hits," said Private First Class Tadsen, 552d MP Company, who had grabbed a ride out to Tower 4 aboard an ammo jeep. The strong point faced the northeast end of Widows Village at the north corner of southwest-northeast Route 316, and the northwest-southeast railway line that separated the Plantation from the 199th LIB base camp.

Tadsen hauled the ammo up the ladder to the sand-bagged, tin-roofed top of the concrete blockhouse. "Tower 4 took a few hits, but not many for all the fire coming at it," he noted. The MPs primarily fired at figures moving between the houses in the ville. Two or three times, however, the VC/NVA tried to come through the bamboo and brush along the railroad tracks. Each charge broke up in the face of heavy fire. "We ran out of ammo three times. In each case, we didn't call for a resupply until we only had a hundred rounds left of linked M60 ammunition, which we were breaking down to use for single shots with our M14s."

At one point, three guerrillas took cover in a hootch only to have Tadsen pump M79 rounds at it until it caught fire. He kept his sights on the place until it burned down but never saw anyone slip out. The MPs were joined by several gung ho 199th LIB troopers, one of whom was wounded while firing from the railroad overpass over Route 316 to the immediate left front of Tower 4. "The guys on the bridge were yelling for help, so I jumped off the tower to run over there. It was about fifteen feet down, and I didn't realize how heavy my flak vest and gear was until I hit the ground," said Tadsen. Keeping low against the foot-high concrete edge of the overpass, Tadsen bandaged the gunshot wound in the back of the GI's calf, then helped him to a gun jeep. "I jumped on the M60 and fired cover until we got back inside the perimeter. We took the casualty to the 199th dispensary, but by the time the medics wheeled him into surgery, the jeep was gone, so I had to walk all the way back. Along the way, I ran into a guy who had brought some food out in a jeep. He had quarts of milk and apples that had been iced down. I wasn't real fond of milk, but I hadn't had any water for hours and I was starved. It tasted like the best meal of my life and got me going again . . ."

14

Widows Village

The counterattack on Widows Village began an hour after sun up. The first unit to go in was led by a new officer, First Lieutenant Henry L. S. Jezek, who after a week of in-country training at his division base camp, had only been in command of the 1st Platoon, B/2-47th Mechanized Infantry, for three weeks at the time of the Tet Offensive. Detached from its parent company, Jezek's platoon, designated as the ready reaction force for the field force headquarters, had conducted fruitless ambush patrols at night, while spending its days securing one of the engineer companies involved in the massive land-clearing operation outside Long Binh.

Lieutenant Jezek's platoon was abruptly pulled inside the base the night before Tet and placed in the post exchange parking lot behind II FFV HQ. Buttoned up in their tracks, the Bravo One troops took no casualties during the rocket barrage. Being new, Jezek, in fact, had no idea that a major enemy attack was under way. Nor was he unduly alarmed when summoned to the operations center at daybreak and given the mission of clearing Widows Village.

He was briefed by an MP colonel. "He said that there was sporadic fire coming from the village," Jezek recalled. "When we went out the gate, the colonel followed us in a jeep to show us exactly where the fire was coming from. We thought that there were maybe a few snipers in there."

Having exited through the southern gate of the Plantation, Lieutenant Jezek, sitting atop his track as Bravo One rolled up Route 316, stared in shock when the ammo dump suddenly exploded with a huge mushroom cloud. It was an omen of things to come, for there was a VC/NVA battalion, not a handful of snipers, hunkered down in Widows Village. The size of the force had been underestimated because the guerrillas had so badly bungled their night attack. "As we subsequently discovered from prisoner interrogations, the enemy battalion commander had been told to launch his attack after several hundred rockets hit the II FFV compound," explained Lieutenant Colonel Peter. "Only ninety rockets came in, however. The VC commander across the street, who had been dutifully counting off these rockets, did not attack when the barrage suddenly stopped. He thought there would be more rockets coming in. There weren't any more because the launching sites had been destroyed by gunships, and in the resulting confusion, that battalion never got off the dime."

Widows Village appeared deserted as Bravo One entered the southwest end. The government-built hamlet was twice as long as it was wide at six hundred by twelve hundred meters. Neatly cut into five pieces along its width by four short roads, it was further subdivided lengthwise by three longer roads that paralleled Route 316.

The little houses in the village were just as neatly laid out, eight rows of twenty houses each. Lieutenant Jezek advanced lengthwise through the village on a two-hundred-meter front with dismounted troopers on line between his four tracks, which were manned only by a driver and .50 gunner apiece. The APCs were abreast, each proceeding down a different lane between the shacks, with the right-flank track on a boundary road that tracked with Route 316.

The line rumbled along slowly. "We were going to flush that sniper and get him," Jezek ruefully remembered.

Bravo One was about a third of the way through the ville when the right-flank track ran up on a line of enemy soldiers in a drainage ditch along Route 316. The man in the commander's hatch, Private Robert A. Huie, cut loose with the .50 even as an RPG slammed into the APC. Jezek ran over and knelt beside the disabled track as he shouldered his M16. "I couldn't see the enemy, but I could see their RPGs flying through the air. They traveled slow enough that you could watch them go past. I looked up at Huie. He was firing. I was firing, too, but when I looked back at Huie, one of those RPGs caught him right in the chest—and it took his head off, along with his left shoulder. I saw it happen. I couldn't believe it. It looked like hamburger meat had been splattered all over the track . . ."

A moment later, Lieutenant Jezek felt a solid punch to his right side, and thinking one of his men had slugged him to get his attention over the cacophony, he turned around. No one was there, and glancing down, he realized that he had been shot. The round had blasted through an ammo pouch, so in addition to the bullet lodged against his hipbone, he had also taken a chunk of metal from a mangled ammo magazine. Feeling no pain, but having a hard time moving his leg, Jezek hit the deck. Something exploded in his face. Stunned, his ears ringing, he learned later that BB-size pellets from a Chinese claymore mine had peppered his cheeks. He was spared further injury because his helmet was low on his forehead, and his flak jacket was zipped all the way up to his chin, protecting his throat.

Leaving the disabled track where it sat, the platoon sergeant got the remaining three APC crews reorganized to return fire from more protected positions. Lieutenant Jezek, lying on a stretcher with all his gear on, was evacuated in an ambulance that arrived from Long Binh.

Jezek was such a bloody-faced mess that the platoon sergeant thought him dead. He would actually return to the field within six weeks. Meanwhile, First Lieutenant Brice H. Barnes's Scout Platoon, HHC/2-47th Mechanized Infantry, 9th Division, was in a blocking position south of Long Binh on Route 15, when an ambulance pulled up and the driver, probably the same medic who had just evacuated Jezek, begged for help in recovering other wounded men who were pinned down in Widows Village.

Barnes tried to explain that he had his own orders and could not just pick up and leave his position. Fortuitously, the battalion commander Lieutenant Colonel John B. Tower—call sign Panther 6—radioed Barnes at that time and instructed him to move up Route 15 to the 90th Replacement Battalion. The Scout Platoon was to secure the 2-47th Mech command vehicles there while Tower went airborne to control the battalion's multiple actions: A/2-47th Mech was moving out to counterattack the enemy who had hit the 199th LIB HQ, while B/2-47th Mech continued clearing sappers from the burning ammo dump, and C/2-47th Mech defended the ARVN III Corps Headquarters in Bien Hoa.

Barnes found the command tracks idling on the highway in Long Binh. "The medic had followed us and continued to plead for assistance," wrote Barnes, who had no idea that the wounded in question were from his own battalion. "I decided to ask the Old Man for permission to perform this mission as the casualties were close by. With an affirmative answer from Panther 6, we raced for Widows Village . . ."

The hamlet was a scene of mass confusion. Several superficially wounded GIs were crouched behind the disabled Bravo One APC, screaming at the reinforcements to take cover. "None of their weapons were operative," said Barnes. "They were in such a panic that they'd forgotten their training on how to clear jammed weapons. I took charge of those people, and they responded. It was just a matter of them seeing some leadership."

Lieutenant Barnes put his eight tracks on line to support his two-platoon, fire-and-maneuver assault. "The morale in the Scout Platoon was tremendous, and that was because of Barnes. He was close to us as individuals, and in combat he was always the first one to go," said Specialist Four William S. McCaskill of this rangy, bespectacled Texan, a superhawkish career officer with a big handlebar mustache. After the assault line cleaned out the ditch from which the closest enemy had been firing, Barnes—subsequently awarded the Distinguished Service Cross—was walking back to his APC to get more CAR15 ammunition when a bypassed enemy soldier popped up in the ditch ten feet to his left. "In what seemed like slow motion he raised his AK-47 and pointed it right at me," wrote Barnes. "Without having to aim, I fired off a round and saw it hit him in the chest. He fell back against the back of the ditch, but started aiming his rifle at me again. After two more well-placed shots, he finally went to his reward, while at the same instant, another VC, just to his left, started to swing his AK-47 on me. As I pulled the trigger to take him out, all I heard was the click indicating that the bolt was locked in the rear position and I was out of ammo. Knowing that I didn't possibly have time to reload, I spun around in a classic pivot kick, knocking the weapon out of his hands and taking him prisoner."

The attack resumed. Barnes brought his APCs forward to continue providing fire support but found their path blocked by the concertina wire strung around the little houses as property boundaries. Enemy soldiers were firing from houses less than a hundred meters ahead and from the cover of the brush and palm trees around some of the dwellings as three staff sergeants crawled forward with wire cutters. "I couldn't believe all the green tracers coming at us," said McCaskill, who used an M79 to cover the wire-clearing team. He lobbed a dozen shells at one window in particular, only to have a boy run out the front door of the shack, followed by a young woman holding a child against her hip. "I started screaming for everybody to stop shooting at that house. I tell you my heart was in my throat when I realized that I had almost killed these people. I thank God to this day that I didn't get a round in that window. . . ."

Lieutenant Barnes bellowed at the woman to come toward his platoon, "but her fear held her back. In order to remove them from the danger area, I ran forward and carried them to safety behind one of the APCs." Barnes had the woman and child under one arm, the boy under the other, and he felt like he was moving in a state of grace as he "heard the crack of small arms all around me and saw the dirt kicked up to either side as bullets came near. When the woman and her two children were secure, we renewed the attack, crushing houses along the way . . ."

The maelstrom was incredible. The tracks pressed forward, pausing to sweep each new row of houses with .50-cal fire while the troops alongside joined in with M16s. Dust and smoke hung in the air, and houses were engulfed in flames from direct M79 hits. Palm trees hung limp and shredded. "As the first house began to burn, I noticed several more civilians hesitantly moving towards the street, totally uncertain of our intentions. The fear in their eyes said that Death was near them, either from the Viet Cong hiding in their houses, or from the maddened GIs," wrote Barnes. Each group of civilians was ushered behind the tracks as they were encountered. Two Cobras appeared, and Barnes, having neither their call signs nor frequency, resorted to hand and arm signals to direct them. "Standing on top of my track, I pulled on my collar, pointing out that I was the ranking man on the ground. I saw the command pilot nod his head in agreement as he made an orbit around our position. On his second pass, I pointed down a row of houses that I wanted him to take under fire, then drew my finger across my throat, to signify slicing, and he nodded agreement again. On his third pass, the firing began. . . ."

The rockets and minigun fire shattered the enemy.

The fight was almost over. During the morning, Captain James O. Lawson's B/4-39th Infantry, 9th Division, had combat assaulted into a clearing in Widows Village directly across the highway from the II FFV HQ. Lawson brought his company abreast on Barnes's left flank, and the enemy collapsed under the weight of this combined attack.

Some of the drainage ditches along the roads were stuffed with enemy bodies. More littered the waist-high grass around the houses, seventy-seven in all by body count. "One VC with an AK-47 was hiding behind a building, and he would jump out and fire off a burst from the hip and then jump back to cover," said Sergeant Jared, who watched the action through binoculars from the Plantation. "This one time he jumped out—and just as he opened fire I saw a 2.75-inch rocket from one of the gunships hit him in the chest. I went into the village after it was secured, and all I found at that spot was the man's leg hanging in a bush."

The enemy retreated. From Tower 4, Tadsen watched in amazement as a guerrilla, moving faster than any human being he had ever seen, outran the Cobra that followed in hot pursuit, firing its nose-mounted minigun and grenade launcher. The VC was sprinting for a small patch of jungle growing along the railway line, and he disappeared into it with the buzz saw chewing up the ground at his heels. The occupants of Tower 4 sniped at other figures that were moving north from the embattled village. Tadsen saw one guerrilla try to give up, apparently because he was out of ammunition. "The VC had a basic load of 120 rounds for an AK-47. When they used up their basic load and couldn't get anymore off the dead, they were instructed to bury their weapon and surrender," Tadsen explained. The guerrilla in question popped from a position from which the cement blockhouse had been taking fire all morning. "Well, I was pretty pissed off that he just thought he could surrender when he ran out of ammo, and as he came running toward the base perimeter, I nailed him with my M14 at two hundred and fifty yards," said the hotheaded MP.

The enemy rear guard was pressed into a little pocket in the northeast end of the ville, which was on slightly higher ground than the rest of Widows Village. Having organized his line for the final push against these diehards, Lieutenant Barnes hustled back to his track to find that Specialist Four Charles A. Kronberg had been shot while manning the .50-cal MG. He had a gaping wound in the back of his head and died in the arms of his close friend, Specialist Four Danny Lawless, while the platoon medic, Specialist Four Mike Keener, tried desperately to save him. "I recall the look of total helplessness in the eyes of Danny Lawless, eyes that pleaded for me to do something," Barnes wrote. "I walked away in sickness that such a fine young man had died in nondescript Widows Village. . . ."

Moments later, a VC with an AK in one hand and a big National Liberation Front flag in the other, sprinted across the last-stand hillock toward a better firing position than the one he had. The VC was caught in mid-stride by a devastating .50-cal MG burst, and was later found with the flag still clutched in a hand that was connected to an arm that was connected only to half a torso.

When the running figure was chopped down, Barnes launched the final attack. The hillock was quickly overrun.

Meanwhile, Captain Gardner, CO, 552d MP Company, had been running ammunition up to Barnes and Lawson in gun jeeps and had been securing the prisoners taken as the assault line progressed through Widows Village. There were about thirty in all, most of them wounded and hastily bandaged and splinted by their own medical cadre.

Tadsen had joined the MPs guarding the prisoners when one of their NCOs, apparently gripped with the idea that the enemy might counterattack and push them back, barked with forced bravado to, "Tie 'em up, or shoot 'em!"

"C'mon, shoot 'em?" Tadsen rejoined.

"Yes! We don't have time to mess with these people!"

The panicked sergeant was ignored. At about that time, an old man drove out of the smoke on a Vespa motorbike and frantically tried to explain to the MPs that his wife and mother were in one of the houses being rocketed by the gunships. The old man was seriously wounded in his ankle. "I sat him down to put a bandage on his wound while he pointed to the house where his family was," said Tadsen. "I tried to get one of the sergeants to temporarily call off the gunships, but then that same pantywaist sergeant who had wanted to shoot the prisoners made me tie this old man up just like a Viet Cong, even while he lay there pleading for his family. I never did find out what happened to them."

The battle was a madhouse. One MP tried to rescue a three-year-old boy caught in the crossfire, but the boy was shot in the head and killed even as the sergeant carried him back. Tadsen saw another group of civilians working their way toward the MPs. "There was a man, a woman, and a teenage girl. They were carrying some of their belongings on their heads," said Tadsen. "The man was wearing a red shirt. It stood out like crazy, and in the confusion, a sergeant first class on one of our gun jeeps fired the M60 at him, blowing his head off at the chin. As we moved forward, I tried to comfort the woman and the girl, but they kicked and scratched and hit me, and I moved on."

The northeast end of the village was virtually obliterated before the last enemy position was overrun. The subsequent mopping up proved traumatic. To begin with, several die-hards had disappeared into the village wells, which were interconnected with tunnels. "We had a number of people come across the highway at this time from the II Field Force compound. They had no business being out there, but they were trying to get themselves a VC KIA for the day," said Tadsen. One of these straphangers, an administrative NCO, looked over the edge of one of the wells to see what was at the bottom of the twelve-foot shaft. "Well, there was a little guy down there with an AK-47, and he shot the sergeant in the face," noted Tadsen, who ran to the scene and found the NCO lying there in shock, a medic bent over him. "I snuck over to the well and dropped a frag down on that VC. I snuck a look, but I don't know if I got him or not because it was too dark to make out the debris at the bottom."

Lieutenant Barnes was sweeping back through the ripped-up ville when one of his dismounted troopers, McCaskill, glanced back and realized the line had missed several enemy packs sitting in a row along a narrow drainage ditch that snaked away from a culvert built into one of the village roads. McCaskill doubled back with two or three others, and kicking the packs away, he realized that several VC had squeezed themselves into the fissure, lying lengthwise with their packs placed overhead to conceal them.

The packs had given them away instead, and at McCaskill's urging, one guerrilla came out of the ditch. "He was just a kid. He was terrified that I was just going to kill him on the spot," remembered McCaskill. "He was jabbering, so I calmed him down as much as I could, trying to tell him to get the others to come on out, too."

The prisoner coaxed a second enemy soldier from the ditch. There was one more in there, but when the VC was halfway out, he suddenly produced a grenade. "We were looking right at each other. I yelled, 'Grenade!' and everybody took off running," said McCaskill. The VC did not throw the grenade after them as feared, but clutched it to his chest, determined not to be taken alive. He wasn't. He was blown to pieces instead. Captain Gardner had just pulled up in a jeep at that moment. When the grenade went off and the startled MPs climbing out of the jeep saw two VC rushing away, they opened up with their M14s—Gardner apparently joined in too with his M16—unaware that they were actually firing at prisoners who were simply trying to escape the diehard with the grenade. "They were unarmed, and they were running side by side with us, but the MPs just went crazy on automatic," said McCaskill, who dove over a roll of concertina wire as he ran back toward his platoon. "The MPs were spraying everywhere, and as soon as I hit the ground, I was rolling over and over, trying to get away from the fire. It was hitting all around me, kicking up the dirt right in front of my face. . . ."

McCaskill had skidded in next to Private First Class James M. Vielbaum, an energetic replacement only two weeks with the Scout Platoon. When the fire died down, McCaskill realized that Vielbaum had accidentally been shot in the throat by the pumped-up, trigger-happy MPs.

Vielbaum was on his hands and knees, blood jetting from his jugular vein in great spurts. He turned wide-eyed to McCaskill, and said, "Bill, can you help me?"

That was all he said. Vielbaum's eyes glazed over, and he slumped down, already dead as McCaskill frantically screamed for the medic. The nearest platoon medic, Doc Metcalf, however, had also been caught in the wild firing, stitched across both legs. Splintered bone jutted from the wounds. The MPs had completely missed the VC, but had blitzed yet a third mech trooper across the chest. He was only bruised, his ammo bandolier having stopped the rounds.

Vielbaum was the third and final U.S. fatality in Widows Village. It was fortunate that McCaskill had dropped his M16 in his scramble for safety because he ran toward the MPs now in a killing fury, screaming like a berserker. Rushing to the scene, Barnes intercepted McCaskill and, telling him to calm down, asked for an exact account of what had happened. "These sons of bitches just killed Vielbaum!" McCaskill choked out, pointing at the MPs who stood in awkward silence. "They were completely out of it. They probably had never had to fire a round in anger before, and then all of a sudden they see what really happens when you start yanking that trigger," remembered Barnes, who told McCaskill to stand aside as he turned to Gardner. "Seeing the absolute white rage that had gripped my troops, some of whom had leveled their weapons, I told the MP captain that his safety in my area could only be guaranteed for the next fifteen seconds. The captain and his sorry bunch of MPs drove off as fast as they could, thereby avoiding what might have been yet another senseless tragedy."

15

A Hard End to a Long Day

The town appeared deserted. The doors and shutters of the little shacks were closed. No one was in the streets. Lieutenant Barnes was on the lead track as the Scout Platoon rolled through shortly after securing Widows Village, having been ordered to reinforce C/2-47th Mech, which was heavily engaged at the ARVN III Corps Headquarters.

The ghost town along the way was actually the village of Ho Nai, which had been built by anti-communist Catholic refugees relocated from the same village in North Vietnam in 1954. The Scout Platoon reached Ho Nai after proceeding up Route 316 and turning west onto Highway 1. As the column rumbled through the western end of town, "[a] lone Vietnamese boy pulled out of a side street on his motor bike, pointed down the street, and shouted, 'Beaucoup VC!'" wrote Captain Arnauld G. Fleming, one of three division information officers riding on the seventh APC in the line after hooking up with the Scouts in Widows Village. "Before we could react to his warning, we heard a loud explosion as one of the APCs in front of us seemed to dissolve in dust and smoke. We were caught in a surprise attack. . . ."

The guerrillas initiated their ambush from a two-story yellow house on the left side of the highway, directly opposite a Catholic church. Barnes had already passed the site, as had the second track in line, when the third took three RPGs. Its front drivetrain disabled, the out-of-control APC zigzagged wildly before running off the road and crashing into a house. Tracks four and five received broadside hits, while track six turned to fire on the yellow house before being silenced in its turn by another RPG.

Tracks seven and eight slammed to a halt. The crew of track six had already "rolled onto the ground behind a thick masonry fence surrounding the church," wrote Fleming, who joined the crew of track seven as they "darted over to the protection of a house that fronted onto the street. We began cover fire for the men behind the fence until they could dash across the street to join us . . . We were separated from the remainder of the platoon by about 500 yards and by at least three enemy rocketeers, a VC machine gunner and an undetermined number of hostile riflemen. . . ."

At the front of the column, Lieutenant Barnes was fanning the crews of the lead two tracks out to secure the immediate area when a grenade rolled in beside his APC. Barnes's flak jacket absorbed most of the blast, but some of the red-hot specks peppered him in his face and left arm.

Having taken up a firing position nearby, Doc Keener was dragged back to Barnes at that point, shot in the head. He had a bullet hole on both sides of his steel helmet just above the ears, and a bloody gash where the round had deflected over the top of his head. Keener wasn't shook up, he was furious and screaming bloody murder.

Barnes shouted at McCaskill and Staff Sergeant Robert W. Schultz, a new squad leader, to secure track three, a hundred and fifty hundred meters behind them. Sprinting straight down the road through a terrifying crossfire, McCaskill ran into the house where the APC had crashed, while Schultz peeled off toward an adjacent shack where he had spotted one of the enemy machine guns. Schultz charged the position, blowing the crew away with a captured AK-47.

Though wounded, Schultz took out another gun position with grenades before being shot and killed. The sergeant was posthumously awarded the Distinguished Service Cross. Meanwhile, McCaskill got things organized in the shack where track three had crashed to a stop. "The 'PC was actually inside the house. It had crashed through the wall, and the crew had been thrown off by the impact. They were strewn around in the rubble, wounded and dazed. I kicked out a board in the building to open up a line of fire into the village itself, and immediately got everybody set up in a defensive position because I thought we was fixin' to get overrun. I set up to face the road. . . ."

The battle lasted four hours. It broke down into two separate firefights, with the sixteen troopers who had scrambled against the side of the shack at the rear of the column fighting their own little war with the ambushers in the yellow house across the highway. "Every time we attempted to move into another area, we were turned back by a deadly hail of fire," noted Fleming. Despite this fire, Specialist Four Lee E. Wilson, a soft-spoken draftee, repeatedly popped around the corner to heave grenades and blast back with his M16. Wilson also ran to the APC they had abandoned in the street to obtain ammunition. "At one point in the fight, Wilson grabbed a [LAW] from [the] track, and moved out into the center of the street in full view of the VC," wrote an awed Fleming. "When he calmly released his rocket toward the ambush site, the VC defenders fired back with an RPG round, just barely missing Wilson. Wilson seemed to vanish under a dense cloud of smoke and dust. Suddenly from out of the smoke, the infantryman came running back to the comparative safety of our position."

Wilson was superficially wounded in the blast, but his LAW seemed to put some pause in the enemy fire. Encouraged, Wilson—earning the Distinguished Service Cross—secured two more LAWs from the APC, and again stood in the open to fire them straight into the VC.

Major Raymond E. Funderburk, the division information officer, found himself in command of this isolated element of the Scout Platoon, HHC/2-47th Mech, 9th Division. "Funderburk [directed] our fire, moving soldiers into better positions and yelling words of encouragement," wrote Fleming. The frontal fire on the yellow house was not completely suppressing the enemy—in fact, the combat photographer in Funderburk's team, First Lieutenant Charles C. Ashton III, was shot twice in the arm—so finally, "[w]ith two riflemen providing covering fire, the major climbed to the roof of our building and began lobbing M-79 grenades onto the roof of the VC stronghold. Piece by piece he completely removed the roof and began working on the second floor, trying to penetrate the enemy hideout below. . . ."

Lieutenant Barnes pushed through the houses hemming in his strung-out column, and after linking up with McCaskill, he pressed on toward Funderburk. It was dusk by then, and the major's group was almost completely out of ammunition. Like manna from heaven, two gunships came on station. "Since we were only 20 to 30 yards from the VC, it was hard for them to pinpoint the target without endangering friendly troops," continued Fleming's narrative. "Funderburk grabbed the radio and began talking them in. He instructed them to circle to the north, line up directly on the big cross atop the church, sweep in across it and blast away at the house across the street. With the foot soldiers cheering them on, the [Huey] gunships came roaring in, skimming the church and launching their rockets directly into the bottom floor of the yellow house. It collapsed in a roar of flame and smoke."

Leaving the damaged tracks, Barnes raced the setting sun back to Long Binh with the rest of the battered Scout Platoon. Lieutenant Colonel Tower's command group had also retired behind the wire for the night, and Barnes had his ten wounded men taken straight to the battalion aid station. "Checking on my remaining soldiers, I was told that Sergeant Schultz had been killed and was still lying in the village of Ho Nai," wrote Barnes who thought he had gotten through this second battle of the day without serious loss. "I reported to the TOC, and told them that I was going back in to retrieve the body. At that point, I was crying, partly from a sense of rage of having any of my men killed, partly for a plea for relief, and partly because I just didn't know how else to deal with the insanity that I had just witnessed."

Tower calmed Barnes down. "Panther 6, knowing exactly what to do, just grabbed and hugged me, telling me that it would serve no useful purpose to expose my men to further harm at that time, that he understood why I needed to go back there, but that I would not return to Ho Nai until the next morning, and that was an order."

The Scout Platoon walked back down Highway 1 the next day. "Sergeant Schultz had been carried out from where he had fallen by some Vietnamese Catholic nuns from the church in Ho Nai," wrote Barnes. "The most beautiful lace handkerchief had been placed over his face. . . ."

The Scout Platoon claimed twenty-six kills in Ho Nai. Specialist McCaskill accounted for the last of these casualties just before the Scouts had mounted up for the hasty withdrawal to Long Binh. "We were milling around there, and I was sitting on the ground, totally exhausted, but still hyped up and trying to be alert," McCaskill remembered. Three Viet Cong suddenly came around the corner of a nearby building, their weapons slung. "These guys were as shocked to see us as I was to see them. Everybody else was oblivious to these guys. They never even saw them. I ripped off about half a magazine on automatic, firing right between the legs of this big guy nicknamed Bear who was between me and the VC. Bear was furious because he thought my weapon had just gone off, but I hit one of them. As he started to go down, the other two grabbed him and jerked him back around the corner. I jumped up and threw a grenade over the top of the building to make sure they didn't come back around. They didn't. They were just trying to get out of the village and had come around the wrong corner. . . ."

16

Forewarned Is
Forearmed

Like the attack on the northwest side of Long Binh, the
attempt to breach the northeast perimeter bogged down
before it ever got started because the assault battalion
moved in along a route being monitored by Specialist Five
Richard D. Vincent's six-man team from Company F, 51st
Infantry (Long-Range Patrol), II FFV. The green-faced,
cammie-clad troopers were ensconced in a clump of high
brush that provided the only cover in a relatively open area
where an engineer road forked from a wide, well-traveled
dirt road six hundred meters north of Ho Nai, the long and
thin hamlet stretching down both sides of Highway 1. The
east half of the village ran past the front perimeter of the
199th LIB base camp, known as the BMB for Brigade Main
Base.

Inserted by helicopter, Vincent's patrol was one of many
covering the various approaches to the BMB. "We just
happened to set up in the right location," noted Vincent, a
tough, stocky twenty-seven-year-old juvenile delinquent
turned career soldier from Camden, New Jersey.

"All of our guys were a little wild," said the F/51st LRP
operations officer. "You don't volunteer for a long-range
patrol company if you're a conservative person. . . ."

Having deployed claymore mines around its position,
Vincent's patrol—Team 3-7—spent a quiet day watching

the engineer road from behind the berm of dirt and brush that had been pushed to the side of it by the bulldozers. The road branched northeast from the main north-south trail that sliced through Ho Nai and connected with Highway 1 a kilometer east of the turnoff to Route 316.

The situation went from routine to heart-thumping sometime after midnight. A chronic snorer, Vincent was used to being nudged awake all night long during patrols. He was dozing lightly when one of his guards—the LRPs operated with three up and three down at night—kicked him. Vincent thought he had been snoring again, but the guard instead wordlessly pointed to the engineer road. There was a VC column moving down it. Lying unseen in the thick brush, Vincent squeezed his radio handset, silently alerting the company TOC, while he counted the figures double-timing past in single file. He stopped counting at eighty because there seemed to be no end to them. When the last guerrilla finally trotted by, and Vincent guessed that there had been a hundred and fifty in all, the team leader slipped onto the engineer road, followed the column to confirm that it had turned onto the main road, then rushed back to his original position to alert the TOC.

Awakened by his ops sergeant, Lieutenant Colonel William C. Maus, commander of F/51st LRP, scrambled to the TOC and got on the horn with Vincent. "He whispered, I mean *whispered,* his report that eighty-plus heavily armed VC had passed his position, headed for Long Binh. You could tell he was scared," recalled Maus. The report came in at 0105. Within minutes, Maus and Captain Howard W. Randall, his S3, climbed aboard one of the helicopters kept on standby for the LRPs at Bien Hoa. Lights out, the Huey orbited above Vincent, who requested an immediate extraction. Maus could not risk sending in a helicopter under the circumstances but was reassured that an infantry-armor force was en route from the 199th Light Infantry Brigade.

During Tet, F/51st LRP was opcon to the 199th LIB. The decision to send the infantry-armor force was made by acting brigade commander Davison and Lieutenant Colonel Kenneth W. Hall, the S3. "I started my tour with the 1st

Division, and I can state absolutely that the Big Red One would not have dispatched an armor force to reinforce us until daylight," reflected Maus. "However, we needed it *then,* not later, and to the credit of Davison and Hall they took the risk and moved the armor out in the dark. The reinforcements ended up stopping the enemy in their tracks. . . ."

In light of the pivotal information provided by Vincent, it is ironic to note that Lieutenant Colonel Maus had almost disobeyed the original order to deploy Team 3-7. The order had come directly from Davison during a conference between Davison, Hall, Maus, and Randall in the 199th LIB TOC two days before Tet. Given the indications of impending enemy attack, Maus already had five teams in early-warning positions outside the BMB. Davison now wanted a sixth team sent out. "My worst fear was to have several widely separated patrols in contact at once, and not be able to support them properly," noted Maus, a fatherly, highly respected West Pointer. Maus objected to the sixth patrol on the grounds that his company was already fully committed, "but Davison was adamant. He just looked at me and squinted his eyes, and said, 'Do it.' That's when I had the thought that, 'Okay, I'll tell you I did, but I won't. I'll just put the patrol on the berm.' "

Maus had responsibility for part of the perimeter berm around the army compound at Bien Hoa. By putting the patrol on the berm, he rationalized that "I wouldn't be a complete liar. However, something about honor, heavily stressed at West Point, wouldn't allow me to deceive." It was thus that Team 3-7 saddled up, though Maus prudently decided to place it closer to Long Binh than his other patrols so that a reaction force could reach it quickly if needed. "The issue at that point was inserting the team safely because of all the woodcutters and farmers around Ho Nai," recalled Randall, concerned about those residents who were not part of the anti-communist majority. "We made ten or fifteen false insertions before we dropped the patrol off, and then we made ten or fifteen more after that so the people in the area wouldn't know where the patrol really was."

* * *

The attack had been anticipated. The avenue of approach was the unknown, and the counterattack that unfolded in response to the warning from that sixth, propitiously placed patrol led to the total destruction of the enemy. "I know the guys out in the field didn't think the battle was a picnic, but in retrospect it really was," said Colonel Davison, the crisp but personable deputy brigade commander who served as the acting 199th LIB commander while the CG was home on leave from January 15 to February 18. "It was a fantastic operation. First of all, we knew they were coming, and were able to place our units accordingly. Second, we had all the fire support we could use, and, third, the troops just fought like hell when the battle was joined. An attacking force has to expect to take more casualties than the defenders, but not the beating the enemy took that night."

Pinned with the Legion of Merit for Tet, Davison was later promoted, and as the army's first black general since WWII, he commanded the 199th LIB from August 1968 to May 1969. Davison, in turn, credited the Tet victory to the 179th Military Intelligence Detachment, 199th LIB, which had, according to a brigade history, "gathered evidence of the attacks and knew the exact date a week ahead. Their forecast was off by a mere three hours because the enemy was delayed in reaching his assembly point. . . ."

The detachment's leading light was Chief Warrant Officer 2 N. Ken Welch, who began piecing this prophetic intelligence picture together as of January 15, when small groups of VC were detected by ground radar and other surveillance means as they moved between War Zone D and Long Binh. Welch correctly interpreted the activity as that of supply parties positioning weapons and ammunition in preparation for an attack. The target came into focus, noted the 199th LIB after-action report, when "VC agents dressed as civilians were spotted in villages inquiring of US and ARVN installations and activities [at Bien Hoa and Long Binh]."

The subsequent movement of larger enemy groups was also detected by ground radar. Forewarned being forearmed, Colonel Davison placed F/51st LRP teams along the approaches to the BMB. "LRPs usually operated at the extreme edges of an area of operations," noted Davison, "but as things appeared to get tighter and tighter, my decision was that we would use them within the ring between the infantry battalions and the BMB."

The LRPs scored several intelligence coups in the week before Tet, including the destruction of a VC reconnaissance team near Ho Nai that was described in the 199th LIB after-action report: "The VC wore US type camouflage clothing, carried US M-16 rifles and had US cigarettes."

Only three nights before Tet, another enemy reconnaissance party was engaged in the hilltop cemetery on the northern fringe of Ho Nai. The VC scattered and slipped away in the dark, leaving behind one dead guerrilla who was found to be carrying a new compass, a new Russian pistol, and a new pair of East German Zeiss binoculars.

Colonel Davison took the binoculars as a souvenir. These indicators of impending attack seem crystal clear after the fact. In reality, they shone out amid all the other activity in the area only because "Welch was the best intelligence officer I ever met," stated Warrant Officer Creamer, who served in the 179th MI Detachment until rotating Stateside two months before Tet. "Welch had a lot of luck, but you have to be ready for luck. If you're not well grounded in what's going on around you, you may get critical information and not give it the appropriate value."

Welch was able to pinpoint the exact timing of the offensive thanks to one of his intelligence agents—a young Vietnamese woman known as Suzy who lived in Ho Nai and did kitchen police work in one of the BMB mess halls. "Suzy's uncle was the mayor of Ho Nai. More importantly, she had a first cousin who commanded a Viet Cong reconnaissance company," noted Creamer, who got the details from Welch when he rejoined the brigade for a second tour. "The cousin visited his family in Ho Nai a week before Tet. He told them that they needed to move out, that the 275th VC Regiment was going to attack right through their living room, so to speak, and he gave them the time and date of the attack. Suzy immediately came and told Welch. If her cousin hadn't had such a big mouth and decided to come warn his family, we never would have known with such exactness what was coming."

* * *

Throughout the war, intelligence available at the command level tended to remain at the command level. Small units, and this included the infantry-armor force sent to Ho Nai, frequently executed mission orders with no knowledge of their critical part in the Big Picture. "Tet was a total surprise for us. We had received no forewarning from higher command," said Lieutenant Colonel William Mastoris, CO, 4-12th Infantry, 199th LIB. Directed to reinforce the LRPs in Ho Nai, Mastoris routinely dispatched Captain Robert L. Tonsetic's Company C, the designated Brigade Ready Reaction Force. "I was awakened by a runner from the Bn TOC who passed a message that a [LRP] Patrol had reported sighting some 80 VC about [five] kilometers [south]east of our FSB," Tonsetic wrote in an informal after-action report. "I checked my map and was not too surprised when the location turned out to be in the vicinity of a contact several nights before in which a similar patrol had engaged a small force of VC and killed one. I was skeptical, however, of the reported 80 VC in this area and thought that [the LRPs] had probably wildly exaggerated the number."

Captain Tonsetic was presently securing FSB Concord, the battalion base camp one klick north of the army compound at Bien Hoa. Mastoris had been instructed to move from War Zone D to FSB Concord three weeks before Tet. "Although [we] did not know it at the time," noted Tonsetic, "this redeployment was the result of a general shift of American forces back toward the populated area. . . ."

The earlier contact cited by Tonsetic was the one in which the LRPs had bagged the VC officer with the binoculars in the cemetery outside Ho Nai. Tonsetic had also been dispatched to that action, and after reconning by fire, his troops had swept the cemetery without incident under the light of flares dropped from an orbiting Huey.

Given the same mission only a few nights later, Captain Tonsetic, expecting another wasted night, was actually to earn the Distinguished Service Cross for his superb leadership during the unexpected battle in Ho Nai.

"Tonsetic was the best soldier I ever soldiered with," said

First Sergeant George L. Holmes, the top sergeant of C/4-12th Infantry.

The son of a Pittsburgh steel worker, Tonsetic was an ROTC graduate who had since served with the Special Forces in Thailand and attended the British Jungle Warfare School in Malaysia. He had a quick mind and an explosive temper. "He was a mad redhead," quipped Holmes. "The captain was not pleasant to be around," said Specialist Four Cliff Kaylor, an antiwar college dropout who served as senior company RTO. "He wasn't the kind of guy you joked with or had a beer with—but when the caps started popping, he was the sanest, coolest man there. He never seemed to make a mistake. He was a dedicated career officer, and very much a believer. He believed in the war, he believed in the army, and he believed in the United States of America."

At the time of the second mount-up, Tonsetic had at his disposal only a five-man command group and the thirty-eight members of the 3d Platoon and Mortar Platoon of C/4-12th Infantry. The 2d Platoon was in ambush positions in a valley east of FSB Concord where movement had been picked up the last few nights by ground radar; and because of the numerous ARVN on Tet leave, the 1st Platoon, along with a cavalry platoon, had been detached to the thinned-down ARVN guard unit at the prisoner of war compound on the south side of Highway 1 just east of Bien Hoa City.

Fortunately, Tonsetic's meager reaction force was beefed up with a platoon from D/17th Cav, 199th LIB. "It took less than twenty minutes to get the M113s out of their berm positions on the perimeter, and get my men mounted," Tonsetic wrote. "As always, we rode atop the vehicles rather than inside. Better to be blown clear off if the track hit a mine or was hit by RPGs. The crews did likewise. Even with seven vehicles, the infantrymen with their rucksacks, weapons, and radios were crowded atop the tracks."

Tonsetic added that the troops "were none too happy to have their sleep disturbed, and there was the usual cursing back and forth as we mounted up." The grunts considered firebase duty a time to relax between operations. This no-sweat attitude was especially pronounced because of the Tet truce, which many units in the boonies thought was still in effect. "I was totally blitzed when the word came to saddle up," said Specialist Four Nick Schneider, a squad leader in Charlie Three. "The platoon sergeant had brought a couple bottles of whiskey out, and my squad and I stayed up partying in one of the perimeter bunkers until almost midnight. . . ."

Captain Tonsetic gave the word, and the column was soon enveloped in dust as it rolled south from FSB Concord. Tonsetic expected to be back by morning. "It seemed incredible to me that there might be a large force of VC so near the Long Binh Base," he wrote. After the column cut through the army compound at Bien Hoa and seemingly secure Dong Lach, Lieutenant Colonel Mastoris—in the TOC at FSB Concord—radioed Tonsetic to hold in place at his first checkpoint, a road junction in the rubber on the eastern edge of Bien Hoa City. "I had my men dismount and we formed a 360° perimeter with the M113s," wrote Tonsetic. "The silence among the rubber trees was eerie. Within five minutes this silence was broken by the thundering roar of 122mm rockets shrieking overhead toward the airfield at Bien Hoa. They sounded like freight trains at full speed ahead. The first rockets hit the fuel dumps of JP4 aviation fuel, and the sky was ablaze several kilometers away."

The rockets got everyone's attention. Shortly thereafter, Mastoris directed Captain Tonsetic to proceed to his second checkpoint, the nearby PW compound on Highway 1. The column idled on the blacktop while Tonsetic spoke briefly with First Lieutenant Howard Tuber of Charlie One at the front gate of the compound. The VC PWs were housed in rows of Quonset huts and surrounded by a chain-link fence and rolls of concertina wire. "[Tuber] was uncomfortable about the size of this facility he had to defend with only one platoon and [with] his inability to communicate with the few Vietnamese who remained on duty," wrote Tonsetic. "I shared his concern, but told him to hold the place at all costs since we couldn't afford to lose 2,000 prisoners. . . ."

* * *

The crackle of another radio message from battalion, and the column rolled on. Tonsetic's third checkpoint was the intersection of the highway and the trail that cut due north to the engineer road where the LRP team was ensconced above Ho Nai. "As we drove towards the village, I heard occasional firecrackers exploding as part of the TET celebration," Tonsetic wrote, unaware that the "firecrackers" might actually have been the opening shots of the ground attacks on Bien Hoa and the Plantation. "[Reaching] our [third] checkpoint, I had already decided to dismount my platoons and move north dismounted, providing frontal and flank security for the column of seven M113s. The road [north] was narrow and bordered on both sides by drainage ditches, [and it] slope[d] downward for some 400 meters towards a small creek [running along the north edge of Ho Nai]. Houses bordered the road for approximately the first 300 meters. There was no room for the armored personnel carriers to maneuver, and they were restricted to moving in column until the culvert over the creek was crossed."

Specialist Schneider accompanied his point team on the road itself while Tonsetic's command group and Platoon Sergeant Orville Wyers's Charlie Three followed single file in the knee-deep drainage ditch on the left side of the road.

The Mortar Platoon, under Platoon Sergeant Clifford Jaynes—both acting platoon leaders were solid NCOs—used the drainage ditch on the right side of the road, the tracks rumbling along slowly between the two infantry files. Lanterns burned in the houses of those Ho Nai residents who had not taken advantage of the warning from the Viet Cong.

Tonsetic also knew nothing of this intelligence. It was now about 0345 on January 31, 1968, and C/4-12th Infantry was unknowingly headed north on the same road which the VC/NVA assault battalion was using to move south toward Long Binh. "We were nearing the culvert when some idiot behind us, probably from the CP group, fired a hand flare," remembered Schneider, furious that his point team could have been exposed. "When the flare went off, we saw several figures run across the road to our front, but we weren't close enough to tell who they were."

Schneider radioed the command group, but Tonsetic—reckoning that whatever small enemy force that had been in the area was long gone—thought that the unidentified troops were probably the LRPs or from the South Vietnamese Popular Forces platoon posted in Ho Nai.

Specialist Schneider was of the same mind, and when he saw upon pressing on that there was a tripod-mounted machine gun sitting on the road in front of the culvert he thought it belonged to the PFs. He realized an instant later that the weapon's flash suppresser was distinctive to the Chinese .51-caliber MG. "There was nobody manning the gun. They were getting ready for their attack and got caught as much by surprise as we did," mused Schneider, a smart, streetwise career NCO from the Bronx who had been up and down in rank but who was something of a natural born leader. Schneider shouted at his point team to hit the deck. Instead, Private First Class Kenneth C. Barber sprang forward, and at a range of ten feet blasted three VC scrambling to put the gun into action with his pump shotgun. "There was a shadowy mob of thirty or forty more troops behind the .51, mostly in the ditch where the ground fell away to the creek running under the culvert," noted Schneider, who rolled to hasty cover on the left side of the road—the rest of his squad opened up from the right side—and quickly burned through two M16 magazines trying to keep the enemy away from the machine gun. "I rolled a hand grenade at it next, and it went in the ditch. I guess that discouraged them. Nobody ever got behind that machine gun. I threw the other three grenades that I carried, then ran back to the lead track, pulled my rucksack off, opened it up, and just threw everything else that I had in there, cooking the grenades off first because the enemy was that close."

Caught off guard, the enemy was hurt in the opening moments of the battle. The guerrillas quickly recovered and their return fire was ferocious. Ducking behind an old civilian truck parked alongside a stucco-walled house, Captain Tonsetic shouldered his CAR15 even as one of his radiomen, a new man, scuttled under the truck in a panic. "Tonsetic was screaming at him and yanking on the handset cord connected to his radio, trying to get him back out," remembered Kaylor, the senior RTO. The lead track was hit by a rocket-propelled grenade and burst into flames. The ammunition inside began exploding. The third ACAV was also put out of action by RPGs. "[T]he undamaged second track sprayed the area to the west and front, suppressing [some of] the heavy VC fire," Tonsetic wrote. "I couldn't see what was going on beyond the house to our left, and concerned about being flanked, I threw hand grenades over the roof to disrupt any enemy in that area. I kept firing my CAR15 at muzzle flashes to the front, but the weapon jammed. I quickly changed magazines. It fired but would not eject spent cartridges without my performing the immediate action sequence each time."

Meanwhile, Kaylor made contact with the 2-40th Field Artillery (105mm), 199th LIB, at Long Binh. "We need a fire mission."

"I can only give you one tube."

"One tube! Why?" exclaimed Kaylor, who was expecting the usual support of a six-gun battery.

"You don't know, do you?" the voice at the other end of the radio answered. "It's going down *everywhere!*"

Specialist Schneider had rejoined his squad on the right side of the road and was rearing up to throw another grenade when he was suddenly knocked to the ground by another RPG. Ignoring the superficial fragment wounds in his face and arm and leg, Schneider—subsequently awarded a BSMv—bandaged a squad member who had been hit in the throat. The trooper stumbled rearward, holding the field dressing firmly against the blood-gushing wound.

As far as Captain Tonsetic could determine in the chaos, the RPGs were being fired from a certain house to the right front of the column. The ACAV on the road next to Tonsetic sported a 106mm recoilless rifle, and he bellowed at the gunner to fire on the house. The weapon remained silent, the gunner either unable to hear Tonsetic or too stunned to react. Instead, several infantrymen turned their fire on the house, and a grenadier ignited the thatch roof with a direct hit. The roof caved in, the whole house was soon burning like a bonfire in the dark, and when the flames engulfed the unfired rocket-propelled grenades inside, the resulting explosion leveled the place.

From their orbiting perch above the battlefield, Lieutenant Colonel Maus and Captain Randall had seen the flashes that signaled the beginning of the rocket attacks. "There were some two dozen launching sites at the maximum range to the north. We saw the 122s launch, and we saw them slamming into Bien Hoa and Long Binh," recalled Randall. The coordinates of the launch sites were instantly reported—"we had worked those northern areas a lot, and we knew exactly where they were," the F/51st LRP operations officer noted—and just as quickly some of the gunships previously scrambled for Team 3-7 went to work. The miniguns of a USAF C47 Spooky added to the devastation. There were secondary explosions, and body parts and destroyed equipment were subsequently discovered during ground sweeps of the area. Meanwhile, Maus maintained constant illumination over Vincent, the cabin of the C&C Huey being stacked knee-high with flares. "Randall and I rigged them up every evening in case we had a night contact," said Maus. "The flares were two feet long and cylindrical in shape, and just like parachutists going out the door, they were hooked to a cable inside the chopper. All you had to do was shove them out, and the pins were pulled by the force of gravity. Each would go down slowly under its parachute, providing an enormous amount of illumination."

The flares gave away the approximate position of the blacked-out Huey, and the enemy turned several heavy machine guns skyward. Bright green tracers snapped past, little dots that seemed to grow into huge glowing orbs as they got closer. "Man, they're shooting *basketballs* at us!" the pilot exclaimed over the intercom.

The door gunners did not return fire, concerned that they might hit the stranded LRPs. At that time, Specialist Vincent and Team 3-7 were deployed in a wagon wheel configuration—the six prone LRPs all faced in a different direction like spokes, their feet touching in the center of the circle—as stray .50-caliber tracers from the infantry-armor force six hundred meters to the south slashed through the brush that concealed them. Vincent managed to get through to the cavalry platoon, and he whispered harshly, his radio handset cupped tight against his mouth, "Hey, mother, lift your goddamned fire—*you're shooting me up, too!*"

"We're in a firefight here—"

"Yeah, well, I'm in the *middle* of the sonofabitch!"

Ironically, Vincent came under no enemy fire. The enemy never stumbled across his hideaway, even as squads of VC/NVA hustled past on the engineer road and a smaller footpath on the other side of Team 3-7 to reinforce the action in Ho Nai. Vincent fired pen-flares over each group and, in coordination with Maus and Randall, brought in the gunships, which roared through heavy ground fire to strafe the enemy with rockets and machine guns.

Most of the gunships were from A/3-17th Air Cav, 1st Aviation Brigade. Forced to make their runs through the interlocking fire of several .51-caliber machine guns, every one of the twenty-three Hueys supporting F/51st LRPs and C/4-12th Infantry ended up taking hits. Lieutenant Colonel Maus's command ship even took fire during an aborted refueling stop at the 199th LIB aviation section pad, then under attack from a small group of VC who had worked their way up to the BMB. "When we went down, we drew fire, and the pilot pulled out," said Randall. "We went over to the 1st Division pad at Di An instead, which was well out of the area and which wasn't being hit. You've only got about two hours of fuel, so we returned to Di An to refuel and get flares throughout the battle."

Meanwhile, when Vincent wasn't calling in the gunships, he was requesting extraction. "Vincent hung in there. He held it together, he did what he was supposed to do—but, boy, did he want out of there," said Maus. Vincent became particularly agitated when one of his LRPs took a bullet in his shoulder, apparently from a gunship. Vincent had the man gulp down a handful of Darvon painkillers as he gripped his handset, calling again for extraction. "I remember trying to calm Vincent down. I promised him a bottle of Chivas Regal when it was all over," said Maus. "I wanted to get them out, but there was no way to land with all those VC running around without putting the aircraft and crew in grave jeopardy. They were really concerned that they were going to be found—and so was I."

Captain Tonsetic had no idea that his reaction force had blocked the main body of an enemy assault battalion. He instead thought that they had prematurely sprung an ambush, and that they needed to withdraw to reorganize, evacuate casualties, and permit the unrestricted use of fire support on the numerically superior guerrilla force. Informed by the battalion operations officer that gunships were en route, Tonsetic told First Sergeant Holmes to start the withdrawal and get the medevacs organized. Four track crewmen had been wounded at that point, along with seven grunts from C/4-12th Infantry.

Captain Tonsetic intended to bring up the rear after remaining in place as long as possible to coordinate the fire support, and the command group, accompanied by an M60 team, moved into the stucco-walled house beside which the truck they had been sheltering behind was parked. "My machine gunner quickly found a side window and began to take the enemy under fire," recounted Tonsetic, who took up a position at the door. "My radio came to life and the lead pilot of a light helicopter gunship team requested that I direct his fires. I asked him if he could see the burning vehicle on the road just north of the village, and he quickly identified this reference point. I requested that he make his passes with rocket and machine-gun fire on an east-west axis intersecting the burning vehicle on the road. The two gunships began their passes as my small group inside the house engaged the enemy with small-arms fire."

The time was approximately 0500. Specialist Schneider was pulling back at the tail end of Charlie Company when the gunships flashed in. "I got hit with shell casings, and I thought for a second that they were shooting at us in the dark. I thought I was kissing my ass good-bye. . . ."

Direct hits from an enemy machine gun shook the little house as Tonsetic directed the gunships. Meanwhile, Holmes got the infantry-armor force reorganized after it fought its way back down the narrow road to the intersection with Highway 1. "Holmes was great. He was the typical old first sergeant," said Tonsetic of this humorously boastful, tattoo-covered, deep-voiced veteran of the Korean War. To avoid power lines along the highway, Holmes—who won the Silver Star for Tet—brought their medevac into an open school yard in southern Ho Nai. "I got the most seriously wounded on board, but when I tried to load the rest, they wouldn't go," he remembered. "This was the first time we'd ever encountered dinks in open battle, and the guys said, 'Hell, we ain't wounded bad. Top, this is too good a fight, we ain't gonna leave you out here now!'"

As soon as the dust-off was completed at 0605, First Sergeant Holmes, who packed a shotgun and a demo bag full of shells, grabbed a squad from Charlie Three and started back up the road to find Captain Tonsetic. The command group was in a precarious position. "We gradually realized that we'd been left behind. We looked out and couldn't see any of our guys. Everyone had pulled back," noted Kaylor. Tonsetic was preparing to follow suit when he unexpectedly heard Holmes calling for him—"You got to fall back, sir, the whole company's back down the road!"—and greatly relieved to have the first sergeant's squad laying down "intense covering fire[,] we ran through the garden next to the house [and headed back] towards the village. We all made it, thanks primarily to the gunships, which continued to pour their deadly fire on the VC positions. . . ."

Randall was on his second tour. It had been his experience that the enemy always broke off attacks before dawn so as to slip away under the cover of darkness. To face U.S. firepower in broad daylight was virtually suicidal. "But when the sun came up that morning, they kept on fighting, and as I said to Maus at the time, 'This is different. They're here to stay. They think they're going to do something,'" remembered Randall. The VC were holding positions in the creek bed running along the north edge of Ho Nai. "You could see them laying there, you could see them shooting. They were fully exposed," Randall continued. "They gave us Cobras at that point, and they went down that ravine with rockets and miniguns, and just literally tore the enemy apart. As soon as one team expended its ammo, another rolled in, then another, and another, and another. . . ."

17

Total Annihilation

The enemy finally broke. From the ravine, they still had to cross a kilometer of open ground to reach the jungle to the north, and gunships swooped down on them like hawks on fleeing mice. The scene reminded Lieutenant Colonel Maus of a rock in a stream as desperate groups of VC flowed past either side of the thick brush concealing Team 3-7. "Other VC were racing right toward the area because it was the closest cover. We went into a low, tight circle to try and keep them out of Vincent's corner," said Randall. The C&C door gunners opened fire, as did Maus—subsequently awarded the DSC for his pivotal role in the destruction of the enemy attack—who leaned into the slipstream with his M16. "We shot, we saw them fall, but I don't know if I personally hit any," Maus recalled. "Randall was concerned that I was going to hit some of our own people, and he finally pushed my weapon up, but I and the door gunners knew exactly where our kids were because their clump of bushes was very distinguishable out there. We fired only at guys who were running. Their main objective was just to get out of there. They were heading back to the jungle, and I don't think they fired on our helicopter."

When a lone VC ran up the engineer road, Vincent and his point man flipped their M16s to automatic and fired him up. "He never saw us behind the berm," said Vincent.

"We just blew him away. We literally blew his brains out. . . ."

Vincent hastily recovered a brand-new 9mm pistol from the body, along with a whistle that was hanging around the dead man's neck and letters stuffed in his pocket. When translated, the letters indicated that the man had been a doctor serving as a captain in the Viet Cong.

The doctor was only the first guerrilla to be killed by LRP Team 3-7. "If the VC came close to that clump of bushes, they dropped," noted Maus. "I counted eleven dead ones directly in front of the team's position."

Vincent won the Silver Star, his men the BSMv. All the while, the team leader was requesting extraction. Despite the risks, the time had come. "The situation was getting out of hand. More and more VC were heading for their position, and eventually some of them were going to make it," said Randall. Maus radioed Vincent that an extraction ship was on the way, and the team blew its claymores. The Huey went in with gunship cover. "The pilot complained that there were so many bodies he couldn't find a level spot," noted Randall. "When the lift ship finally touched down, I saw enemy soldiers run right by it, trying to get away, trying to get the hell out of there even as our team clambered aboard. It was chaos, absolute chaos. . . ."

With Vincent out of harm's way, Maus and Randall checked on their more distant patrols which had reported during the night that "they had mortars or heavy machine guns digging in by them, or they had a company run by them," as Randall put it. Maus had passed the information to the 199th LIB as it came in. "If the team wasn't in danger, we left them there to keep reporting," Randall said. "When we determined that the enemy was still in position near these teams, we stayed up all day, running more gunships and artillery and air strikes. . . ."

There had been light action during the night at the brigade base camp. Slipping past the infantry-armor force tying up the main assault battalion, small groups of infiltrators were able to take the brigade helipad on the northwest side of the base under fire. An element of the provisional rifle company created in the 7th Support Battalion to act as a reaction force "was sent to the area of the helipad to suppress the attacking force," noted a 199th LIB after-action report. "On the north side of the perimeter[,] small arms fire was received from an unknown number of VC who were located in the huts and houses of HO NAI village which hugs the base perimeter. The perimeter defense [forces] reacted quickly and saturated the area with small arms and automatic weapons fire to silence the enemy action."

Another group set up an automatic weapon in a tower among the hootches just east of the BMB. Lieutenant Colonel Henry R. Meyer, CO, 2-40th Field Artillery, had two 105mm howitzers from Battery A in position on the east perimeter. "I recall being pinned down between the [gun] sections and the perimeter fence and yelling [directions] back to the gun crews," wrote Meyer, who had the flare-illuminated tower in his binoculars.

"The gun[s] scored six direct hits on the tower and enemy firing ceased," noted the 199th LIB report.

Lieutenant Colonel Meyer accompanied the howitzer section which displaced by truck to the 12th Aviation Group helipad to silence those sappers who had taken the area under fire after penetrating the Long Binh Ammunition Depot. The VC were ensconced in the thick undergrowth behind the Plantation. The after-action report records that Meyer "ordered a Beehive round be fired. One Beehive round was fired. Enemy fire ceased and the howitzer section returned to its primary position. . . ."

A Phantom also knifed in to napalm the area, and when engineers cleared the brush, eighteen bodies were found. Meanwhile, an assault launched to open the PW compound was handily repulsed by Lieutenant Tuber of C/4-12th Infantry and his attached D/17th Cav platoon. They stacked up twenty-six VC/NVA, along with a civilian blown off his Vespa while trying to flee the area. "There were two ACAVs right on the gate, and that's what saved the day," noted Captain Henry Morris, CO, F/2-11 ACR, which rolled into the PW compound during the next night. Several VC had been taken prisoner. "The ARVN guards were holding one's head underwater in a barrel for minutes at a time to get him to 'talk,'" recalled Morris. "The ARVN were dragging another prisoner behind a jeep on a chain. The ground inside the compound was gravel not grass, and it was hard to believe that the clump at the end of the chain was still alive or even human. It looked like hamburger. I was appalled, but I had no command over the ARVN, and I did not intervene—and that's bothered me ever since."

The counterattack commenced shortly after Captain Tonsetic rejoined the main body of Charlie Company at the mouth of the road cutting through Ho Nai. "Since we were not being pressed by the enemy at this point, I [thought] that we should regain the initiative and attack to the north immediately," he wrote. "The armored cavalry platoon leader was reluctant to advance up the narrow road in another assault, and I was inclined to agree with him. Instead, we moved his recoilless rifle vehicle forward and fired several rounds of HE and Flechette down the road to cover a ground assault by my two infantry platoons."

The advance began at 0615. Tonsetic had been informed that Company B, 2-3d Infantry, was proceeding south on the same road from an overnight position several klicks to the north. The linkup of the two units would crush whatever remained of the enemy assault force in Ho Nai.

The Cobras were presently strafing the retreating enemy, and Charlie Company made it to the scene of its pre-dawn battle without incident. It was now 0650. "[We] came under intense [AK-47] and 60mm mortar fire from an enemy force which had entrenched itself some 100 meters north of [the] creek which ran perpendicular to the road," wrote Tonsetic. One GI was wounded "before we were able to mass our M79 grenade fire on the mortar position and destroy it. We then had another helicopter gunship team on station and it raked the enemy positions with rockets and machine-gun fire. I saw several enemy soldiers attempting to reach some covered position, but they were cut down as they ran."

Charlie Company started forward again, only to be surprised by a diehard who popped up from the creek bed with a machine pistol, shot a grunt in the face, then ducked back and forth under the culvert bridge to blast away at the GIs on both sides of the road. Captain Tonsetic's command group took cover behind the burned-out ACAV, and the FO lieutenant and his recon sergeant tried vainly to lob hand grenades into the ravine. The lieutenant took a fragment in the shoulder, probably from one of their own grenades.

Specialist Schneider sent Private First Class Alfred J. Lewis—who was armed with an XM148 over-and-under—to the left while the rest of his squad laid down cover fire. Having worked his way to a good firing position, Lewis rose up to pump a 40mm shell at the culvert—and was instantly cut down by someone to his rear who mistook him for a Viet Cong.

Hearing the shout for a medic, First Sergeant Holmes ran to the scene with the aid bag of a pinned-down medic. Lewis had been shot in the back of the head. His forehead was blown open. "It's no use," Holmes said when Schneider joined him. "There's nothing we can do for him. . . ."

Though wounded troops may have died after being medevacked, Lewis was the only Charlie Company GI killed outright at Ho Nai. Meanwhile, the diehard had crawled into some thick vegetation on the left side of the road. Eight grenades bounced in after him. "He was blown in half at the waist. I saw his upper body come flying out of the underbrush in an arc at least ten feet high and twenty feet across," Captain Tonsetic noted with grim satisfaction. Tonsetic sent his wounded to the medevac point back down the road then. "I was terribly worried about the soldier who had been shot in the face, and after the battle I went to the hospital to find him. When I went to his bed it was empty and I thought he had died. However, on checking with a nurse I found him sitting on a bench outside the ward. The round had passed through his mouth, taking out some teeth, and exited through his cheek. He could talk, though not too clearly. I told him plastic surgeons could fix his face with no problem. He said he was just glad to be alive."

The battle continued. Those enemy soldiers not put to flight by the gunships rallied in the hilltop cemetery three hundred meters north of the culvert bridge. Charlie Company, pushing up to the edge of the creek bed, engaged them in a cacophonous exchange of fire. During the melee, Tonsetic caught sight of a lone VC who raced across the road to join his comrades in the cemetery just as one of his M79 grenadiers lobbed another shell toward the strong point. Thinking the guerrilla had to be the unluckiest man on the battlefield, Tonsetic watched incredulously as he ran right under the falling shell. It hit him on the top of his head, shattering his skull like a spooned-out egg.

It was now 0730. Captain Tonsetic radioed B-TOC to check on the progress of B/2-3d Infantry, which was supposedly moving south to link up with C/4-12th Infantry. "I was told that they had halted some 2000 meters to the north and were digging in. I failed to understand the rationale of this on the part of their commander, and became quite angry. I felt we had the enemy in a squeeze if he would only move south as I pushed toward the north."

Tonsetic was "somewhat mollified when my Bn S3 radioed me that a task force from the [2-47th Mechanized Infantry, 9th Division] was speeding to my location . . ."

Meanwhile, Cobras rolled in on the cemetery, diving unscathed through green tracers from VC who continued to fire in the face of the miniguns and rockets. The whole area was soon covered by a cloud of dust and smoke. Tonsetic noted that "[b]etween the gunship runs, we could see enemy soldiers crawling and running from position to position, trying to reorganize their hasty defensive positions. . . ."

There was a spontaneous cease-fire at one point when a civilian came down the road on a Vespa. His wife clung to him on the back of the motorbike—which was loaded with all their earthly belongings—and the pair breezed right through the battle as GIs and Viet Cong alike held their fire. The firefight roared back to life as soon as the Vespa sputtered over the culvert bridge to safety.

Another apparition emerged from the smoke. It was a lone guerrilla, naked except for a pair of shorts, who jogged toward Charlie Company with his arms held high. He survived, the grunts too astonished to fire him up, though several overwrought GIs did kick and punch him as they led him to the captain. "The prisoner was urgently trying to communicate something to us," remembered Tonsetic, who, lacking an interpreter—his Vietnamese scout was on leave for Tet—simply had the man escorted rearward. The

VC was subsequently interrogated at brigade, and as Tonsetic understood it, the prisoner claimed that he was the assault battalion commander and that he had dashed down from the cemetery to surrender what remained of his men before they were all killed. "I don't know if the report was substantiated or not, but it was probably credible."

The battle that might not have needed to happen began almost as soon as the mech infantry rumbled up the main road. "The M113s could not cross the creek except at the culvert due to steep banks along the stream," noted Tonsetic. Major William W. Jones, S3, 2-47th Mech, had brought forward twelve APCs. "[Jones and I] decided that what was left of my [two platoons], some 25 men, would attack north on the west side of the road, while the dismounted [mech troopers] would attack on the east side of the road. Once we had crossed the stream and gained a foothold, the armored M113s, with the major's vehicle in the lead, would be brought forward across the culvert and [would then] fan out on both sides of the road to provide covering fire for the infantry's final assault on the entrenched enemy force."

The mech force had arrived around 0800. The attack commenced ten minutes later, the grunts clambering down one side of the creek bed and up the other. There were thirty or forty bodies strewn down the ditch. Captain Tonsetic had just emerged from it when Kaylor, the senior RTO, heard a shot crack past from behind. Spinning around, Kaylor caught a flash of movement in the vines draped down the embankment to one side of the culvert, and shouting excitedly—"Watch my tracer!"—he sighted his M16 on the spot, thinking that another diehard might have a little hole behind the overhanging vegetation. Some twenty keyed-up grunts joined in, firing like crazy, and a dead guerrilla in black pajamas tumbled out of the hiding place.

Major Jones started bringing his APCs across as A/2-47th Mech and C/4-12th Infantry plunged on into the cemetery.

Captain Tonsetic's command group was about ten meters behind the assault line, using the left shoulder of the road for meager cover. The mech troops on the right side were moving so quickly they bypassed an open-topped, grave-size bunker partially covered by scrub brush. An enemy soldier popped up from the dugout. "He was behind the 9th Division guys, but to our right front," said Kaylor. "The VC just suddenly appeared as if by magic—and he shot the nearest mech trooper in the back at point-blank range."

The GI lurched forward dead. The VC swung his AK-47 on Kaylor next. The RTO had already shouldered his M16. "I shot first. I pulled off a three-round burst, and I'll never forget the sight—his hair went straight up from the concussion of the rounds, and his head just exploded. . . ."

There were more enemy soldiers in the position. Dropping against the raised road, Tonsetic was firing his CAR15 when he saw one of his radiomen, Private First Class Robert S. "Archie" Archibald—a sharp soldier, and an articulate, likable, soft-spoken young man—cross the road and advance straight at the VC. Archibald was limping. He had twisted his ankle jumping from a track when they first reached the village during the night, and relieved of his twenty-five-pound radio, he had tagged along with the command group as an extra rifleman during the battle.

Archibald didn't know what he was getting into when he first approached the bunker. "I saw a 9th Division trooper gesturing rapidly at the grave before he turned and ran," he later wrote. "Since I couldn't understand exactly what he was saying, I proceeded toward the grave to investigate what had gotten him so excited."

Archibald was halfway there when a bareheaded guerrilla rose up from the grave and let loose with a half-aimed AK-47 burst in the general direction of the shouting 9th Division GI. Caught by surprise, Archibald instinctively brought his weapon up and pulled the trigger. Nothing happened. "It was at that moment that I realized the weapon I had was still on safety," he noted. Worse, it was not even his weapon. His M16 had jammed when the command group was cut off in the house before dawn, and he had ended up with a shotgun. "I had never fired a shotgun before and didn't really know where the safety release was located. . . ."

Continuing forward even as he wrangled with the shotgun, Archibald had closed the gap between himself and the bunker to ten or fifteen feet when the guerrilla suddenly noticed him. The VC stared straight at Archibald, who found the safety at that moment. He promptly fired off a round from the hip, and realized to his shock that although the enemy soldier was perfectly centered in the spray pattern of the blast—the radioman-turned-rifleman saw a half circle of pellets kick up dirt at the forward edge of the dugout—he survived unscathed. The VC was stunned, however, and instead of blasting Archibald with his AK, he dropped back to cover giving the trooper time to back up, firing all the way, until he reached a shallow ditch running down the right side of the road into which he ducked for cover.

"Great, I'm safe," Archibald thought, "Someone else with more firepower can take care of this guy. . . ."

Everyone was hunkered down, however, waiting for someone else to be the hero. Dismayed, Archibald later wrote that he "waited for a short period of time, and then decided that 'I guess this is why I get paid. . . .'"

The cemetery entranceway was to Archibald's right front, and he rushed from the ditch to one of the battle-damaged concrete pillars. The guerrilla in the bunker had ducked back down. Archibald slowly advanced toward the position. The VC reemerged. They fired at each other—both missed—and Archibald scrambled back behind the pillar. "While standing there, I had an overwhelming feeling that 'I must move and move *now*,'" he recounted. Just as he took a half step to his left—getting most of his right leg behind cover—it felt like someone yanked on his right trouser leg at hip level. "I felt heat spread across the leg. I called out that I thought I was hit. However, as I waited the quick splash of heat rapidly went away and I didn't see any blood. Several days later back at base camp, I was changing fatigues. It was only then that I realized that I had actually been hit. My trousers had two small holes, and my boxer shorts had a three-inch tear. My leg had a thin line of blood—but what would have happened if I hadn't moved?"

The shotgun wasn't doing the job. Archibald reached for a grenade, but found that he had used all of his frags earlier in the battle. He asked the grunts nearest him in the roadside ditch if they had any grenades. None did, but the word went out and grenades were soon being lobbed man-to-man up the line to Archibald. The first grenade he threw landed right in the bunker, and relaxing, thinking the job done, he was utterly amazed when the enemy managed to flip the grenade back out in his direction before it exploded. The concrete pillar protected him from the blast.

Archibald pulled the pin on a second grenade, released the safety handle, counted one thousand *one,* one thousand *two*—the frag had a four-second fuse—made another perfect throw, and sprang forward as it exploded inside the bunker. "Archie ran right up to it and just hosed that hole down with his twelve-gauge shotgun," said Kaylor. "In a few seconds, he had worked the hole at every angle, pumping off shot after shot. He just filled it with buckshot."

There were four or five dead VC in the position. Limping back across the road to rejoin the command group, Archibald was surprised when First Sergeant Holmes grabbed his hand and shook it. "Good job, Arch!"

Until then, the radioman didn't think he'd done anything special. "[Now I thought] maybe I'd get a Bronze Star," Archibald wrote. "But my first priority was to stop my hands from shaking and catch up with the rest of the unit. We had started sweeping up the hill again. . . ."

Archibald was shocked when awarded the Distinguished Service Cross while still in Vietnam. He was cited not only for knocking out one bunker but for eliminating eight more VC/NVA during the push through the rest of the cemetery. "[W]e threw him several additional grenades so that he could continue his deadly work," wrote Tonsetic. "As we fired our M16s on full automatic at the enemy positions [to cover him], Archibald would creep forward and grenade the positions. . . . I never witnessed a more fearless and heroic effort on the part of an individual soldier."

Archibald thought the total of twelve kills credited to him exaggerated. In any event, noted this modest hero, the rest of the sweep was a team effort—First Sergeant Holmes joined him at one point—and the shell-shocked enemy had little fight left in them near the end. "It was weird," said Holmes. "When we ran up to their holes, they just looked up with blank eyes before we blew them away. . . ."

Major Jones made it forward as the melee was petering out, and at Tonsetic's direction, his tracks ran over and caved in several suspected enemy positions. Seven dazed prisoners were policed up. Medevacs landed in the cemetery, and wounded VC were loaded aboard with the GIs. Jones and Tonsetic decided to push on toward B/2-3d Infantry, a klick up the road. When Tonsetic called the Bravo Company commander, "[h]e complained that his unit had been under fire from our direction and had suffered one KIA." The implication was that the GI had been killed by friendly fire. "I explained that there were still enemy between our location and his, and that we needed to clear the area and link up. We would stay in radio contact throughout the move[,] and [he agreed that] his men would fire only at clearly visible enemy soldiers," Tonsetic wrote. "We moved out and after some light fighting with a few fleeing enemy soldiers, we reached the [blocking] position. The company commander of [B/2-3d] Infantry, whose force had dug itself in on the cleared hilltop, met us, still complaining of the one casualty he had suffered. I was still angry that the unit had not moved to my assistance the night before, but didn't press the point. Rather, I suggested that we now radio our respective battalion commanders and request further instructions."

To Tonsetic's regret, Major Jones was instructed to take his hard-hitting force to Bien Hoa. Pulling back as ordered, Charlie Company and B/2-3d Infantry were digging in on the northern edge of Ho Nai by late afternoon. At dusk they were warned to be prepared for a possible second wave. "I was apprehensive about our capability to withstand a major attack. Moreover, I was concerned that [there] might still be enemy units hidden in the village which could add to our problems," wrote Tonsetic, who was relieved when C/2-3d Infantry arrived around midnight to reinforce the perimeter. "The company moved through our positions and took a portion of the perimeter to our [west, where it] engaged a few enemy soldiers trying to exfiltrate the village. Three VC were killed in this exchange. Occasional aerial flares kept the perimeter illuminated on and off for the remainder of the night. Sleep was sporadic and restless."

On February 1, a house-by-house search was conducted through Ho Nai. Happily, the enemy was gone, leaving only their dead, who were searched in their turn. Captured documents included an operations order and map for the attack on Long Binh. The enemy assault force had been annihilated. Total casualties in the Long Binh area during the first three days of Tet were recorded as 9 U.S. KIA and 78 U.S. WIA against 47 enemy prisoners and an incredible but not unreasonable body count of 775 VC/NVA.

It was estimated that fifty civilians were killed and two hundred injured in the Battle of Long Binh. During the February 1 sweep through Ho Nai, Captain Tonsetic was approached by a French priest who "ask[ed] me for some soldiers to escort a burial party which wanted to bury some civilian casualties from the heavy fighting on the first night, as well as some victims of VC reprisals." The priest explained to Tonsetic that Ho Nai was primarily populated by Catholic refugees who had fled North Vietnam. "Suffice to say, the VC had a special vengeance in mind for these people [during Tet]," wrote Tonsetic. "I granted the Priest's request, and sent a squad to guard the burial party."

Given control of the Ho Nai operation, the 2-3d Infantry commander flew into the village later that afternoon to confer with the three company commanders there. He told them that the VC offensive was nationwide and that heavy fighting continued in the Saigon Circle. "Intelligence indicated that the enemy forces had been severely mauled, however, and many units were in disarray. Nonetheless, at least one regiment was reported to still be in our general area," Tonsetic paraphrased the briefing. The battalion commander "ordered his own two companies to continue to defend the village while my own unit was ordered to march north about 2000 meters to the high ground occupied by his own company during the first night's fighting. The idea was to establish a blocking position to engage any movement of enemy forces through the area."

Joined by the force from the PW compound, Tonsetic dug in on the scrubby, rocky-soiled hillock with three C/4-12th Infantry and two D/17th Cav platoons. The north-south road bisected the perimeter. The enemy attacked the position for six hours during the night of February 1–2, and ran into such a wall of fire as to shatter what remained of the VC/NVA at Long Binh. The battle began when enemy soldiers were spotted crossing the road to the north, and Tonsetic ordered the crew of an 81mm mortar that had been helicoptered in just before nightfall to commence firing. "The enemy returned small-arms and machine-gun fire, trying to silence the mortar," he wrote. "The crew hugged the ground, rising to their knees to drop the mortar rounds into the mortar tube, [and they broke] up the enemy assault from the north rather effectively, firing their entire sixty rounds in about twenty minutes."

Captain Tonsetic called in artillery and silenced a second enemy force that began firing on the west perimeter, even as a major attack from a third force developed on the east perimeter. Silhouetted against the skyline on the hillock, two ACAVs were hit by RPGs. The enemy were so close in the surrounding jungle that they could be heard as they shouted orders back and forth. Shadows darted toward the perimeter, but M16 and M60 fire scythed through them and M79 rounds flashed amongst them.

The attack fell apart just as a gunship team arrived. The Hueys strafed the enemy as they rushed back toward the jungle. Shortly thereafter, a C47 flareship came on station, turning night to day. "This flareship, equipped with a minigun, took up the work of the gunships when the latter departed to rearm and refuel," wrote Tonsetic. "Enemy tracers arched skyward trying to reach the flareship, but its altitude made it all but invulnerable."

Tonsetic decided to risk a medevac attempt under this suppressive fire. More than a dozen infantrymen and track crewmen had been seriously wounded. Two Hueys answered the call. "I directed them to land inside our perimeter from the south as this was the only area from which we had no enemy pressure," wrote Tonsetic, who dispatched a member of his command group to mark a landing zone with strobe lights. "[T]he lead helicopter touched down inside the perimeter, but the trail ship landed outside the perimeter. I desperately communicated his precarious position to him and he took off in a hail of enemy fire. Meanwhile, the loading of the most seriously wounded continued on the first helicopter. Among those was the soldier who I had sent to mark the LZ. He had been shot in the shoulder during the loading operation. As the lead dustoff took off, a surge of enemy fire was directed at it, but it took off, suffering only minor damage. I then directed the second ship in, landing it safely on the second attempt. Throughout the medevacs, the flareship continued to suppress the enemy with its minigun fire."

After coordination between Tonsetic and an FAC orbiting the hillock, the enemy in the jungle to the east were hit by two F4s out of Bien Hoa. "[T]he Phantoms screamed over the treeline, dropping their napalm canisters and creating an inferno which to my mind no enemy could escape," wrote Tonsetic. The napalm seared the faces of the troops on the perimeter. "I remember lying there, feeling sorry for whoever was in that treeline," said Kaylor, the RTO. "We could see Viet Cong running out on fire, and dropping."

Coming around again, the Phantoms went down the treeline with their 20mm automatic cannons. Meanwhile, C/2-3d Infantry, accompanied by ten ACAVs, was moving up the road from Ho Nai. "About thirty minutes after the air strike, the lead soldiers in the relief column could be seen approaching our perimeter," wrote Tonsetic. The awesome amount of gunship fire on the column's flanks looked like a moving red curtain. "The M113s were [also] firing suppressive fire on both sides of the road and the enemy was only able to return light fire. Two soldiers in the relief column were wounded. As the column entered the perimeter, I knew the battle was over at last. The remainder of the night was quiet with only occasional artillery flares illuminating the position and surrounding jungle."

Epilogue

A New War

The scene around Captain Tonsetic and C/4-12th Infantry on February 2, 1968 was out of a painting by Goya. The morning fog shrouded their hillock, as did smoke from the two blasted and gutted ACAVs. The air was acrid with the smell of cordite, napalm, and roasted flesh, and the GIs who swept the battered jungle to the east counted approximately fifty enemy soldiers who were burned beyond recognition.

Three dazed and scorched Viet Cong wandered into the perimeter during the morning to be medevacked.

The relief force returned to Ho Nai. Tonsetic and Charlie Company loaded up on the remaining tracks from D/17th Cav and returned to FSB Concord. Meeting them at the gate, Lieutenant Colonel Mastoris—beaming at the job they had done, relieved beyond words at their light casualties—rushed to Tonsetic and wrapped him in a bear hug. Mastoris turned to the grimy, exhausted troops and exclaimed, "The mess hall's open. Free beer for everyone!"

Captain Tonsetic was as tired as his troops, and as proud as Mastoris. He was also "overcome with a deep sense of melancholy," he later wrote. They had won their battle, but it seemed a battle that should never have occurred if they were indeed winning the war. "The enemy was no longer the elusive shadows we had pursued through the jungles of War Zone D. He was real and could challenge us on our own ground. The war would continue for me for months to come, but our purpose and cause in Vietnam would become less and less clear . . ."

The communists had gambled and they had lost. The Tet Offensive was nothing less than a shattering military disaster for Hanoi. Everything went wrong for the enemy. Their costly campaign of feint and diversion leading up to Tet may have distracted COMUSMACV, but General Weyand —the key figure in the battle for the Saigon Circle—had not been deceived. Allied maneuver units had been redeployed from the Cambodian border to the environs of Saigon. The security forces at key enemy objectives like Bien Hoa, Long Binh, and Tan Son Nhut were in a red alert posture when the attacks began. The surprise that the Viet Cong achieved in other locations, most notably downtown Saigon, was not decisive. The ARVN did not fall to pieces. The urban population did not spontaneously rally to the revolution. The communists tried to hit everything at once instead of massing their forces. Many assault units bounced off their objectives for lack of weight. What the enemy did seize, they could not keep. The Viet Cong were pushed out of most towns within days, sometimes within hours, and street fighting only continued for any length of time in Hue and in the Cholon section of Saigon.

In the first two weeks of Tet, a thousand U.S. and two thousand ARVN troops were killed. During this same period, MACV reported that 32,000 VC/NVA had been killed and 5,800 captured. Though these latter figures are exaggerated, they do speak to the terrible price the guerrillas paid for emerging from the jungle to take on the military might of the United States in open battle.

Firepower alone did not win the battles of Tet. It also took good soldiers and good leaders. Troop morale was still high at that time in the war. The officer and NCO corps had not yet been eroded by multiple combat tours, lowered standards, and accelerated promotions. When Tet erupted, the U.S. Army was still the best army in the world, and finally called to do what it had been trained to do, January 31, 1968, was its proudest day in Vietnam. Thirteen soldiers won the Distinguished Service Cross in and around Saigon that day—Lieutenant Colonels Maus and Otis, Captains Otis and Tonsetic, Lieutenants Barnes, Gallo, and Galloway, Sergeants Brewer and Schultz, Specialists Crowell and Wilson, and Privates Archibald and Healey—and their citations are testimony to the excellence of the units that saved the capital. Taken by surprise in some cases, faced with a numerically superior enemy in most, these units plunged into battle not only with overwhelming mobility and firepower but with well-schooled, quick-thinking officers who led from the front, and young troops imbued with an aggressive fighting spirit that was unlike anything seen in the latter years of the Vietnam War.

Most officers felt that Tet was a great allied victory. The army had thoroughly trounced the enemy, showing that the communists did not have what it took to win on the battlefield. Nevertheless, the fact that the communists had been able to launch such a massive offensive discredited General Westmoreland and the Johnson Administration—three years of search-and-destroy operations, and the communists were as powerful as ever. Tet was a military victory but psychological defeat for the U.S. not simply because of defeatist reporting—and those officers who had seen their units triumph during Tet would be dismayed at how the battles played on the home front—but because the offensive forced America to take stock of what would be required to defeat an enemy as resolute and willing to absorb casualties as the VC and NVA. What was required was more than what the American public decided it was willing to sacrifice for a regime on the other side of the world of nebulous strategic value to the United States.

The public might have tolerated a long war had Saigon shown itself to be a worthy ally. It did not. Corruption permeated the government; and despite its tenacious showing during Tet, the ARVN, led in the main by officers whose careers advanced according to their political connections not their battlefield successes, never matured into a force that could stand on its own. There were some good units —the rangers, the airborne, the 1st ARVN Infantry Division—but a few good units does not an army make, and from beginning to end the ARVN remained a paper tiger in comparison to the VC and NVA.

Ironically, Tet was the beginning of the end for the Viet Cong. Decimated during Tet, the guerrilla army was further wrecked during a second wave of virtually suicidal attacks launched on Saigon in May and June. By 1969, the VC had been almost entirely replaced on the battlefield by the regulars of the North Vietnamese Army.

Many of the guerrillas killed in these conventional battles were veterans of years or decades of revolutionary warfare. These dedicated cadre were needlessly sacrificed by impatient leaders in Hanoi. As Tet showed, the guerrillas could not win conventional battles against U.S. firepower. They did not need to. After three years of big-unit operations, U.S. forces were spinning their wheels, unable to force the enemy to fight their way, and public support for this inconclusive war was in decline even before Tet. The communists were prepared to fight forever, America was not, and it did not require the wholesale sacrifice of the Viet Cong in epic battles to drive the point home. Eventually, inevitably, the U.S. would have withdrawn from Vietnam, even without the butchery of the Tet Offensive.

Glossary

AB air base
ABD airborne division
ACAV armored cavalry assault vehicle
ACR armored cavalry regiment
ADC assistant division commander
AK-47 standard communist 7.62mm automatic rifle
AO area of operations
APC armored personnel carrier
ARP aerorifle platoon
ARVN Army of the Republic of Vietnam

BEQ bachelor enlisted quarters
BMB brigade main base
BOQ bachelor officers quarters
B-TOC battalion tactical operations center

C&C command and control helicopter
CAR15 5.56mm submachine gun used by officers
CG commanding general
Chinook CH47 transport helicopter
CMD Capital Military District
CO commanding officer
Cobra AH1G helicopter gunship
COMUSMACV commander, U.S. Military Assistance Command Vietnam
CORDS Civilian Operations and Revolutionary Development Support
COSVN Central Office for South Vietnam
CP command post
CSC Central Security Control

GLOSSARY

CVC combat vehicle communications (radio helmet for armor crews)

DMZ demilitarized zone
DOD Department of Defense
D-TOC Division Tactical Operations Center
Duster M42 combat vehicle with twin 40mm cannons

FA field artillery
FAC forward air controller
FFV Field Force Vietnam
FO forward observer
FSB fire support base

G1 personnel officer at division or corps level
G2 intelligence officer at division or corps level
G3 operations officer at division or corps level
G4 logistics officer at division or corps level

HAC Headquarters Area Command
HHC headquarters & headquarters company
HQ headquarters
Huey the UH1 series of helicopters

JDOC Joint Defense Operations Center
JGS Joint General Staff

KIA killed in action
Klick kilometer

LAW 66mm light antitank weapon
LF local force
LIB light infantry brigade
LNO liaison officer
LP listening post
LRP long-range patrol

M14 nonstandard U.S. 7.62mm automatic rifle
M16 standard U.S. 5.56mm automatic rifle
M60 standard U.S. 7.62mm machine gun
M79 standard U.S. 40mm grenade launcher

GLOSSARY

MACV Military Assistance Command Vietnam
MF main force
MG machine gun
MI military intelligence
MP military police
MSG Marine Security Guard
MSR main supply route

NCO noncommissioned officer
NCOIC noncommissioned officer in charge
NVA North Vietnamese Army

OIC officer in charge
OSA Office of the Special Assistant

PF popular forces
Phantom F4 jet
PM provost marshal
POL petroleum oil lubricants
PW prisoner of war

QC Quan Canh (VNAF security police)
QRT Quick Reaction Team
Quad-50 truck mounted with four .50-caliber machine guns

RA regular army
Raven H23 scout helicopter
RF regional forces
ROE rules of engagement
RPG rocket-propelled grenade
RTO radio-telephone operator
RVN Republic of Vietnam (South Vietnam)
RVNAF Republic of Vietnam Armed Forces

S1 personnel officer at battalion or brigade level
S2 intelligence officer at battalion or brigade level
S3 operations officer at battalion or brigade level
S4 logistics officer at battalion or brigade level
SAT Security Alert Team
SKS communist carbine

GLOSSARY

Skyraider   prop-driven A1E fighter-bomber
SP   security police
SPS   security police squadron
Super Saber   F100 jet

TC   tank or track commander
TCK-TKN   Tong Cong Kich-Tong Khoi Nghia (General Offensive-General Uprising)
TF   task force
TOC   tactical operations center
Track   nickname for the tracked armored personnel carrier
TSNSA   Tan Son Nhut Sensitive Area

USA   United States Army
USAF   United States Air Force
USARV   U.S. Army Vietnam
USMC   United States Marine Corps

V-100   XM706 security vehicle with twin .30-caliber machine guns in a revolving turret
VC   Viet Cong
Ville   village
VNAF   Vietnamese Air Force

WIA   wounded in action

XM148   M16 rifle mounted with a 40mm grenade launcher
XO   executive officer

Sources

Interviews

This book could not have been written without the participation of numerous Tet Offensive veterans who were willing not only to describe their memories of the campaign but to dig up old letters, photos, and reports. Space limitations have prevented me from including in the text all of those veterans with whom I corresponded or spoke with by phone. Those featured in the book were given the opportunity to review the rough draft for accuracy. Below is a list, by unit, of all those who contributed.

MACV; II FFV; and miscellaneous units: Lt. Gen. Edward C. Peter (Ret.); Cols. Leonard Hasse (Ret.), Robert J. Laflam (Ret.), William C. Maus (Ret.), Howard W. Randall (Ret.), William S. Schroeder (Ret.), and George M. Tronsrue (Ret.); Maj. Thomas A. Tadsen, USANG; CW4 Charles R. Rogers (Ret.); Sgt. Maj. Richard D. Vincent (Ret.); Sfc. Aruealin Dean Moak (Ret.); David A. Jared, and Gilbert B. Kelbaugh.

9th Infantry Division: Brig. Gen. Hugh J. Bartley (Ret.); Cols. Brice H. Barnes, USAR (Ret.), Henry L. S. Jezek, USANG, and Michael D. Mahler (Ret.); Maj. Theodore R. Moen, Michigan National Guard; Philip Beal, Stephen Forcade, William S. McCaskill, and Gerald L. McLean.

25th Infantry Division: Gen. Glenn K. Otis (Ret.); Lt. Gen. John R. Thurman III (Ret.); Cols. Leland H. Burgess (Ret.), Thomas E. Fleming (Ret.), and Charles K. Flint (Ret.); Lt. Cols. Dale D. Dow (Ret.), Malcolm D. Otis (Ret.), Leo B. Virant II (Ret.), and Michael E. Wikan (Ret.); Sgt. Maj. Willie H. Porter (Ret.); Sfc. Glen T. Pike (Ret.);

SOURCES

MSgt. Gary D. Brewer, USAF (Ret.); Dwight W. Birdwell, Russell H. Boehm, Frank Cuff, Rolland Fletcher, Dean A. Foss, Joseph A. Gallo, David W. Garrod, Ken Hardesty, Richard Hawk, Thomas F. Higgins, Anthony E. Kozlinski, Albert J. Porter, Philip T. Randazzo, John Rourke, Michael D. Siegel, Steve Uram, Donald L. Weyer, and Robert D. Wolford.

101st Airborne Division: Lt. Gen. David E. Grange (Ret.); Maj. Gen. Frank B. Clay (Ret.); Brig. Gens. J. Keith Kellogg, and Ran L. Phillips (Ret.); Cols. Paul Robblee (Ret.), Richard L. St. John (Ret.), and William P. Tallon (Ret.); Lt. Col. George William Lanahan (Ret.); and James I. Scheiner.

199th Light Infantry Brigade: Maj. Gen. Frederic E. Davison (Ret.); Cols. John K. Gibler (Ret.), William Mastoris (Ret.), and Robert L. Tonsetic (Ret.); Lt. Cols. James F. MacGill (Ret.), and Henry R. Meyer (Ret.); Capt. Stanley A. McLaughlin (Med. Ret.); CW3 James W. Creamer, USAR (Ret.); 1st Sgts. George L. Holmes (Ret.), and Nick Schneider (Ret.); Sfc. Joe R. Meyer (Ret.); Robert S. Archibald, Cliff Kaylor, Al Schlenker, Robert Stanard, and C. Dale Tracy.

11th Armored Cavalry Regiment: Maj. Gen. Neal Creighton (Ret.); Cols. Frederic J. Delamain (Ret.), Donald W. Derrah (Ret.), John H. Getgood (Ret.), and Robert C. Palmer (Ret.); Lt. Cols. Henry Morris (Ret.), and Anderson H. Walters (Ret.); CW4 Eldon E. Nygaard, USAR; Cmd. Sgt. Maj. Donald E. Horn (Ret.); and Anthony N. Stanfa.

18th Military Police Brigade: Cols. Arnold Daxe (Ret.), Richard E. George (Ret.), and Nevin R. Williams, USAR (Ret.); Lt. Col. Gerald L. Waltman (Ret.); MSgt. Robert J. Woods (Ret.); and John R. Van Wagner.

7th U. S. Air Force: Cols. Carl B. DeNisio (Ret.), Melvin G. Grover (Ret.), Harold A. Ogden (Ret.), and Martin E. Strones, USAF Reserve (Ret.); Lt. Cols. Carl A. Bender (Ret.), and Kenton D. Miller (Ret.); Senior MSgts. Bernard C. Gifford (Ret.), and William Piazza (Ret.); MSgts. Robert A Knox (Ret.), and Robert L. Ruth (Ret.); David C. Chunn, John F. Langley, John A. Novak, Steve Rivers, and Thomas N. Tessier.

SOURCES

Veterans Organizations

Assistance was provided by John Sperry of the Mobile Riverine Force Association (9th Infantry Division); Jerry Headley, John D. Boyle, and Joseph S. Grasso of the 25th Infantry Division Association; and Col. Nicholas A. Keck (Ret.) and Technical Sgt. Rick Maitland (Ret.) of the Air Force Security Police Association.

Documents

"After Action Report, Long Binh/Saigon, TET CAMPAIGN; 199th Infantry Brigade (Separate) (Light), 12 January–19 February 1968."

"Battle of Tan Son Nhut" (G3 staff, II Field Force Vietnam).

"Combat After Action Report (Operation Uniontown). Headquarters, 4th Battalion, 12th Infantry, 199th Infantry Brigade (Sep) (Light), 14 January–17 February 1968."

"Combat After Action Report—TET OFFENSIVE, Headquarters, II Field Force Vietnam, Period 31 January–18 February 1968."

"Commanders Combat Note Number 20. Headquarters, 25th Infantry Division, 29 November 1968."

"Historical Account of the Military Police Corps Regiment, Assault on the American Embassy, TET—1968." (SSgt. Thomas L. Johnson, and Mary R. Himes, March 16, 1983).

"Incident/Information/Occurrence Report; Number 1-68 Viet Cong Attack on American Embassy 31 January 1968" (Marine Security Guards, American Embassy, Saigon).

"Operational Report—Lessons Learned, Headquarters, II Field Force Vietnam, Period Ending 30 April 1968."

"Operational Report/Lessons Learned, PM, USAHAC, 15 February 68."

SOURCES

"Recommendation for the Presidential Unit Citation. Headquarters, 3d Squadron, 4th Cavalry, 25th Infantry Division."

"Summation of Combat Activities Involving Military Police During the Period 30 January to 6 February 1968, RVN."

"Task Force Ware After Action Report, 31 Jan–18 Feb 1968."

Untitled after-action report of the 3d Security Police Squadron, USAF, regarding attack on Bien Hoa Air Base, January 31, 1968.

Periodicals

"Currahees Kill Over 150 Reds." *The Screaming Eagle* (newspaper of the 101st Airborne Division), February 23, 1968, 1.

Dees, Joseph L. "The Viet Cong Attack that Failed." *Department of State Newsletter,* May 1968, 22–30.

Devitt, Lt. Col. J.W., ed. *The Hurricane; A Publication of II Field Force Vietnam,* April 1968.

Fleming, Capt. Arnauld G. "Info officer leads infantrymen in 4-hour fight." *The Old Reliable* (newspaper of the 9th Infantry Division), February 14, 1968, 6.

Funderburk, Maj. Raymond E., ed. *Octofoil; 9th Infantry Division in Vietnam,* April, May, June, 1968.

Pisor, Robert L. "Saigon's Fighting MPs." *Army,* April 1968, 37–41.

Sheehan, Chaplain (Capt.) Donald J., USAF. "Battle of Bunker Hill 10." *The Airman,* June 1968, 10–11.

Speedy, Col. Jack, USA. "Charlie Company to the Rescue." *Vietnam,* June 1990, 22–28.

Books

Arnold, James R. *Tet Offensive 1968; Turning Point in Vietnam.* London: Osprey Publishing, Ltd., 1990.

SOURCES

Bergerud, Eric M. *Red Thunder, Tropic Lightning; The World of a Combat Division in Vietnam.* Boulder, Col.: Westview Press, 1993.

Boettcher, Thomas D. *Vietnam; The Valor and the Sorrow.* Boston: Little, Brown and Company, 1985.

Braestrup, Peter. *Big Story; How the American Press and Television Reported and Interpreted the Crisis of Tet 1968 in Vietnam and Washington.* New Haven: Yale University Press, 1983.

Davidson, Lt. Gen. Phillip B., USA (Ret.) *Vietnam at War; The History: 1946–1975.* Novato, Calif.: Presidio Press, 1988.

Ford, Gary Douglas. *4/4: A LRP's Narrative.* New York: Ivy Books, 1993.

Fox, Lt. Col. Roger P., USAF (Ret.) *Air Base Defense in the Republic of Vietnam 1961–1973.* Washington, D.C.: Office of Air Force History, United States Air Force, 1979.

Gleim, Albert F. *Distinguished Service Cross Awards of the Vietnam War.* Ft. Myer, Va.: Planchet Press, 1993.

Hall, Don C. and Annette R. *I Served.* Bellevue, Wash.: A.D. Hall Publishing Co., 1994.

Mahler, Col. Michael D., USA (Ret.). *Ringed in Steel; Armored Cavalry, Vietnam 1967–68.* Novato, Calif.: Presidio Press, 1986.

Oberdorfer, Don. *Tet!* New York: De Capo Press, Inc., 1984.

Palmer, Brig. Gen. Dave Richard, USA. *Summons of the Trumpet; A History of the Vietnam War from a Military Man's Viewpoint.* San Rafael, Calif.: Presidio Press, 1978.

Sheehan, Neil. *A Bright Shining Lie; John Paul Vann and America in Vietnam.* New York: Random House, 1988.

Son, Lt. Col. Pham Van. *The Viet Cong "Tet" Offensive (1968).* Saigon: Printing and Publications Center (A.G./Joint General Staff) RVNAF, 1969.

Starry, Gen. Donn A., USA. *Mounted Combat in Vietnam.* Washington, D.C.: Department of the Army, 1978.

SOURCES

Stanton, Shelby L. *The Rise and Fall of an American Army; U.S. Ground Forces in Vietnam, 1965–1973.* Novato, Calif.: Presidio Press, 1985.

Westmoreland, Gen. William C., USA (Ret.). *A Soldier Reports.* Garden City, N.Y.: Doubleday & Company, Inc., 1976.

Wirtz, James J. *The Tet Offensive; Intelligence Failure in War.* Ithaca, N.Y.: Cornell University, 1991.

Index

INDEX